The Devil's Party

The Devil's Party

Critical Counter-interpretations of Shakespearian Drama

HARRIETT HAWKINS

CLARENDON PRESS · OXFORD
1985

Oxford University Press, Walton Street, Oxford OX2 6DP

London New York Toronto
Delhi Bombay Calcutta Madras Karachi
Kuala Lumpur Singapore Hong Kong Tokyo
Nairobi Dar es Salaam Cape Town
Melbourne Auckland

and associated companies in
Beirut Berlin Ibadan Mexico City Nicosia

Oxford is a trade mark of Oxford University Press

Published in the United States
by Oxford University Press, New York

British Library Cataloguing in Publication Data

Hawkins, Harriett
The Devil's Party: critical counter-interpretations of
Shakespearian drama.
1. Shakespeare, William
– Criticism and interpretation.
I. Title
822.3'3 PR2976
ISBN 0-19-812814-2

Set by Grestun Graphics, Abingdon
Printed in Great Britain at
the University Press, Oxford
by David Stanford,
Printer to the University

For Eric Buckley

Acknowledgements

I hope this short survey of critical counter-interpretations of Shakespearian drama will be of practical use to teachers and students, as well as Shakespeare specialists. Although it offers no solutions to the major problems posed, the questions raised may provide a number of topics for fruitful discussion.

I am particularly indebted, throughout this book, to Norman Rabkin's discussion of the current 'crisis of confidence' in Shakespeare criticism (see *Shakespeare and the Problem of Meaning* (Chicago, 1981)), and to Richard Levin's critical account of recent trends in the reinterpretation of Elizabethan drama in *New Readings vs. Old Plays* (Chicago, 1979). My own conclusions about current trends in the criticism of Shakespearian drama are based on the books, journals, and articles I reviewed for Volumes 33 (1980), 34 (1981), and 35 (1982) of *Shakespeare Survey*, and are, therefore, likely to seem old-fashioned to readers especially interested in recent theoretical criticism *per se*. For the fact is that – as John Bayley and Terence Hawkes (among others) have observed – the intercontinental explosion in critical theory has had only a peripheral impact on critical discussions of Shakespearian drama in particular. And the reasons why the names of so many modern critical theorists are conspicuously absent from so many publications devoted to Shakespeare may be of methodological, ideological, historical, and critical interest in their own right, and thus merit a great deal more consideration than they are given in this book. One hopes that some modern Dryden will emerge to tell us why certain modern theories, applicable elsewhere (rather like the French theories discussed in *The Essay of Dramatic Poesy*) are not relevant, or applicable, to Shakespeare's plays, and to say why others are. Because of what seemed to me to be their obvious relevance to past and present critical discussions of Shakespearian drama, the major arguments about critical methodology in this book are based on the theories of K. R. Popper, T. S. Kuhn, E. H. Gombrich, E. D. Hirsch, Morris Weitz, and Harold Bloom.

I have previously discussed some of the problems posed in Chapters 1 and 2 (with reference to some of Shakespeare's contemporaries) in an article on 'The Morality of Elizabethan Drama', in *English Renaissance Studies Presented to Dame Helen Gardner*, ed. John Carey (Oxford, 1980), pp. 12–32; and a section of Chapter 4 was used as an essay in *Reconciliations: Studies in Honor of Richard Harter Fogle*, ed. Mary Lynn Johnson and Seraphia Leyda (Salzburg, 1984). Early versions of parts of Chapter 3 were originally presented as short papers at meetings of the American Shakespeare Association and the International Shakespeare Association, and were published in *Shakespearean Comedy*, ed. Maurice Charney (*New York Literary Forum*, 5–6 (1980), pp. 37–46), and in *Shakespeare, Man of the Theater*, ed. Kenneth Muir, Jay L. Halio, and D. J. Palmer (Newark, London, and Toronto, 1983), pp. 105–13. Some of the points scatter-shot throughout this book — along with its Blakean title — were used in an article, '"The Devil's Party": Virtues and Vices in *Measure for Measure*', in *Shakespeare Survey*, 31 (1978), 105–13. I am grateful to the Open University for permission to reprint sections of a radio lecture, '*Measure for Measure*: Some Open Questions', first broadcast on 24 June 1984. Although some overlap was necessary, I have tried to avoid reiterating the extended arguments made with reference to major artistic protests against sexual, social, and cosmic injustice in Chaucer and Webster, as well as in Shakespeare, in Chapter 1 ('Poetic Injustice') and Chapter 2 ('The Victim's Side'), of *Poetic Freedom and Poetic Truth: Chaucer, Shakespeare, Marlowe, Milton* (Oxford, 1976).

Shakespeare references are to Peter Alexander's edition of *The Complete Works of Shakespeare* (London, 1981). Quotations from Aristotle's *Poetics*, Sidney's *Apology for Poetry*, and other critical landmarks are from Walter Jackson Bate's *Criticism: The Major Texts* (New York, 1970). For the purposes of quick reference, quotations from Shakespeare's earlier critics are from the World's Classics edition of *Shakespeare Criticism, A Selection, 1623–1840*, ed. D. Nichol Smith (London, 1916) — for more extensive and comprehensive quotations from early criticisms of Shakespeare, see *Shakespeare: The Critical Heritage*, in the successive volumes edited by Brian Vickers. Quotations from Plato are from *The Republic*, translated by Desmond Lee (Harmondsworth, revised edition, 1974).

In its manifest indebtedness to major arguments — and counter-arguments — posited by Shakespeare himself, as well as by Plato, Aristotle, Augustine, Sidney, Dr Johnson, Shelley, and some of the best of all twentieth-century critics of Shakespearian drama, this could accurately be described as the least original book on the subject that ever has been published. Conversely, however, it could be most enthusiastically recommended by virtue of the brilliance and enduring relevance of the original insights and ideas quoted in it. In any case, ''Tis dangerous when the baser nature comes/Between the pass and fell incensed points/Of mighty opposites', and in the course of interposing my own arguments between some of the mightiest of all opposites in the history of literary criticism, I have often had occasion to raise a comradely glass (or two) to Rosencrantz and Guildenstern.

For references, offprints, stimulating conversations, and invaluable criticisms of my own criticism, I am grateful to Robin Bulow, Dan Davin, Dame Helen Gardner, Cicely Havely, Terence Hawkes, Hugh Lloyd-Jones, Marguerite McDonald, Joe Muir, Kenneth Muir, Paul Turner, and Werner Habicht. And I am still, and most, indebted to the John Simon Guggenheim Foundation for a grant which allowed me to begin work on this book back in 1975.

H. H.

Linacre College, Oxford

Contents

Introduction. In Pursuit of the Fox: Some Examples
of Critical Action and Reaction   1

Chapter 1. **The Questions of Mimesis and Morality:**
Some 'Footnotes to Plato'   14

i. The Question of Representation in
Shakespearian Drama and Criticism: How
Does a Play Look?   17

ii. The Question of Morality in Shakespearian
Drama and Criticism: The 'Screw-guns'
of Plato   38
Notes   55

Chapter 2. **The 'Books' and 'Counterbooks' of**
Shakespearian Drama and Criticism   61

i. 'The Art of the Insoluble': Some Open
Questions in *Measure for Measure* and
Hamlet   61

ii. 'On the Other Hand': The 'Counterbooks'
of Criticism   83

iii. In Particular: What Neo-Classical Criticism
Has to Tell About What Shakespeare
Does Not Do   93
Notes   102

Chapter 3. **'Conjectures and Refutations': The Positive**
Uses of Negative Feedback in Criticism and
Performance   109

i. The Burden of Disproof   109

ii. The Popperian Alternative   124

iii. Some Dramatic and Critical Constructions
and Misconstructions: The Problem of the
Obvious   133
Notes   137

Contents

Chapter 4.   **Some Current Themes for Critical
Disputation**   143

i.   Female Virtues and Vices in Shakespearian
Drama and Criticism   143

ii.   The Poetic and Critical 'Rape of Lucrece'   149

iii.   Some Recent Examples of the Dialectical
Process   164

iv.   Shakespeare's Construction and
Characterization: The Questions of
Technique and of Vision   172

   Notes   183

Index   191

Introduction

In Pursuit of the Fox: Some Examples of Critical Action and Reaction

The fox knows many things. The hedgehog knows one big thing.

Archilochus

General criticism . . . is more than commonly absurd with respect to Shakespeare, who must be accompanied step by step, and scene by scene, in his gradual developments of characters and passions, and whose finer features must be singly pointed out, if we would do complete justice to his genuine beauties.

Joseph Warton

The form is mechanic, when on any given material we impress a pre-determined form, not necessarily arising out of the properties of the material; — as when to a mass of wet clay we give whatever shape we wish it to retain when hardened. The organic form, on the other hand, is innate; it shapes, as it develops, itself from within, and the fullness of its development is one and the same with the perfection of its outward form. Such as the life is, such is the form. Nature, the prime genial artist, inexhaustible in diverse powers, is equally inexhaustible in forms . . . and even such is the appropriate excellence of her chosen poet, of our own Shakespeare.

Samuel Taylor Coleridge

An *Encyclopaedia of Pseudo-Sciences* might define critical method as *the systematic (q.v.) application of foreign substances to literature; any series of devices by which critics may treat different works of art as much alike as possible.*

Randall Jarrell

In ancient discussions of poetic mimesis and morality, as in certain recent discussions of Shakespearian tragedy and comedy, critical arguments (and counter-arguments) concerning the meaning and effect of drama and poetry have sometimes reflected the nature of art, but have just as often been at odds with it. For instance, the axioms of neo-classical criticism, which included the ubiquitously applied 'example theory' as well as the theory of poetic justice, were dialectically devised, not to explain any specific plays or poems, but rather to answer a succession of Platonic attacks on drama and poetry for arousing immoral and irrational passions, sympathies, and even admiration for sinners; and for showing manifest instances of cosmic and social *injustice* (see Chapter 1). For that matter, although the dicta of neo-classical criticism (concerning the decorums of language and structure, as well as the moral premises governing portrayals of comic and tragic characters) did, of course, influence certain major neo-classical playwrights, they were so remote from Shakespeare's own dramatic practice that Dr Johnson, in effect, turned the critical process into reverse and used the various axioms of neo-classical theory to show precisely what Shakespeare does *not* do, even as he used Shakespeare's 'just representations of general nature' as the criteria by which to attack the formal tenets of neo-classical theory itself (see Chapter 2).

In the Romantic period, poets and critics went on to praise Shakespeare for doing precisely what Plato, and his neo-classical successors, had argued that dramatists ought not to do. Shelley deemed it a good thing that poets like Shakespeare and Milton extended their sympathies even unto sinners, while Keats especially admired Shakespeare because he wrote without a direct moral purpose, and extolled the 'negative capability' of the chameleon artist who can take as much delight 'in conceiving an Iago as an Imogen'. It is, as Hazlitt and Shelley argued, by leaving good and evil to fight it out with each other on the stage, and in our minds (just as they do on their old prize-fighting stage, the world), that Shakespeare encourages us to experience all the pains and pleasures of our species as our own. At their best, the arguments posited by Romantic critics up to and including A. C. Bradley came — to my mind, anyway — closer to describing what Shakespeare's art really does do, than any other school of criticism before or since. But at its worst, Romantic criticism did tend to over-sentimentalize Shakespeare's characters and plays.

Much twentieth-century criticism, like much of the greatest twentieth-century poetry, was written in reaction to Romantic criticism and poetry. As satire, detachment, and irony began to dominate in poetry, a critical premium was placed on adopting a detached, judicious, censorious — anything *but* a Romantic — attitude towards Shakespeare's characters. Eliot's asides noting that Hamlet died somewhat 'too pleased with himself' and that Othello died 'cheering himself up' were developed and extended, over and over again, in the countless critical tirades against the vices and follies of Shakespeare's tragic heroes and heroines that were published in the nineteen-forties, fifties, and sixties. In England, F. R. Leavis and his followers pitilessly vivisected Othello, Antony, and Hamlet. And in America, there were essays on the indiscretions of Desdemona and the misdemeanours of Juliet (both of whom, it was argued, got just what was coming to them for disobeying their fathers). When necessary, mid-twentieth-century scholars could refer back to Renaissance critical theory in order to buttress their arguments that the characters in Elizabethan comedy and tragedy alike were intended to have been seen, by their original audience – and therefore should be seen by the judicious modern spectator as well – to exemplify the errors and vices that all of us should deplore and eschew. Thus, while arguing in opposition to Romantic critics, innumerable twentieth-century scholars insisted that a judgemental and censorious attitude towards Shakespeare's characters was historically, as well as critically, correct; and that neither a right-thinking Elizabethan audience, nor a critically informed and judicious modern spectator would, or should, have extended any undue sympathy or admiration to Shakespeare's tragic heroes, heroines, victims, or villains.

This criticism proved, however, to be all too obviously at odds with the fact that Shakespearian drama itself actually does allow the audience to experience any number of differing emotions simultaneously, and may elicit any number of different responses (e.g. pity and terror and aesthetic admiration and moral disapproval) towards those of its characters who 'make defect perfection', and whose very vices may become them, in dramatic portrayals that 'nothing extenuate' *nor* 'aught set down in malice'. By contrast, many mid-twentieth-century critics of Shakespeare and his contemporaries insisted that we should limit ourselves to one point of view, to one response, and that a judgemental one.

A reaction to such dogmatic and authoritarian interpretations of Shakespeare's plays was inevitable. And indeed, the best recent theoretical discussions of literature – regardless of the differing premises on which they are based – have all posited the same liberating point: which is that we might as well freely and frankly acknowledge the openness of literary form, effects, and responses. Recent criticism thus brings us back to a concern with the multiplicity of dramatic and poetic effects and responses that were originally recognized, even as they were condemned, by Plato, in his arguments that the greatest art may, and often does, simultaneously elicit conflicting and contradictory moral and emotional responses — within even the wisest and most judicious of individuals — towards a single character or 'object in the realm of vision' (see Chapter 2).

The central object in our realm of vision here — that is, Shakespearian criticism itself — is currently the subject of conflicting and contradictory arguments and responses. A whole book could, therefore, be devoted to positing various reasons why this may well be the best of times for criticism in general, and for critical studies of Shakespeare in particular. Alternatively, one could summon equally impressive arguments that ours is the worst of times for both. I shall accentuate the positive case in certain sections of this book, but there can be no victory for it until the case for the prosecution of modern criticism has been confronted head on.

. . . . .

Anyone familiar with the irate reviews, letters, and arguments currently being published in the *Times Literary Supplement* (or the *London* and *New York Review of Books*), or who has read the successive laments concerning the diminished status of literary studies that regularly appear in the *Newsletter* of the Modern Language Association of America, will know the context of the current controversy about criticism. There is, on the one hand, a strident over-confidence that makes wildly excessive claims for the autonomy and virtue of modern critical theory, and, on the other hand, a sense of whistling in the dark, of a wholesale collapse of confidence in the validity of any critical theory, ancient or modern. Both in publications, and in private conversations, Shakespearian scholars and critics deplore the fact that the over-production resulting from institutional pressures to publish has made it practically impossible to keep up with more than a fraction of the books and articles that annually roll off the academic assembly-line.[1] Conversely, however, there is also a hitherto unheard of premium being placed on critical 'readings' of all kinds. In a controversial book entitled *Re-Reading English*, and in arguments in favour of redesigning the traditional curricula for schools and universities, there are statements that go so far as to assert that what counts is not what students read, but how well they can read it — you might as well study *King Kong* as *King Lear*, since what matters is not the script involved, but the critical expertise, or the ideological virtues, manifested in your own 'reading' of whatever it is you are reading.[2] So far as readings of

Shakespeare's plays in particular are concerned, this, above all, is the age of the 'new reading' derived from some external 'approach'. There are Marxist readings of Shakespeare, Christian readings of Shakespeare, and Freudian readings of Shakespeare, amongst the host of other readings clamouring for our attention in advertisements, in libraries, and in bookshops.

In its multiplicity and openness, the modern range and variety of approach is all to the good. What — arguably anyway — is doing immeasurable harm to Shakespeare studies is the compartmentalization of theses, books, articles, and seminars in terms of the stock approaches now being systematically and mechanically imposed on Shakespeare's diverse plays, 'as when to a mass of wet clay we give whatever shape we wish it to retain when hardened'. As opposed to openness and multiplicity, the principle of the governing thesis or approach itself tends to determine the arguments and dictate the conclusions arrived at in various books and articles (see Chapters 3 and 4). Thus the 'approach' being advocated often assumes more importance than the works of art ostensibly being approached through it. As Geoffrey Hartman has observed, we are 'made aware of the institutional character of psychoanalysis' in criticism wherein 'Freud becomes scripture as interpreter': 'That the patient — in this case the text — survives is something of a miracle.'[3] In certain instances, critics propounding a Freudian approach to Shakespeare cite only the works of Freud and the works of other psychoanalytic critics, even as critics propounding a 'Christian approach' cite only other critics of the same persuasion, and so on. A major reason why advocates of certain approaches to Shakespeare often tend to disregard even the most obvious arguments against their own interpretative premises and theses may be that they do not know that there are, or do not believe that there could be, any valid arguments against them. It therefore seems worthwhile to stress, even at risk of labouring, the most obvious reasons why so many (if not all?) of the best critics have agreed that there never has been, and never will be, any one sign in which to conquer Shakespeare, and have consistently argued that his works defy (rather than lend themselves to) interpretation in terms of a single theological, psychological, or ideological frame of reference. Conversely, however, there are excellent reasons for arguing that *any* theory or approach may serve as a perfectly legitimate starting-point — the mistake is to think of one's own, or anyone else's theories (however distinguished their proponents and impeccable their intellectual pedigrees), as if they were finish-lines. Or, as Sir Karl Popper has argued, any and all sources of knowledge and insight are welcome, but they are also equally likely to mislead us, and should, therefore, constantly be subject to critical challenge, to revision, to refutation (see Chapter 3).

But why is there no unified field theory that can comprehend all the works of Shakespeare? Why is it impossible to explain his plays in terms of the critical, psychological, theological, or ideological axioms of his own time, or of ours?

In the First Plenary Lecture delivered at the International Shakespeare Association Congress in 1976, Alistair Cooke accurately described Shakespeare as the 'king of the foxes'.[4] Cooke's reference was to the distinction between two kinds of artists that Sir Isaiah Berlin had derived from a line of Archilochus. In his famous essay on Tolstoy, *The Hedgehog and the Fox* (London, 1953), Berlin used Archilochus' distinction between the fox (who 'knows many things'), and the hedgehog (who 'knows one big thing'), to describe two fundamentally different kinds of artists, thinkers, and human beings generally. In his knowledge of so many things, his mastery of so many different tricks, Shakespeare is comparable to the fox. In their knowledge of the 'one big thing', their mastery of the one big trick, certain artists and thinkers, like Dostoevsky, Freud, or Marx, can be compared to the hedgehog. Berlin's distinction was not intended to imply that either form of art or thought is intrinsically superior to the other — just that they represent different forms of thought, art, insight.

Given the nature of their subject, there is, however, no question which category the best critics of Shakespeare belong in: they have always had to learn 'many things' in the course of pursuing the fox from one, into yet another, part of the forest of art.[5] Conversely, hedgehog-like approaches to Shakespeare almost inevitably run into trouble precisely in so far as they treat the many things communicated in and by his works, as if they were, or ought to have been, or could finally be explained in terms of, the one big thing known to, and communicated to us, by someone else — by, say, St Paul or by Freud or by Marx. Marxist criticisms of Shakespeare can serve as a preliminary illustration of these points.

Few people familiar with (for instance) Georg Lukács's discussions of Shakespearian drama would deny that Marxist perspectives on certain plays can be revelatory. Indeed, as Kenneth Muir has demonstrated in his article on '*Timon of Athens* and the Cash-Nexus', Karl Marx himself was a card-carrying Shakespearian. Marx admired

Shakespeare immensely and quoted him repeatedly. Lukács and Marx alike followed the fox.[6] Yet the reverse holds true of the conclusions propounded in Elliot Krieger's *A Marxist Study of Shakespeare's Comedies.* What we have here looks suspiciously like an ideological steamroller in operation:

[In *The Merchant of Venice*] the emphasis on harmony, especially through its association with heavenly hierarchies . . . protects the social position of the ruling class.

[*As You Like It*] articulates an ideological process, whereby the ruling class uses Nature, or its own translation and redefinition of *nature*, to justify its freedom from labour and the subordination of, or struggle against, other social classes.

[In *Twelfth Night*] the ruling class ideology that 'all is fortune', that fortune creates and determines nature, is meant to keep people, especially servants, blind to the opposite proposition: that people create nature . . . as they bring about changes in the social order.[7]

It should be noted that the hierarchical premises that Krieger concludes are most significant in shaping the action of the various comedies he discusses are perhaps most dramatically articulated by Shakespeare himself, in the single sentence and stage direction (see *King Lear*, III. vii. 79) wherein Regan utters the ideologically loaded exclamation, 'Give me thy sword. A peasant stand up thus', even as she takes the sword and stabs Cornwall's servant 'from behind'. And, obviously, Regan's insistence upon upholding the hegemony of the ruling class, and her use of hierarchical premises to justify the subordination of, and struggle against, the lower orders, is here attacked with all the moral force at Shakespeare's command. But, then, so is the rejection, or overthrow, of hierarchical principles whereby daughters should honour their fathers, and subjects should honour their King. The presence of shifting, changing, clashing, and conflicting ideological pressures, and principles, and premises throughout Shakespearian drama makes it very difficult to determine which, if any of them, has won a given battle, to say nothing of the war. For that matter, a Marxist critic with different ideological interests could write a study of Shakespearian comedy — as it were in dialectical opposition to Krieger's — stressing differing contexts in which the author himself most effectively sends up, or puts down, aristocratic assumptions concerning hierarchical distinctions (as he does, gently but generally, in *Love's Labour's Lost*, or in celebrating the 'bourgeois' virtues of *The Merry Wives of Windsor*, and in his portrayal of the caddish Bertram's claims concerning his aristocratic 'honour' in *All's Well That Ends Well*). Yet this counter-study might, in turn, be attacked on the grounds that it failed to give due weight to Shakespeare's affirmation of aristocratic values in, say, the Fifth Act of *The Merchant of Venice*. And so we come full circle. The very existence of so *many* ideological counter-currents would seem to suggest that to ask whether Shakespeare's plays and characters do (or do not) affirm the hierarchical assumptions of the ruling class is comparable to asking whether gentlemen do (or do not) prefer blondes, since the only true answer to either question necessarily has to be: 'Some do; some don't'.[8]

Such are the ways of the fox, that even in *Coriolanus,* a play most explicitly concerned with class-warfare and thus (as Brecht clearly recognized) of particular interest when looked at from a Marxist perspective, the criticisms that Shakespeare directs, in turn, at the Patricians, the Tribunes, and the Plebeians alike make it almost impossible to pin down the author's own ideological stance.[9] Why should this be true? It could be argued that Shakespeare had to hedge his ideological bets in an art made tongue-tied by authority; but it could also be argued that he scored points against, as well as in favour of, the various attacks levelled by one class at another, in order to assure that the complex social, political, and economic questions involved in *Coriolanus* were correctly posed (see Chapter 3). In any case, 'the difficulty is not in grasping the idea' that Shakespeare's plays 'are bound up with certain forms of social development. It lies rather in understanding why they still constitute for us a source of aesthetic enjoyment and in certain respects prevail as the standard and model beyond attainment' – see Marx's conclusions about 'the relation of Greek art, and that of Shakespeare's time, to our own' (in *Grundrisse*) in *Karl Marx, Selected Writings*, ed. David McLellan (Oxford, 1977), pp. 359–60.

In any event, there seems to be no good reason why we should assume that, because a given approach, or ideological perspective, does in fact illuminate one play, it should, therefore, prove equally relevant to all the others.[10] Perhaps largely because of the ever-increasing pressure to publish, what appears to be a purely academic (as opposed to a genuinely critical) premium has been placed on the sheer applicability of various theories and approaches. Thus, the more publications in which a given theory may be propounded, and the more literary works to which it may be applied, the better that theory appears to be. Yet it might, with far more justification, be argued that a theory which is not deemed refutable by anything that might occur in the complete works of Shakespeare, cannot, therefore, be of any particular use in explaining the altogether different events and effects that do occur in individual works. The Shakespearian dialectic operates internally; and with effects that differ from scene to scene, and from play to play. It is the critical dialectic that tends to impose its own acts of uniformity on Shakespeare's various works. Moreover, the odds are very good that, by the time a theory has been applied to every Shakespearian character, or to every play, a theory diametrically opposed to it will already have emerged.

Looked at from an historical perspective, the antithetical nature of successive interpretations of Shakespearian drama would seem to suggest that the dialectical process itself often tends to dictate major changes in critical priorities, assumptions, concerns (see Chapter 4). Discussing *The Structure of Scientific Revolutions*, T. S. Kuhn has noted the ways in which various explanatory paradigms have been stretched to their outer-limits of applicability, finally exhausted, and subsequently replaced by new paradigms.[11] The same holds true for literary criticism generally, and for Shakespearian studies in particular. As Maynard Mack has reminded us,

During a bare half-century we have seen the School of Character Analysis, very much in the ascendant when I went to university, ousted by the School of Imagery and New Criticism, and both of these, during especially the last decade, giving ground steadily to what I will call the School of Performance, since its chief tenet seems to be that Shakespeare's plays are only to be known aright in actual productions. Meantime, ever more visible in the wings, though perhaps not yet quite ready to seize centre-stage, the School of Psychoanalysis, with Tarquin's ravishing strides, comes on apace.[12]

And so a series of previous critical paradigms have been, and are now being, replaced by the various approaches clamouring for priority right now. What's good about the situation nowadays is that no single paradigm or approach wields unchallenged power: Shakespeare's plays are currently open to any number of interpretative perspectives. What's bad about the present situation is the way a single approach may wield tyrannical power over its own adherents in books and articles that slavishly apply whatever theory currently seems to be most fashionable to whatever plays it has not previously been applied. As I shall argue later on, it might be far more fruitful to consider the reasons why a theory that does illuminate certain works, does *not* apply to others.

Thus our various approaches might prove genuinely liberating — as incentives to critical thought rather than substitutes for it.

For the truth is that, given the richness of the plays themselves, nothing could be easier than to find in them some lines, characters, or situations that might appear to confirm practically any theory about them that any one of us might, conceivably, wish to posit — that is, so long as we ignore any contradictory evidence, or alternative explanations for the same features of the work being discussed (see Chapter 3). Thus, although one certainly can see the point of Frank Kermode's eloquent arguments that the survival of a masterpiece like *King Lear* may finally depend on its malleability, its inclusiveness, its capacity to accommodate successive, and diametrically opposite, interpretations,[13] it could, conversely, be argued that the inclusiveness of Shakespeare's plays works both ways, and that the status and survival of *King Lear* as an independent and primary source of wisdom and insight into the ways of our world (as opposed to an eminently pliable subject for successive critical commentaries on and theatrical adaptations of it) may well depend on its exceptions, its resistance, its ability to challenge and ultimately refute, and thus outlive, by defying and denying, *all* the one-sided interpretations that have been, and may yet be, imposed upon it. To see great literature as a primary source of wisdom may seem critically outmoded. Yet that is the way the Renaissance thought about the literature of classical antiquity. For that matter, Freud and Marx both saw, and cited, literature as a major source of wisdom in the same way that we now see, and cite, the works of Freud and Marx. So why can't we use literature in the same way they did? The neo-medieval, neo-scholastic notion that literary works serve, primarily, as subjects for endless commentaries and allegorical interpretations (and therefore all texts are but pre-texts for criticism) is not one whit more original. And when all is said and done, there could be more truths discovered (not devised) in Shakespeare's fictions than in any, or all, of our critical fictions about them. Even if not, we could surely learn just as much — and possibly a lot more — about his (and about our own) fictions by using Shakespeare's plays to challenge currently fashionable, as well as historically fashionable, theories about life and art, than we will ever learn by using them simply to confirm whatever theories we already happen to hold.

It is often said that criticism of reigning critical axioms and approaches threatens to put us out of business; yet — as the history of Shakespeare criticism can serve to demonstrate — the fact is that the reverse holds true: it is what keeps critics in business. In criticism, as in physics, there can be no action without reaction, and (as I hope both recent and historical examples of the processes of critical action and reaction will demonstrate) in criticism, as in science, 'negative feedback' is what may finally prove of most positive use in assuring that the advancement of learning will continue.

In criticism, as in science, to present the extant evidence against a given theory may be a positive action. In certain instances, only one obvious contradiction to a given rule, or theory, can serve to challenge any number of confirmations of it, even as the generalization, 'All swans are white', would – no matter how many white swans had been sighted – be called into question by the sighting of a single black swan. Yet the sighting of that one black swan would serve to advance our knowledge of the truth if it is in fact the case that 'Not all swans are white' (an observation that would open up scientific speculation by raising the question, 'Why not?'). In cases of this kind, *Major est vis instantiae negativae.* 'To conclude, upon an enumeration of particulars, without instance contradictory, is no conclusion, but a conjecture.' So wrote Bacon.[14] And (although, in Chapter 3, I have paraphrased Karl Popper in order to discuss the method's critical ramifications) the method of confronting a given theory or generalization with various instances, or with a single 'instance contradictory', is the one most frequently employed by Shakespeare himself, who is forever citing the one black swan,[15] even as he characteristically tends to confront the best possible case in favour of someone or something with the strongest (not the weakest) arguments that could possibly be levelled against it – and vice versa. The major question posed by many recent critical and directorial interpretations of his plays, as well as by the most ancient of all critical arguments about dramatic mimesis and morality, is whether Shakespeare's is, in fact, the kind of art we really want, or whether we believe it to be critically desirable (or possible) to make a hedgehog type of artist from our fox. As we shall see in the next several chapters, there is no way to evade the following Platonic questions: What kind of dramatic reality, or morality, do *we* finally deem to be of most importance? Are the messy, complicated, and sometimes contradictory political, sexual, emotional, social, artistic, and moral realities that Shakespearian drama actually reflects, to be preferred to – or, preferably reinterpreted and reread in accordance with – the social, political, sexual, or religious orthodoxies that critics and directors have concluded that they, ideally, *ought* to reflect?

Notes

1. On the problem of quantity, John Gross wrote in a prophetic strain in *The Rise and Fall of the Man of Letters* (London, 1969), p. 294:

> To stick to the example of Pope: a generation or so ago very little of real note had been added to what the eighteenth-century critics had to say. Today there are, I suppose, at least half-a-dozen full-length critical studies which are worth reading, while a leading American scholar has edited an anthology entitled *44 Essential Articles on Pope.* None of this represents wasted labour. But what are we all going to do when there are forty-four essential *books*?

Gross, of course, was writing in what now seems an age before the deluge. Forty-six critical books devoted, exclusively, to Shakespeare were received for review by *Shakespeare Survey* between late 1979 and early 1982, and to keep up with the articles devoted to him – to say nothing of his contemporaries – is a sisyphean task in itself. On these and other related issues, see Helen Gardner, *In Defence of the Imagination* (Oxford, 1982), p. 157: 'One serious result of this over-production is that it has become impossible to keep up with "the literature of the subject" and many who give up trying to do so in despair may miss work that is of real value and importance.'

2. See *Re-Reading English,* ed. Peter Widdowson (London, 1982), and the letters to the editor following Tom Paulin's critical review of it, 'Faculty at War', in the *London Review of Books,* 17–30 June 1982, p. 14. Here is Paulin's account of the critical issues involved:

> The contributors are collectively of the opinion that English literature is a dying subject and they argue that it can be revived by adopting a 'socialist pedagogy' and introducing into the syllabus 'other forms of writing and cultural production than the canon of Literature', ... it is now time to challenge various 'hierarchical' and 'élitist' conceptions of literature and to demolish the bourgeois ideology which has been 'naturalised' as literary value. It is essential, they argue, to demystify this myth of literary value 'as a universal and immanent category'. They wish to develop 'a politics of reading' and to redefine the term 'text' in order to admit newspaper reports, songs and even mass demonstrations as subjects for tutorial discussion. Texts no longer have to be books: indeed, 'it may be more democratic to study *Coronation Street* than *Middlemarch.*'

However one looks at them, it seems undeniably true that the issues involved in these arguments (*pro* as well as *con*) are of paramount critical, pedagogical, and social importance. I have had my say on some of these issues in a paper, 'From *King Lear* to *King Kong* and Back', delivered at the Oberlin College symposium on 'High Art and Popular Genres' in April, 1984.

3. See Geoffrey Hartman's introduction to *Psychoanalysis and the Question of the Text, Selected Papers from the English Institute* (1976–7), pp. xii, xv. See also Hartman's discussion of the differing problems faced by modern critics in *Criticism in the Wilderness* (New Haven, 1980).

4. See Alistair Cooke, 'Shakespeare in America', in *Shakespeare: Pattern of Excelling Nature,* ed. David Bevington and J. L. Halio (Newark and London, 1978), pp. 17–25.

5. For arguments that Dr Johnson derived some of his best critical insights from Shakespeare himself, see James Black, 'Johnson, Shakespeare, and the Dyer's Hand', in *Pattern of Excelling Nature,* pp. 152–63.

6. See Georg Lukác's discussions of Shakespeare in *The Historical Novel*

(Harmondsworth, 1969), and Kenneth Muir, '*Timon of Athens* and the Cash-Nexus', in *The Singularity of Shakespeare and Other Essays* (Liverpool, 1977), pp. 56-75.

7. See Elliot Krieger, *A Marxist Study of Shakespeare's Comedies* (London, 1979), pp. 10, 96, 130. Krieger makes some interesting points about *The Merchant of Venice*, but when he makes virtually identical points about Shakespeare's other comedies, he appears to be writing criticism by formula. The reigning principle of the thesis, or the book-length critical study propounding – and invariably confirming – a single theory about 'Shakespeare and X' virtually forces critics to make the message to be derived from Shakespeare's various works sound utterly predictable. See Norman Rabkin's criticisms of the academic premium placed on reductiveness (by the principle of the thesis itself) in *Shakespeare and the Problem of Meaning* (Chicago and London, 1981), pp. 19-25.

8. See Ian Donaldson, *The World Upside-Down* (Oxford, 1970), for a fascinating discussion of the various ways in which dramatic examples of social and moral inversion and levelling occur throughout English comedy from Jonson to Fielding. And see also Cicely Havely's rich discussion of 'Society in Lear's Kingdom', *Proteus* 1 (1978), 49-62.

9. See Jan Kott, '*Coriolanus* or Shakespearian Contradictions', in *Shakespeare our Contemporary* (London, 1967), pp. 141-2. Brecht was preparing for the production of an adapted version of *Coriolanus*: 'His reading of the play was antitraditional and didactic. He saw in it a drama of the people betrayed by their fascist leader.' 'As written by Shakespeare, [*Coriolanus*] could not wholly satisfy either aristocrats, or republicans . . . The play annoyed those who believed in the masses, and those who despised them.'

10. The major point that Nicholas Grene makes with reference to comedies by Shakespeare, Jonson, and Molière, would seem valid with reference to Shakespearian drama generally. As Grene observes, there are various ways through which playwrights establish differing dramatic 'contracts' whereby members of the audience agree, for the duration of a play, to accept a given frame of reference. These contracts are neither fixed, nor universal; rather they are provisional, temporary agreements to share certain assumptions which might well not be shared at another time. Thus, one comedy may celebrate, and one tragedy may extol, what another comedy ridicules, and another tragedy deplores. See Grene's *Shakespeare, Jonson, Molière: The Comic Contract* (London, 1980).

11. See T. S. Kuhn, *The Structure of Scientific Revolutions* (Chicago, 1962); and his article on 'The Logic of Discovery or Psychology of Research?' as well as his 'Reflections on my Critics', in *Criticism and the Growth of Knowledge*, ed. Imre Lakatos and Alan Musgrave (Cambridge, 1977), pp. 1-23, 231-78.

12. See Maynard Mack, *Rescuing Shakespeare* (Oxford, 1979), p. 3.

13. See Frank Kermode's essays on 'The Patience of Shakespeare' and the 'Survival of the Classic', in *Renaissance Essays: Shakespeare, Spenser, Donne* (London, 1973).

14. On these points, see Anthony Quinton, *Francis Bacon* (Oxford, 1980), pp. 51, 56: 'In establishing any true axiom, the negative instance is the more powerful'. 'G. H. von Wright, the most thorough and scrupulous of contemporary students of induction says about this: "Laws of nature are not verifiable . . . but they are falsifiable . . . It is the immortal merit of Bacon to have fully appreciated the importance of this asymmetry in the logical structure of laws".'

15. See (for instance) *King Lear*, IV. vi, 207-9: 'Thou hast one daughter/Who redeems nature from the general curse/Which twain have brought her to'.

Chapter 1

The Questions of Mimesis and Morality:
Some 'Footnotes to Plato'

On Mimesis

'What I mean is this. If you look at a bed, or anything else, sideways or endways or from some other angle, does it make any difference to the bed? Isn't it merely that it *looks* different, without *being* different? . . .'

'Yes, it's the same bed but it looks different.'

'Then consider — when the painter makes his representation, does he do so by reference to the object as it actually is or to its superficial appearance? Is his representation one of an apparition or of the truth?'

'Of an apparition.'

Plato, *The Republic*

I have learned that it is not possible to paint any definite object, say, a rose, so that I, or any other intelligent critic, shall not be able to decide . . . at what period it was painted, or, more or less, at what place on the earth. The artist has meant to create either a picture of a rose in the abstract, or the portrait of a particular rose; it is never in the least his intention to give us a Chinese, Persian, or Dutch, or . . . a pure Empire rose. If I told him that this was what he had done, he . . . might be angry with me. He would say: 'I have painted a rose.' Still he cannot help it. I am thus so far superior to the artist that I can mete him with a measure of which he himself knows nothing. At the same time I could not paint, and hardly see or conceive, a rose myself. I might imitate any of their creations. I might say: 'I will paint a rose in the Chinese or Dutch or in the rococo manner.' But I should never have the courage to paint a rose as it looks. For how does a rose look?

Isak Dinesen, 'The Poet'

On Morality

We are therefore quite right to refuse to admit [the poet] to a properly run state, because he wakens and encourages and strengthens the lower elements in the mind to the detriment of reason, which is like giving power and political control to the worst elements in a state and ruining the best elements. The dramatic poet produces a similarly bad state of affairs in the mind of the individual, by encouraging the unreasoning part of it, . . . and by creating images far removed from the truth.

Plato, *The Republic*

I was constantly troubled about philosophic questions. I would say to my fellow-students at the Art School, 'Poetry and sculpture exist to keep our passions alive'; and somebody would say, 'We would be much better without our passions.'

W. B. Yeats, *Autobiography*

In his pincer-like attack on poetry and drama in terms of (a) their 'low degree of truth', and (b) for arousing passions at odds with moral and rational judgement, and (c) for having a bad effect on education and society in general, Plato unlocked the Pandora's box from which mutually contradictory arguments have swarmed into and around, and back and forth, and between, successive critical discussions of imaginative literature throughout the Western world, and down through the centuries ever since. Even as Aristotle's influence has pervaded subsequent discussions of dramatic structure, genre, and cathartic effect, the following questions have shadowed critical discussions of poetic and dramatic mimesis and morality ever since Plato raised them in *The Republic*:

How can you justify the use of poetry for educational purposes *if* it evokes responses at odds with morality and reason, and is untrue? Ought we to approve of fictional characters whom we should be ashamed to resemble? Does poetry encourage an undue tolerance of human vice, error and folly? May not the more glamorous sinners portrayed on the stage inspire us to emulate their bad behaviour? And when it depicts sex, anger, and grief, does not poetry 'water passions which ought to be left to wither, and make them control us when we ought, in the interest of our greater welfare, to control them'? Should poets be allowed to imply that the gods are sometimes unjust to men? For that matter, should we not 'forbid them to suggest that unjust men are sometimes happy and prosperous, and just men sometimes wretched', and indeed require their poems and plays to have 'the opposite moral'?

'We shall', Plato conceded, 'be glad', if their defenders can, conclusively, prove that drama and poetry 'not only give pleasure', but also 'bring lasting benefit to human life and human society'. But 'in the absence of such proof . . . Our theme shall be that such poetry has no serious value or claim to truth, and we shall warn its hearers to fear its effects on the constitution of their inner selves.'[1] These same Platonic themes, and the identical Platonic warnings, have resounded in critical discussions of drama and poetry from the time when Shakespeare wrote his plays to ours.

To begin at the beginning of Elizabethan literary criticism, the battle-lines of countless subsequent controversies were drawn when Sir Philip Sidney defended imaginative literature against the various charges levelled against it in Stephen Gosson's *The School of Abuse.* 'Now then go we', wrote Sidney, 'to the most important imputations laid to the poor poets':

For aught I can yet learn, they are these. First, that there being many other more fruitful knowledges, a man might better spend his time in them than in [poetry]. Secondly, that it is the mother of lies. Thirdly, that it is the nurse of abuse, infecting us with many pestilent desires, with a siren's sweetness drawing the mind to the serpent's tale of sinful fancy, . . . And lastly, and chiefly, they cry out with an open mouth, as if they outshot Robin Hood, that Plato banished them out of his Commonwealth.[2]

Although Sidney presented his defence of poetry with great eloquence, elegance, and wit, the 'most important imputations' he had to contend with have — so far as I know — never been satisfactorily refuted. For behind what, at first glance, might appear to be Gosson's facile and Philistine objections to poetry, loomed the Goliath of Western European philosophy. The case for the prosecution of poetry that Sidney confronted had been lifted, virtually intact, from Books 3 and 10 of *The Republic,* and ultimately rested on the most formidable series of arguments ever directed against art.[3] To appreciate the complexity of the challenge Sidney faced, try to defend the teaching of, say, *Antony and Cleopatra* against the Platonic charge that it might evoke passions and sympathies quite at odds with rational judgement (or orthodox morality), and see if you can, *simultaneously,* refute the Platonic contentions that, since dramatic representations are shadows, not realities (*The Republic,* X. 561), the watching, reading, or studying of them is a waste of time better spent acquiring more 'fruitful knowledges'. How can one *prove* that some 'squeaking Cleopatra' boying greatness 'in th' posture of a whore' (*Antony and Cleopatra,* V. ii. 219-20) does not 'only give pleasure', but also brings 'lasting benefit' to society?[4]

Part i
The Question of Representation in Shakespearian Drama and Criticism: How Does a Play Look?

In the lines just quoted from *Antony and Cleopatra,* as elsewhere, Shakespeare seems to have delighted in treating the premiss that poetical fictions are falsehoods in a paradoxical, ironical way.

> I never may believe
> These antique fables, nor these fairy toys.
> . . . .
> The best in this kind are but shadows;
>
> (*A Midsummer-Night's Dream,* V. i. 2–3, 210)

So says Theseus. But are we supposed to believe, or to believe in, Theseus? He is, himself, a character resurrected from an antique fable, who, in the context of Shakespeare's own 'fairy toy', has no more – albeit no less – reality than Oberon, King of Shadows. A comparable conundrum occurs in *Timon of Athens* (I. i. 217-24). 'How now, poet!', says Apemantus, the philosopher,

Poet. How now, philosopher!
Apemantus. Thou liest.
Poet. Art not one?
Apemantus. Yes.
Poet. Then I lie not.
Apemantus. Art not a poet?
Poet. Yes.
Apemantus. Then thou liest.

In earnest and in jest, in his comedies and tragedies alike, Shakespeare creates what amount to poetic equivalents of the classical 'Paradox of the Liar' (Epimenides, the Cretan, says: 'All Cretans always lie'). If a poet's own fictions contain the assertions that poetic representations are baseless fabrications comparable to the frenzies of lunatics or lovers, that poets are liars, etc., then are those assertions to be interpreted as true or false?

'I do not know what "poetical" is', says Audrey, 'Is it honest in deed and word? Is it a true thing?'

Touchstone. No, truly; for the truest poetry is the most feigning, and lovers are given to poetry; and what they swear in poetry may be said as lovers they do feign.
Audrey. Do you wish, then, that the gods had made me poetical?

Touchstone. I do, truly, for thou swear'st to me thou art honest; now, if thou wert a poet, I might have some hope thou didst feign.

(*As You Like It*, III. iii. 16-22)

Given Touchstone's premiss that the 'truest poetry is the most feigning', then if poets claim to be honestly telling the truth, we can assume that they are lying; but — by exactly the same token — if a true poet asserts that 'the truest poetry is the most feigning', can we not assume that this statement is false? Moreover, there are certain occasions when (like lovers' vows) poetic fictions seem to be so true that we believe them, although we *know* they are feigned. In art, as in life, the belief — or the willing suspension of disbelief — in something, may be a reality, although what is believed in may be false: 'When my love swears that she is made of truth,/I do believe her, though I know she lies' (Sonnet 138). *Query*: Is this a poetical fiction, or a psychological fact?[5] In any case, the fact that poetical fictions may be believed to be true, and may elicit real responses, was what Plato found so objectionable about them. Moreover, essentially the same objections could be, and have been, made with reference to critical fictions *about* poetical fictions: may they not engender a comparably erroneous belief — or a willing suspension of disbelief — in theories that are false? May they not be so far removed from, that they distort or falsify the very realities they claim to represent? Once raised, the questions Plato posed with reference to poetic and dramatic mimesis lead straight to a sequence of cognate questions concerning criticism's claims to educational value and to truth. Thus, the cases for the defence and the prosecution of poetry are inextricably linked to the cases for the defence and the prosecution of criticism.

For instance: it is almost impossible to ask the question, *what, if any, truths and realities do, or should, the fictions of Shakespearian drama reflect?* without summoning forth a cohort of related questions in an endless, exponential succession:

Do Shakespeare's plays, by avowed purpose, and in effect, 'hold the mirror up' to nature itself? If so, what is the nature of the nature that *Hamlet* holds the mirror up to? And does it, or does it not, most dramatically differ from the 'nature' that Shakespeare has reflected, or refracted, in *As You Like It*, or *King Lear*? Or does his poetry 'better nature', showing 'artificial strife' that lives in his writings 'livelier than life' (*Timon of Athens* I. i. 40-1)? Or are the best and the worst of Shakespeare's comedies and tragedies, 'but shadows' of the poet's private fancies and frenzies? Or is their primary reference to other literature ('The story is extant, and written in very choice Italian')? Or are they the abstract and brief chronicles of reigning assumptions concerning the ways of the world that held sway back in Shakespeare's day, but have long since been deposed? If so, are his plays most accurately seen as a series of dramatic illusions about other illusions, as poetical lies about life?

These questions, in turn, give rise to cognate questions concerning critical interpretations of Shakespeare's works. Do they, in purpose and effect, point to the truth about a play as it really is? Or are they most accurately seen, at their best, as a fascinating series of critical illusions about Shakespeare's dramatic illusions, or, at their worst, as an interminable sequence of commentaries primarily addressed to other critical commentaries, and thus, quite literally, self-consuming artefacts, in that they are of no significance to anyone except another critic?[6]

Can critical interpretations themselves reflect anything except the intellectual fashions or presuppositions or preoccupations of the critic's own age? Have critics who would swear that they had said something profoundly true about Shakespeare's *Hamlet*, actually given us their own Romantic, or late-Victorian, or Modernist, or Post-Structuralist pseudo-Hamlets which will be seen, and probably sneered at, as such, by successive generations of commentators who will, in turn, rewrite, misread, or deconstruct *Hamlet* to suit themselves and their own age? If this is the case, then shouldn't we frankly admit that critical interpretations are the products of our personal, or historically determined fancies (or frenzies), and that we ourselves read, or write, critical essays about *Hamlet* primarily to judge the critic's ingenuity, or to display our own — as distinct from, and sometimes opposed to, Shakespeare's own — imaginative vision, or rhetorical skill, or technical virtuosity? On the other hand, doesn't this admission leave criticism itself wide open to attack from some of the heaviest artillery that Plato directed against poetry — that is, on the grounds that critics at best produce only 'a superficial likeness of any subject they treat, including human excellence' (X. 429) and that their work 'has no serious value or claim to truth', and is, therefore, of no 'lasting benefit to human life [or] human society' (X. 438-9).

The answers we give to the questions of literary and critical mimesis have obvious professional consequences for poets, students, critics, and teachers alike. For instance: if literary works are nothing but fictions about fictions, or self-reflexive displays of the author's ingenuity — and ditto for critical interpretations of them — then it is hard to see, and far harder to explain to a sceptical outsider (e.g. a budget-conscious administrator, a heavily-burdened taxpayer — or an admirer of Plato's *Republic*), just exactly why any of us should be paid for so pointlessly — albeit harmlessly — diverting ourselves by endlessly showing-off to, and/ or misreading, each other. Viewed with a cynical eye, such premisses place us in a position dangerously analogous to that of someone who demands payment and prestige for the artful reading and writing of horoscopes, while simultaneously insisting that there is no truth in the tenets of astrology itself (there may well be a flaw in this analogy, but it's hard to pin down what it is).

I must, and do, most sincerely apologize for having oversimplified, to the point of parodying, some very sophisticated arguments; but it seemed necessary to do so in order to stress the fact that the philosophically overwhelming question, 'What, if any, reality is revealed or reflected in art?' cannot finally be divorced from the professionally loaded question, 'What, if any, reality is revealed or reflected in literary criticism?' If there is little, if anything, of enduring validity to be derived from them, then why on earth should we (or our students) shun delights and live laborious days in order to produce, or keep up with, an ever-increasing volume of commentary on Shakespeare's fictions? For that matter, even as works of art have been accused of distorting, or falsifying, or serving as feeble substitutions for life, literary criticism has been accused of distorting, falsifying, and serving as a dubious (albeit pretentious) substitute for art.

For instance, in his justifiably famous — and increasingly pertinent — essay entitled 'The Age of Criticism', the poet and novelist, Randall Jarrell, observed that although the best twentieth-century criticism 'is as good as anyone could wish', a huge body of it amounts to an 'astonishingly graceless, joyless, humourless, long-winded, niggling, blinkered, methodical, self-important, cliché-ridden, prestige-obsessed, almost-autonomous criticism' that gives a very odd impression of the critic's response to the subject concerned — 'one that might be given this exaggerated emblematic form: "Good Lord, you don't think I *like* to read, do you? Reading is a serious business, not something you fool around with in your spare time."' And whereas real audiences or readers are 'almost as wild a species as writers', some critics are 'so domesticated as to seem institutions — as they stand there between reader and writer, so different from either, they remind one of the Wall standing between Pyramus and Thisbe'.[7]

Anyone familiar with Richard Levin's work — or who has attempted to read through the immense volume of commentaries published in any given year – must needs agree that what Jarrell had to say about criticism in general is all too true of all too many critical books and essays on Shakespearian drama (and could well prove true of this one). To put Jarrell's case about writers and audiences in psychological terms, although Shakespeare's art generally tends to 'uncondition' the audience's responses to characters and conflicts of altogether different kinds, much recent criticism tends to 'condition' or 're-condition' them by erecting judgemental, theoretical, theological, ideological, or psychological 'walls' between the admirers of Shakespeare's characters, and the objects of their admiration. Over the past several decades, for instance, we have been repeatedly informed that Shakespeare's heroes and heroines ought to be critically judged in terms of severely moralistic frames of reference, like these:

If Cleopatra 'makes hungry,/Where most she satisfies', she inverts the promise of the Beatitudes to fill those who hunger after righteousness (*Matthew*, 5:6) . . . [while] Antony may also be judged by the standard of divine love, [in that] his passion for Cleopatra falls short of Christian *caritas*, the movement of the soul towards God.

Juliet reveals in unmistakable terms that her love for Romeo is rooted in passion. . . . She hungers . . . violently for Romeo's body (and in the stridency of her imagination comes very close to panting like an animal). . . . The ugliness which to an Elizabethan audience would have been implicit in the rawness of her sexual hunger is the ugliness which arises from the perversion of her natural capacity to love.

[Desdemona is guilty of] self-righteousness . . . moral hypocrisy . . . [and a] . . . proud denial of the body's claims. . . . [She is] potentially, if not actually, unfaithful to Othello. . . . She cannot face her own feminine frailty . . . [and] shrinks from the reality of the whore within her.

Brutus is a dramatic illustration of the hollowness, presumption, and moral sickness inherent in the secular concept of virtue-reason's sufficiency. . . . [His mind is] deranged . . . demented. . . . [His] 'constancy' . . . is clearly evil and results in spiritual death. . . . Brutus commits unmitigated acts of savagery as a result of his having broken all ties with humanity.

Sadly enough, most spectators have . . . taken at face value . . . [the] play's tragic sentimentality. . . . They fail to see that as a hero Romeo lies midway between the surrealist horror of the homicidal Richard III, and the bathos of Pyramus. . . . Like Richard, also, Romeo is a catalyst of disaster, and something close to a mass murderer.

[Hamlet] is a soul lost in damnable error . . . a serpent-like scourge . . . a profane fool. . . . At the play's ending . . . he becomes himself the minister, rather, of a poisoned chalice, and in that sense a fellow celebrant with Claudius in a Black Mass.

Pericles is not an impeccable man; Cymbeline is not abused by his wicked queen; Posthumus and Imogen are not star-crossed lovers; . . . Hermione and Polixenes are not more sinned against than sinning; Perdita and Florizel, Miranda and Ferdinand are not idyllic youth in all its reinvigorating springtime freshness . . . although they all wear this outward mask and try to convince themselves and us of its putative sincerity.[8]

To anyone familiar with Shakespearian drama, but not with twentieth-century criticism of that drama, the above arguments (all of them appeared in different books and articles published since 1965) might well appear to have come from a single, wildly eccentric thesis arguing that, however attractive they might appear to be, we should not extend any admiration or sympathy to any of Shakespeare's heroes or heroines. Conversely, one might well wonder why so many critics, writing in the comparatively permissive nineteen-sixties, would want to sound so much more self-righteous, sanctimonious, censorious, and moralistic than their Romantic, Victorian, and post-Victorian precursors.

The reason is that much mid-twentieth-century criticism was written in dialectical opposition to A. C. Bradley's conclusions concerning Shakespearian tragedy in particular — and to Romantic criticism of Elizabethan drama in general. Where Romantic critics had tended to minimize, rationalize, or explain away the very thing that makes Shakespeare's heroes tragic, and not pathetic — that is, 'the evil in them'[9] — twentieth-century critics insisted that if Shakespeare's heroes, heroines, or victims showed the slightest sign of error or folly, they should not be pitied or admired, but morally castigated and critically put in their place. And ditto for the heroes, heroines, and victims of Shakespearian comedy and romance. By the same token, where Romantic critics had lauded the passionate rebels and sinners of Elizabethan drama, twentieth-century critics condemned them, and proclaimed as morally orthodox the identical plays that had previously been found radically heterodox. Therefore, no matter who your favourite Elizabethan playwright may be, and no matter what kinds of plays he may have written, you need only glance through the scholarly books and articles published in the nineteen-forties, fifties, and sixties, to find at least one discussion of him that sounds very much like this:

Earlier critics have erroneously described X as if he were an Elizabethan Byron, who launched a daring attack on orthodox morality: 'Glorifying and identifying with characters who dare everything to the limits of imagination, X describes his passionate sinners as if he loved them'. This is sentimental nonsense. When they are analysed in terms of their historical context, it is clear that a basic morality-play structure underlies X's plays, and that his 'passionate sinners' are unequivocally condemned. Any *thinking* Elizabethan would have realized that instead of 'throwing down the gauntlet' to the established social, political, and moral order, X dramatically upholds the orthodoxies of his age.

Here are some examples of the critical formula parodied above. Tourneur's plays, writes L. G. Salingar (*The Revenger's Tragedy* was then attributed to Tourneur), have too often been described as if Tourneur had written 'Romantic poetry of the decadence'. Quite the contrary, Salingar insists: 'The dramatic influence' working in harmony with Tourneur's 'narrowly traditionalist outlook' is that of 'the Moralities'. Marlowe, writes W. L. Godshalk, 'was not creating protagonists with whom he expected us to identify', he was trying 'to force his audience to perceive the evils resulting from human pride'. Godshalk therefore takes to task those critics 'for whom the playwright is a kind of pre-Romantic, perhaps an Elizabethan Keats'. Hazlitt, says Mark Stavig, was wrong to conclude that Ford 'delighted in melodramatic plots, licentious scenes, and revolt against the established moral order'; Ford's true intention obviously was to 'add melodramatic and satiric elements to his basically morality-play structure'. And although Willard Farnham, a pioneer in the study of the medieval influence on Elizabethan drama, described *Tamburlaine* as 'a medieval tragedy reversed, a rebellious violation of all that *De Casibus* tragedy had set out to convey', Roy W. Battenhouse concludes that we can say, 'with some assurance', that the 'morality element' in the Tamburlaine story was what interested 'thinking men of Marlowe's day'.[10]

Here we have different twentieth-century scholars, writing about altogether different plays, according to formulas which guarantee their arrival at the identical conclusions that (a) Shakespearian Character X is far more to be censured than pitied or admired; and (b) that the works of Elizabethan Playwright X were in no way at odds with 'the established moral order'. Both formulas seem, primarily, designed to preclude any 'Romantic' sympathy and admiration for the hero and, simultaneously, seem eerily devised to defend the whole body of Elizabethan drama against the Platonic charges that it might arouse passions and sympathies at odds with moral judgement. It is, as it were,

in opposition to the Platonic contention that poets and playwrights
ought *not* to portray their heroes in ways contradictory to ideal
morality, that a chorus of modern commentators has insisted that the
ultimate reality reflected by Elizabethan drama *is* the ideal morality to
which its heroes and heroines woefully fail to conform, and by which
they should be critically judged. Here, for instance, are Plato's conclusions about the original Theseus:

> We must therefore neither believe nor allow the story of the dreadful
> rapes attempted by Theseus, son of Poseidon ... or any of the other
> lies now told about the terrible and wicked things which other sons of
> gods and heroes are said to have dared to do. We must compel our poets
> to say either that they never did these things or that they are not the
> sons of gods; we cannot allow them to assert both. And they must not
> try to persuade our young men that ... heroes are no better than
> ordinary mortals.
>
> (*The Republic*, III. 147–8)

And here are a modern critic's conclusions about Shakespeare's Theseus
(see Levin, *New Readings vs. Old Plays*, p. 80):

> [In *A Midsummer-Night's Dream*] the dramatist is deliberately pointing
> up [Theseus's] perfidy and fraud.... If his first words suggest his
> reputation for unfaithfulness and unnatural patterns of affection, his
> later behavior in the opening scene is designed to add to that image of
> viciousness.... [He] is tyrannically unmerciful ... [and] neglect[s]
> his duties as a ruler.... The final action of the play, the fairy blessing
> ... [is] a ghastly reminder of the fate of the issue of [Theseus's] bride
> bed.... This scene would have been potentially the most ironic one
> within the drama.

Looked at with reference to *A Midsummer-Night's Dream*, these assertions might seem manifestly absurd. Yet looked at as a line of
defence against Platonic attacks on the drama, to insist that the primary
response that Shakespeare — or any other playwright — intended us to
adopt towards his heroes is a judgemental one, and so prove his plays to
be morally didactic, is to do that playwright a great service. It is, at one
stroke of the pen, to remove him from the Devil's party, and place him
squarely on the side of the angels in his own morality-play.

Conversely, in a series of manifestos profoundly opposed to the
Platonic contention that poetry ought not to (as well as modern contentions that plays by Shakespeare and his contemporaries do not)
arouse any undue sympathy or admiration for sinners, Shelley, Blake,
Hazlitt, and other Romantic writers argued that it was a good thing

that the greatest poets, like Shakespeare and Milton, had given their very devils their due. Defending poetic passion and energy as *necessarily* opposed to abstract rationality throughout his *Marriage of Heaven and Hell*, Blake concluded that 'the reason Milton wrote in fetters when he wrote of Angels & God, and at liberty when of Devils & Hell, is because he was a true Poet and of the Devil's party without knowing it.' In his own 'Defence of Poetry', as well as his essay 'On the Devil, and Devils', Shelley concluded that the excellence of poetry consists in its 'awakening the sympathy of men':

The great secret of morals is love: or a going out of our own nature. . . . A man, to be greatly good, must imagine intensely and comprehensively: he must put himself in the place of another and of many others; the pains and pleasures of his species must be his own.[11]

Thus Shelley argues that it is a morally good thing that poetry arouses the responses Plato said it ought not to arouse, and praises poets for doing what Plato banished them from the Republic for doing. Romantic criticism thus provides us with one kind of answer to Plato's assertion that poetry has a 'terrible power' to corrupt us (X. 436). Scholarly arguments that the Elizabethan drama upholds orthodoxy, that its characters serve, primarily, as noxious examples of how not to behave, represent an *altogether* different way to answer Plato's charges. The same arguments, of course, constituted the standard case for the defence that was posited against Platonic attack after Platonic attack on the drama from the time of Sidney on through the seventeenth and into the eighteenth century.

Modern commentators on Elizabethan drama could, therefore, claim historical support for their own arguments by citing the neo-classical (as distinct from and opposed to the 'Romantic') defence of the drama, whereby its comic and tragic characters alike serve as minatory examples of the vices and follies which the audience, having witnessed their ridiculous or horrific consequences, will henceforth deplore and eschew in real life (see below, pp. 97-9). To Plato's rhetorical question, 'Can we approve of . . . impertinences of the rank and file against those in authority, in prose or verse?' (III. 145), these critics insist that poets ought to, and do, impose severe judgements and punishments on characters who rebel against established authority. Plato also claims that 'poets and story-tellers are in error in matters of the greatest human importance': 'They have said that unjust men are often happy, and just men wretched. . . . We must forbid them to say this sort of thing, and require their poems and stories to have quite the opposite moral' (III. 148-9). The orthodox defence of poets and story-tellers claims that they *do* provide us with the opposite moral. Therefore, tragic and comic heroes and heroines, victims and villains alike are alleged to have been dramatically pilloried for their passionate or foolish misdeeds.

Yet the orthodox — as opposed to the Romantic — case for the defence tends to beg, rather than answer, certain major questions raised by Plato's most repressive assertions. Might not rebellions against authority (on the stage, as in life) sometimes be morally justified? Are poets 'in error' when they say that unjust men are sometimes happy and just men wretched? Or are they simply telling the truth? — 'The good ended happily and the bad unhappily', observed Wilde's Miss Prism: 'That is what fiction means.' So far as dramatic protests against temporal injustice (as opposed to dramatic affirmations of poetic or 'providential' justice) are concerned, the historical truth would seem to be that, as Shakespeare's plays frequently — and rightly — remind us, 'Some innocents scape not the thunderbolt', 'Some rise by sin, and some by virtue fall', and 'to do good' is, in this world, 'sometime/ Accounted dangerous folly'. If this be error, when looked at in terms of what, ideally, ought to be true, it seems truth itself when viewed in the light of human experience. Yet the very fact that certain dramatic representations would seem to be irrefutably true to the way things actually are, renders them eternally vulnerable to attack on the grounds that they are, therefore, untrue to what, ideally or morally, ought to be true: 'The Good and the Bad perishing promiscuously in the best of Shakespear's Tragedies', wrote John Dennis, 'there can be either none or very weak Instruction in them: For such promiscuous Events call the Government of Providence into Question, and by Scepticks and Libertines are resolv'd into Chance.'[12] Even Dr Johnson, who, throughout his *Preface to Shakespeare*, brilliantly countered other neo-classical criticisms of Shakespearian drama on the basis of its 'just representations of general nature', felt morally obliged to concede that Shakespeare's 'first defect' is 'that to which may be imputed most of the evil in books and men': 'He sacrifices virtue to convenience ... he makes no just distribution of good or evil, nor is he always careful to shew in the virtuous [characters] a disapprobation of the wicked.'

The arguments of Dennis and Dr Johnson clearly reflect the discrepancy between two classical requirements (1) 'follow nature' and (2) 'show the reward of virtue and the punishment of vice' — which well-nigh inevitably results in contradictory arguments concerning mimesis and morality in Shakespearian drama. For instance (and *pace* Dennis and Johnson), in the middle of the twentieth century a whole cohort of critics set out to reinterpret the complete works of Shakespeare and his contemporaries (and their medieval predecessors, and their Restoration successors), in order to make them affirm (rather than call into question) the 'Government of Providence'. But in arguing that certain works exemplify the Providential reward of virtue and punishment of vice, these critics necessarily had to deprive Shakespeare (and Chaucer and Webster *et al.*) of their moral right – as well as their imaginative liberty, and their artistic power – to confront us with, and protest against, manifest instances of sexual and social and cosmic injustice. By insisting that Shakespeare's heroes and victims and villains alike must have got just punishments for their foolish, or passionate, misdeeds, this criticism, in effect, divested Shakespeare's tragedies of the primal pity and terror that may constitute their major moral impact, as well as their central claim to truth – or so it will be argued later on. Their arguments also posed serious methodological problems.

Discussing those 'Providentialist' interpretations of Elizabethan plays, which (it seems to me) could as easily rationalize the histories of Hitler (who described himself as an instrument of Providence at a Munich rally) and Stalin, as those of Richard III and Tamburlaine, C. T. Watts observes that they all run aground against conflicting logical premises. If death is the punishment for his wicked characters, then why did Shakespeare insist that Cordelia die along with them? Watts cites G. I. Duthie, who answers that 'God moves in a mysterious way – he deals strangely with the Cordelias of this world. His methods are inscrutable.' It is, Watts concludes, 'traditional' for Providentialist critics to use this 'heads-we-win-and-tails-you-lose procedure; but the logic . . . remains self-contradictory. One premiss is that God's goodness can clearly be inferred from events on earth, and the other is that it can not. The antitheist could employ equivalent logic to opposite effect by letting the death of Cordelia be evidence of a malevolent deity and the punishment of evil-doers be evidence of his inscrutability'. Moreover, as Robert Ornstein has observed, the fact is that, 'just as the apologist for the stage can find a moral in the most prurient play, . . . the pious can interpret the resolution of any dramatic fable as a demonstration of Providence.'[13]

The primary reality – and the kind of morality – that we ourselves find reflected in Elizabethan plays may well depend on what we, personally, believe (or have been critically conditioned to believe) that Shakespeare and his contemporaries *ought* to have represented in them. Thus, critics who look for examples of providential justice can cite them ('The gods are just, and of our pleasant vices/Make instruments to plague us') with the same ease that critics who look for examples of cosmic and temporal injustice can cite *them* ('As flies to wanton boys are we to th' gods — /They kill us for their sport'); whilst scholars who seek affirmations of Elizabethan social, religious, and political ortho-doxies will find them as surely as scholars looking for heterodox views will discover them. The reality (or morality) that admiring commen-tators of different critical persuasions have sought, and found, in Shakespearian drama almost inevitably corresponds to, and confirms their own assumptions concerning the realities great drama ideally should reflect. But — as the rare exceptions to this rule (i.e. the very best critics) can serve to remind us — the desire, or need, to find confirmations of our favourite critical theories is by no means the only desire, or need, that Shakespearian drama can, or ought to satisfy.

In his essay on 'Literature as an Equipment for Living', Kenneth Burke has observed that readers and audiences turn to art in order to satisfy a host of differing emotional and psychological needs, and thus expect it to serve any number of differing purposes. Burke's general categories of needs and purposes are 'consolation, vengeance, admon-ition, exhortation, foretelling'.[14] And Shakespearian drama is unrivalled in its capacity to serve a well-nigh comprehensive range of psychological, emotional, aesthetic, and moral purposes. Therefore, almost anyone familiar with Shakespeare's plays could quote any number of lines — even as Kenneth Burke quotes popular proverbs — that could satisfy an audience's desire, or need, for

Consolation: There is providence in the fall of a sparrow.

                    Sweet are the uses of adversity,
                    Which, like the toad, ugly and venomous,
                    Wears yet a precious jewel in his head.

Exhortation: Men must endure
                    Their going hence, even as their coming hither:
                    Ripeness is all. Come on.

                    There is a tide in the affairs of men
                    Which, taken at the flood, leads on to fortune;
                    Omitted, all the voyage of their life
                    Is bound in shallows and in miseries.

Admonition: That man that hath a tongue, I say, is no man,
                If with his tongue he cannot win a woman.

                Striving to better, oft we mar what's well.

                Small have continual plodders ever won,
                Save base authority from others' books.

Revenge: Foul deeds will rise,
       Though all the earth o'erwhelm them, to men's eyes.

                He is justly serv'd:
                It is a poison temper'd by himself.

Prophecy: If you prick us, do we not bleed? If you tickle us,
                do we not laugh? If you poison us, do we not die?
                And if you wrong us, shall we not revenge? If we are
                like you in the rest, we will resemble you in that.

Burke's categories clearly overlap. Valentine's conclusion that 'That man that hath a tongue' is 'no man,' 'If with his tongue he cannot win a woman', could serve, simultaneously, as an inspiring exhortation to men, and as a dire warning to women. And Shylock's great speech about revenge could serve, simultaneously, as an admonition and a prophecy, in so far as people — and groups of people — who have been laughed at, mocked at, threatened, disgruntled, humiliated, and hindered on account of their religion, or their racial or national origins, are likely, when given the opportunity, to exact their pound of flesh.[15] Regardless of whether the words 'we' and 'us' are used with reference to Jews, or Christians — or Arabs, or Catholics, or Protestants, or Blacks — or to human beings in general, the answer to Shylock's question, 'If you wrong us, shall we not revenge?' is (in desire if not in fact) more likely to be 'Yes' than 'No'. There are — as Shakespeare's works remind us — exceptional cases, but statistically, as well as morally, the 'rarer' action is in virtue than in vengeance. Looked at as an admonition, Shylock's speech would seem to suggest that there are sound practical, as well as obvious moral, reasons for never doing unto others anything that you would not have them do unto you, or unto your progeny: 'The villainy you teach me I will execute; and it shall go hard but I will better the instruction.'

But the moral and social arguments in favour of the golden rule, and against revenge, have been known, and preached, for centuries. And if 'to do good were as easy as to know what were good to do', the human race would have done it long ere now. 'I can', Portia says (and so can any one of us), 'easier teach twenty what were good to be done than to be one of the twenty to follow mine own teaching' (*The Merchant of Venice*, I. ii. 13-15). It is, for instance, easy to argue that people, or dramatic characters, ought to leave vengeance to God, until someone has grievously wronged us, or ours, in which case it is not altogether inconceivable that we — or that any individual, or nation, or group — will subsequently respond with a vindictive ferocity comparable to Shylock's.

The difficulty of following moral instructions has obvious ramifications so far as the actual moral impact of the drama is concerned, since, as Portia reminds us, knowing what ought to be done and actually doing it are two entirely different things. Like a great sermon, a play may splendidly confirm and affirm the highest morality. Yet it does not follow from this that the dramatist who propounds it, or the divine who preaches it, or the audience that has both intellectually and emotionally apprehended it, is subsequently, or necessarily, going to behave accordingly. Indeed, the historical evidence of the manifest inefficacy of imaginative literature in affecting a discernible reformation of human vices and follies would seem to outweigh any arguments in favour of its efficacy. 'I must freely confess', laments Swift's Gulliver, in the letter to his cousin Sympson that is prefixed to all editions of his *Travels*, 'that since my last return some corruptions of my yahoo nature have revived in me by conversing with a few of your species . . . else I should never have attempted so absurd a project as that of reforming the yahoo race in this kingdom; but I have now done with all such visionary schemes for ever.'

Pray bring to your mind how often I desired you to consider, when you insisted on the motive of public good, that the yahoos were a species of animals utterly incapable of amendment by precepts or examples, and so it hath proved; for instead of seeing a full stop put to all abuses and corruptions, at least in this little island, as I had reason to expect: behold, after above six months' warning, I cannot learn that my book hath produced one single effect according to mine intentions: I desired you would let me know by a letter when party and faction were extinguished; judges learned and upright; pleaders honest and modest, with some tincture of common sense . . . the young nobility's education entirely changed; . . . the female yahoos abounding in virtue, honour, truth, and good sense; courts and levees of great ministers thoroughly weeded and swept; wit, merit and learning rewarded; all disgracers of the press in prose and verse condemned to . . . quench their thirst with their own ink. These, and a thousand other reformations, I firmly counted upon by your encouragement; as indeed they were plainly deducible from the precepts delivered in my book. And, it must be owned, that seven months were a sufficent time to correct every vice and folly to which yahoos are subject, if their natures had been capable of the least disposition to virtue or wisdom; . . .

Some twenty centuries earlier, Plato had concluded that years of studying Homer had not resulted in any discernible improvement of Athenian morals, manners, and institutions:

> 'My dear Homer', we shall say, 'if our definition of representation is wrong and you are not merely manufacturing copies at third remove from reality, but are a stage nearer the truth about human excellence, and really capable of judging what kind of conduct will make the individual or the community better or worse, tell us any state whose constitution you have reformed. . . . What city attributes the benefit of its legal system to your skill? . . . Would the contemporaries of Homer and Hesiod have let them continue as wandering minstrels, if they had really been able to make them better men?'
>
> (*The Republic*, X. 427–9)

But if imaginative literature hasn't demonstrably succeeded in reforming the human race, neither has the study of moral philosophy — or anything else. Although, in his *Apology for Poetry*, Sidney argued that the 'ending end of all earthly learning is to move men to virtuous action' — to 'well doing, and not well knowing only,' he elsewhere acknowledged that, in certain instances, the study of Plato himself would prove of no avail, save, perhaps, in positing the truths ultimately overridden by the very truth they were designed to counter. Thus,

> Your words, my friend (right healthful caustics) blame
> My young mind marred, whom Love doth windlass so,
> That mine own writings like bad servants show
> My wits, quick in vain thoughts, in virtue lame;
> That Plato I read for nought, but if he tame
> Such coltish gyres. . . .
> . . . .
> Sure you say well; your wisdom's golden mine
> Dig deep with learning's spade; now tell me this,
> Hath this world ought so fair as Stella is?
>
> (*Astrophel and Stella*, Sonnet 21)

By the same token,

> It is most true that eyes are form'd to serve
> The inward light, and that the heavenly part
> Ought to be king, from whose rules who do swerve,
> Rebels to Nature, strive for their own smart.

It is most true, what we call Cupid's dart
An image is, which for ourselves we carve;
And, fools, adore in temple of our heart,
Till that good god make church and churchman starve.
True, that true Beauty Virtue is indeed,
Whereof this beauty can be but a shade,
Which elements with mortal mixture breed.
True, that on earth we are but pilgrims made,
And should in soul up to our country move.
True, and yet true that I must Stella love.

(*Astrophel and Stella*, Sonnet 5)

It is also true that there is no reason why any rational being should suffer from the pangs of unrequited love, but even those who know what 'is most true' still do. And so, as Portia puts it, 'The brain may devise laws for the blood, but a hot temper leaps o'er a cold decree; such a hare is madness the youth, to skip o'er the meshes of good counsel the cripple.'

Thus drama and poetry may call into question the hegemony of reason over passion. For call them by whatever names you wish — Apollonian *v.* Dionysian, Apollonius *v.* Lamia, Houynhnhm *v.* Yahoo, Roman *v.* Egyptian, Classical *v.* Romantic, Superego *v.* Id — the intellectual, rational, moral, and spiritual, *and* the emotional and irrational and imaginative and biological needs of the human race all have, have had, and presumably will continue to have, their own special claims, and powers, and effects. Therefore the greatest playwrights of any age may dramatically counter the valid claims of one set of motives with the equally powerful, and sometimes equally valid, claims of another:

Morality, applied
To timely practice, keeps the soul in tune,
At whose sweet music all our actions dance.
But this is form of books, and school-tradition;
It physics not the sickness of a mind
Broken with griefs: . . .

(John Ford, *The Broken Heart*, II. ii. 8-13)

So far as the 'form of books and school tradition' is concerned, as Kenneth Burke has also observed, 'We usually take it for granted' that people who read inspirational and didactic books 'are students' who will attempt to 'apply the recipes given'. 'Nothing of the sort', Burke concludes, 'I'll wager that, in by far the great majority of cases, such readers make no serious attempt to apply the book's recipes.' The real appeal of the book 'resides in the fact' that the reader, *while reading it*, has experienced a symbolic achievement of the goal (see Burke, p. 105). And the same holds true, perhaps, of reading about, or seeing on the stage, the granting of mercy, the achievement of revenge, the achievement of sexual or political success, or virtue's triumph over social injustice and political corruption. The line between the uses of literature as a 'recipe' for living and an incitement to virtuous (or any other kind of) action, and the use of it as a substitute for living, a surrogate for action, is a fine one.

Independently of whatever incentives to moral (or immoral) action they may (or may not) involve, Burke concludes that art forms like comedy, tragedy, satire, and romance *can* serve to 'equip us for living' by enabling us to 'size up situations in various ways and in keeping with correspondingly various attitudes' (p. 109). Following Burke's line of reasoning, one could make a good case for the educational value of Shakespearian drama on the grounds that there is no other source of knowledge that enables us to 'size up' so many different situations (in correspondingly various ways), in anything like such a brief amount of time, and thus so efficiently equips us the better to enjoy life – or to endure it. To posit the temporal question in Johnsonian terms, precisely how long would it take for us – or our students – to apprehend for ourselves, or to learn from other sources, the same things about, or so many different things about, 'the real state of sublunary nature', as we can learn from those Shakespearian scenes through which 'a hermit may estimate the transactions of mankind, and a confessor predict the progress of the passions'? For instance: is there any source we could recommend to a hermit, or a confessor, or a student, that so concisely and effectively charts – and from which one can predict – the progress of certain human passions so accurately as this one?

Antony. These strong Egyptian fetters I must break,
   Or lose myself in dotage.
                        (*Antony and Cleopatra*, I. ii. 113–14)
                        . . . . . .

Cleopatra.   If you find him sad,
   Say I am dancing; if in mirth, report
   That I am sudden sick. Quick and return.
Charmian. Madam, methinks, if you did love him dearly,
   You do not hold the method to enforce
   The like from him.
Cleopatra.   What should I do I do not?

Charmian. In each thing give him way; cross him in nothing.
Cleopatra. Thou teachest like a fool — the way to lose him.

                                              (I. iii. 3-10)

                        . . . . . .

Maecenas. Now Antony must leave her utterly.
Enobarbus. Never!   He will not. . . . Other women cloy
   The appetites they feed, but she makes hungry
   Where most she satisfies;

                                              (II. ii. 237-42)

                        . . . . . .

Cleopatra.   That time? O times
   I laugh'd him out of patience; and that night
   I laugh'd him into patience; and next morn,
   Ere the ninth hour, I drunk him to his bed,

                        (II. iv. 18-21)

                        . . . . . .

Enobarbus. Octavia is of a holy, cold, and still conversation.
Menas. Who would not have his wife so?
Enobarbus. Not he that himself is not so; which is Mark Antony . . .
   Antony will use his affection where it is; he married but his
   occasion here.

                                              (II. vi. 119-27)

One might, perhaps, arrive at similar conclusions from reading Ovid,
Proust, Stendhal and de Laclos, or from a series of direct, and possibly
traumatic, experiences; but even a recluse, who had *no other source
of information* about the subject, could earn a little money writing
practical, realistic 'Advice to the Lovelorn' solely on the basis of the
lines quoted above which suggest, among other things, that:

1. Success in the great game of love necessarily depends on adapting
your techniques of play to the other player involved. The reasons why
Antony can never leave her utterly have as much to do with his own
nature as with Cleopatra's consummate artistry — another kind of man
(like Menas) would clearly have preferred a wife like Octavia.
2. 'Like tends to attract like', although total predictability will cloy,
and to bore certain lovers is to lose them: you must appeal to the
imagination. Indeed, the show business maxims, 'always keep them
guessing' and 'leave them wanting more' are equally applicable to those
who trade in love. This is why adopting contrary attitudes may prove
far more effective than making predictably sympathetic responses and
gestures.
3. In certain situations (like Octavia's) your very best efforts, good
looks, and manifest virtues will avail you nothing. You can score any
number of moral or social points, but you will not finally win if you are

up against emotional and imaginative and sexual affinities, inclinations, and affections. In these cases you had better cut your losses and concede. And so forth, and so on. One might argue that it is a pity that some of these points hold true, and that, morally speaking, they obviously ought to be true. Yet it is hard to deny that, in certain instances, they certainly do, and will, hold true.[16] Of course, to defend Shakespeare's plays on the basis of their psychological realism is to leave some aspects of some of them wide open to attack on moral grounds. Yet his works could be the best account we've got of how, so placed, human beings actually do behave. *Could* Shakespeare accurately be described as the world's greatest behavioural psychologist? Of what other authors could Lord Lyttelton's statement be made without seeming quite ridiculous?

If human nature were destroyed, and no monument were left of it except his works, other beings might know *what man was* from [Shakespeare's] writings.[17]

Tallulah Bankhead's father would seem to have arrived at similar conclusions when he told his daughters that 'if they knew Shakespeare and the Bible and could shoot craps', that was all the education they were ever likely to need.[18]

The idea that Shakespeare's plays are worth studying because of their accurate portrayals of the ways of this world and the beings who inhabit it, is as time-honoured as it is obvious. It seems to be a major reason why Dryden, Johnson, and countless other critics once saw fit to describe his works, alongside Homer's, in terms of their just representations of general nature. It also suggests that there may be valid, rather than spurious, or snobbish, or purely academic reasons for those historical distinctions between world-class, first-class, master-class, second-class, yeomen, apprentice, and hack writers, in so far as such distinctions have been based on the quantity and quality of insights which those authors have communicated — and still communicate — about the 'real state of sublunary nature'; about the 'progress of the passions' that agitate, adorn, and disgrace human nature; about the arts (and nature) of poetry, of drama, of politics, power, love; about oneself, about other people, about other works of art, etc. This would lend strong support to the traditional curricular assumption that students who have read the greatest authors will, in fact, be better enabled to enjoy life and endure it, than students who have spent the same amount of time studying minor texts, or who have devoted their time to studying critical theories concerning major and minor texts. So far as our recording angel is concerned,

> Let him, that is yet unacquainted with the power of *Shakespeare*, and who desires to feel the highest pleasure that the drama can give, read every play from the first scene to the last, with utter negligence of all his commentators.

(Dr Johnson, *Preface to Shakespeare, Shakespeare Criticism*, p. 114)

Dr Johnson is here referring to textual commentators, but the same points surely hold true of critical commentaries as well. And if the aesthetic and intellectual and emotional profit and delights afforded us by Shakespeare himself amount to inestimably more than any one of us can dream up to say about him, or than we may learn from all the commentaries-on-commentaries on his plays put together, then the burden of proof lies on the critic (and in this case it weighs heavily on me) to make clear why on earth anyone should bother to write, or to read, this particular kind of book.

There is (alas) no point in arguing that a play by Shakespeare, or that literary criticism — or scholarship, or art, or beauty, or anything else — is its own excuse for being. Like the colour and fragrance and thorns of a rose, the beauty, truth, and challenges posed by art (or criticism) are instruments of survival in an essentially competitive world that all too willingly lets things die. If the scent and colour of the rose does not attract to it the following of insects necessary to transmit its properties and allow for cross-fertilization, or if its protective thorns are not strong or numerous enough to defend it from its natural enemies, then the rose will perish. And the same holds true for a poem, or a play, or an essay in criticism. Their short-term and long-term survival alike depend on attracting an audience, and transmitting their particular merits to that audience, and so on to a subsequent generation — even as Shakespeare's masterpieces have so successfully done.

So far as Shakespearian criticism is concerned, the competition for survival is increasingly ferocious. Like the survival of a play, the survival of a critical book or article ultimately depends on the number and quality of admirers that the information and insights in it can attract, and keep on attracting. To give just one example, A. C. Bradley's book on *Shakespearean Tragedy* has, in turn, been lauded and maligned, but it has triumphantly survived an onslaught of hostile criticism and still thrives at least as well as, if not better than, even its most distinguished competitors — whilst any number of its less than distinguished competitors have long since perished on the vine. All judgement is comparative, and there are no absolute values in criticism or in art. But there certainly are relative values, and we cannot, finally, evade the issue of artistic and critical distinction, or get round the obvious fact that Bradley's discussion of Shakespearian tragedy is, to innumerable other discussions of the same subject, as *King Lear* is to *Gorboduc*: by practically any standard of comparison, it's better.

The same, of course, holds true for productions of Shakespeare's plays. 'Who', asks Ernst Gombrich, 'can deny that there are supreme and less good performances, hopeless ones and inspired ones even within the limits of the prescribed text?':

It follows from this example that there is latitude but not license in understanding. There may be different performances of equal validity, but there are certainly many more demonstrably false ones. ... The neglect or even denial of values seems to me the greatest danger in that trend towards the dehumanisation of the humanities of which I spoke. ... [A scholar] may be able to prove beyond doubt that two potsherds once belonged to the same pot, but if the pot is neither rare nor beautiful he may be confronted with the dread reaction: 'So what?'[19]

Perhaps significantly, virtually identical questions of relevance and relative value also arise in the following advice to a young scientist:

It can be said with complete confidence that any scientist of any age who *wants to make important discoveries must study important problems*. ... It is not enough that a problem should be 'interesting' – almost any problem is interesting if it is studied in sufficient depth . . . the problem must be such that it *matters* . . . to science generally or to mankind.[20]

Would this be good advice to give to an aspiring young critic as well? Are short-term and long-run judgements of critical works, scientific theories, and works of art alike, finally based on their explanatory or exploratory range and value, their informational content, their ability to 'save' certain phenomena that would otherwise be unaccounted for? Is criticism to art what art is to life – a more or less important, and occasionally crucial, source of positive, or negative, feedback? Assuming that the answer to these questions is 'Yes', then are there, in fact, any *critical* problems that are matters of importance, not only to critics generally, but to humankind? If so, then this, surely, is the most tenacious and perplexing of them all: *what, if any, psychological or moral effect – for good or evil, for better or for worse – does imaginative literature actually have on its audience?*

Part ii.
The Question of Morality in Shakespearian Drama and Criticism: The 'Screw-guns' of Plato

Jest send in your Chiefs an' surrender — it's worse if
  you fights or you runs:
You can go where you please, you can skid up the trees,
  but you don't get away from the guns!

Kipling, 'Screw-guns'

And then there is the story of how Zeus stayed awake, when all
the other . . . gods were asleep, with some plan in mind, but forgot
it easily enough when his desire for sex was roused: he was indeed
so struck by Hera's appearance that he wanted to make love to
her on the spot, without going indoors, saying that he had never
desired her so much since the days when they first used to make
love 'without their parents' knowledge'. . . . [S]uch lies are
positively harmful. For those who hear them will be lenient
toward their own shortcomings.

Plato, *The Republic*

Agrippa.   Royal wench!
She made great Caesar lay his sword to bed.
He ploughed her, and she cropp'd.
Enobarbus.   I saw her once
Hop forty paces through the public street;
And, having lost her breath, she spoke, and panted,
That she did make defect perfection,
And breathless, pow'r breathe forth.
. . . .
. . . . for vilest things
Become themselves in her, that the holy priests
Bless her when she is riggish.

Shakespeare, *Antony and Cleopatra*

While men consider good and evil as springing from the same root,
they will spare the one for the sake of the other, and in judging,
if not of others at least of themselves, will be apt to estimate their
virtues by their vices. To this fatal error all those will contribute,
who confound the colours of right and wrong, and instead of
helping to settle their boundaries, mix them with so much art,
that no common mind is able to disunite them.

Dr Johnson, *The Rambler*

It is almost impossible to ask what relationship Shakespeare's (or any
other) art has to 'nature' without asking whether it has any significant
effect on the audience, and then asking what kind — and how, or

whether, we can ever finally know what kind — of psychological, or moral, effect it has had on any one, or all, of us. The aesthetic and moral questions raised by Shakespeare's dramatic portrayals of conflicts and characters of altogether different kinds are perhaps most concisely posited in his own account of the multifarious powers that reside in the products of Nature herself:

> And from her womb children of diverse kind
> We sucking on her natural bosom find;
> Many for many virtues excellent,
> None but for some, and yet all different.
> O mickle is the powerful grace that lies
> In plants, herbs, stones, and their true qualities;
> For nought so vile that on the earth doth live
> But to the earth some special good doth give;
> Nor aught so good but, strain'd from that fair use
> Revolts from true birth, stumbling on abuse:
> Virtue itself turns vice, being misapplied,
> And vice sometime's by action dignified.
> Within the infant rind of this weak flower
> Poison hath residence, and medicine power;
> For this, being smelt, with that part cheers each part;
> Being tasted, slays all senses with the heart.
> Two such opposed kings encamp them still
> In man as well as herbs — grace and rude will;
> And where the worser is predominant,
> Full soon the canker death eats up that plant.
>
> (*Romeo and Juliet*, II. iii. 11–30)

Down through the centuries, critics of various persuasions have wondered whether there really are, or ought to be, some clear lines of demarcation between our emotional and moral responses to Shakespeare's characters 'of diverse kind'. Can we, aesthetically at least, conclude that 'nought so vile' in Shakespeare's art doth live, but to that art 'some special good doth give'? If so, does the same point hold true morally? His plays obviously include many characters, 'for many virtues excellent'. But what about those cases wherein 'vice sometime's by action dignified'? One cannot read the works of Shakespeare without encountering characters towards whom one's personal responses, or the responses of audiences generally, never quite cohere in so far as rational and moral judgements of their follies, passions, vices, high crimes, or misdemeanours, are countered by emotional or aesthetic responses that are, at some points indisputably and, in certain cases, irrevocably favourable.

.

Do all plays that contain characters of this kind finally assume — in the mind of the audience, if not in the intent of the author — the form of a morality play, or *psychomachia*? Are there fatal Cleopatras, Venus fly-traps in the garden of art, who may finally catch us in their strong toils of grace, since that is where our greatest pleasure lies? Do such characters inspire the most judicious, as well as the most impressionable, members of the audience to fly after their sails, leaving all rational, moral, and practical considerations behind, and thus cause an audience to lose the decisive psychological, or moral, battle of Actium in very much the same way, and for the same reasons, that Antony lost the one in Shakespeare's play? Whether they do, or do not, serve as role-models, or in any way incite impressionable members of the audience to emulate them in real life, do the more glorious, glamorous, amusing, or sympathetically portrayed sinners encourage us to tolerate, condone, enjoy, or approve of things that we should otherwise rightly deplore? Or are any poisons in residence in the drama turned into medicinal drugs, in that its sinners serve the innocent, as well as the guilty creatures sitting at a play, as minatory examples, instructive images of self-destructive passions, vices, sins, follies, or errors of judgement, or mistaken priorities, which the spectator, having witnessed their dire consequences, will henceforth determine to eschew? If this is true, precisely when does the instruction take place?

Is there, or should there be, a critical moment of truth when one's own better judgement, or some wiser critic's good counsel, finally takes precedence over those emotional responses experienced at that point of poetic or dramatic impact when a given character 'did make defect perfection'? Do we, or can we, or should we at least *try* to, censor our own emotional reactions to Shakespeare's passionate sinners and (critically adapting Hamlet's terminology) join in a 'general censure' of their obvious faults, or their 'one defect', or of that 'vicious mole of nature in them' — and in all of us? — or whatever it is in them, or in our responses to them, that breaks down all the 'pales and forts of reason'? Or does a critical emphasis on moral virtue itself turn vice, being misapplied? Should critics really feel obliged to instruct their audience that, say, the passionate relationship between Antony and Cleopatra falls woefully short of Christian *caritas*, or that, sadly enough, too many spectators have been 'taken in' by the 'tragic sentimentality' of *Romeo and Juliet*, or that 'Once we can break free from the mesmerizing power of Prospero's all-too-often successful attempt to dazzle us with his halo [we see that] from beginning to end Prospero is bent on vengeance', or that once we can dispel 'romantic notions' that certain characters are portrayed as 'innocent victims', we will see that these characters have actually been 'hiding behind their masks of innocence, chastity, purity, benevolence' and that we have been 'taken in by appearances'?[21]

It is hard to believe that, without having been critically counselled to do so, any admirer of Shakespearian drama – or for that matter, any jury in real life – would condemn Juliet, Desdemona, Hamlet, or Prospero, as mercilessly as certain twentieth-century critics have condemned them in print. But apart from a dialectical reaction to Romantic criticism, why should modern scholars have considered themselves obliged to write about Shakespeare's tragic and comic heroes and heroines as if they were their Prosecuting Attorneys unless they were worried that Shakespeare's own portrayals of them might be evoking an undue tolerance towards whatever vices or follies they might exemplify – e.g. Juliet's sexuality (or defiance of parental authority), Othello's pride, or Hamlet's desire for a *bella vendetta*? The most fundamental critical question raised by all such commentaries is that, if or when it *is* 'taken at face value', the tragic sentimentality of Shakespeare's own portrayals of these characters is what stands in the way of our rational and moral judgements of passions and actions that ought to be seen as utterly deplorable, and if Shakespeare's poetry is so 'marvellous that there is a temptation (which we should resist)' to 'drink it in'[22] to the point where we are far too intoxicated to consider it rationally, then precisely who is at fault? Is his audience to blame for its admiring, or sympathetic, responses to Shakespeare's protagonists? Or is the poet himself to blame for having portrayed them in such a glamorous, sympathetic, or sentimental way? And if an audience's favourable responses to Romeo, Juliet, and Prospero are altogether misplaced, then what about the admiration, pity, and affection often extended to villains like Richard III, and Macbeth, whose motives and actions are manifestly more nefarious than theirs?

These questions are as old as criticism itself. The most important of them all were raised in *The Republic*. What is interesting is that even now, twenty-two centuries later, there is no sign of an agreement – much less a consensus – concerning the correct answer to any one of them.

'Is it really right', Plato asked, for us 'to admire, when we see him on the stage, a man we should ourselves be ashamed to resemble? Is it reasonable to feel enjoyment and admiration rather than disgust?'

Plato, of course, concluded that 'It seems most unreasonable' (*The Republic*, X. 436). And so have many modern critics of Shakespeare:

Now admiration is an alien word in the description of the emotional response to the destroying force in a tragic character. . . . Actually it is apparent that Bradley does admire Shakespeare's villains and heroes alike if their sins or their passions are only great enough. [But admiration ought not to be part of a moral response to violations of moral law.] [23]

Here we have agreement with Plato across the millenia: audiences ought not to admire art's sinners and villains. The catch is that some of us (not only A. C. Bradley) occasionally do. But why should this be true? And if it is true, what ought to be done about it? For that matter, why do people tend to admire some of Shakespeare's villains (like Macbeth and Richard III) and find others (like Cornwall) absolutely disgusting? And if we ought not to feel any more admiration for Richard, or Macbeth, than for Cornwall, who is to blame if we do?

Even those modern critics who deplore the audience's – or reader's – injudicious responses to imaginative literature as much as Plato did, dare not follow his argument to the logical conclusion that would, at one stroke, put poets and critics alike out of business. Where Plato concluded that poetry itself is to blame for the irrational passions and sympathies it arouses, and ought, therefore, to be banned, these critics insist that the audience's or the reader's responses are blameworthy and should, therefore, be critically censured, controlled, or banned. Yet the same fundamental issue is involved in both sets of conclusions, and that is the issue of censorship, whether it be of art, or of the audience's responses to art, in so far as it arouses admirations and sympathies at odds with a rational, moral, critical, or analytical judgement of the vices and follies of the characters portrayed.

Can the extension of admiration and sympathy even unto sinners be defended? It seems to me that one can defend Bradley's pity for a tragic sinner like Macbeth, whose suffering is as great as his villainy, on the grounds that it constitutes a form of charity. Admiration, however, is unlike pity, or compassion, or approbation, in that (arguably anyway) it does not, in itself constitute a 'moral' response. Admiration, in the original sense of the word, presupposes wonder, a kind of awe, that can exist quite independently of moral approbation. It is, for instance, possible to extend our moral approbation to certain rather boring characters, like Ben Jonson's Bonario, without admiring them in the Latinate sense of the term. And it is also possible to admire some people, or some things, even as we morally disapprove of them. One can admire a matador, or a champion boxer, while disapproving of bull-fights, or boxing, and admire the skill and energy manifested when a cat captures and kills its prey, while hating to see its prey played with and killed. Watching certain villains, like Richard III, or Volpone, is comparable to watching the matador, or the cat. In the case of Richard III, it is virtually impossible to dissociate an admiration of his wit, his courage, and his intelligence, from an admiration of his nefarious carryings-on, because they are so dramatically associated with each other that distinguishing between them is comparable, in difficulty, to dissociating a matador's grace and courage from the way he fights, and kills, the bull – or to making a clear distinction between the dancer and the dance. It therefore seems possible to feel admiration for him, but practically impossible to posit a moral defence of the admiration extended (by people like myself) to a jolly, thriving villain like Richard, who – markedly unlike Macbeth – is not shown to suffer as much as his victims, but positively enjoys being wicked, and takes it for granted that we in the audience will very much enjoy watching him being wicked.

Indeed, Elizabethan audiences would appear to have been fascinated by characters who are gleefully determined to be as villainous as they possibly can. 'Admir'd I am of those who hate me most', gloats the murderous Machevill who introduces us to *The Jew of Malta*; and 'Give us Barabas!' might well be the most obvious, albeit the most blasphemous, of all curtain-calls with which to acclaim the superstar of Marlowe's contest in outrageous villainy. Moreover, however minatory, and morally reassuring, it may be to watch villains like Barabas, or Richard, or Volpone, or Middleton's De Flores, get what they have coming to them in the end, the primary pleasure they give us may be in watching them being wicked enough to do, or get, whatever they most want to do or get (their revenge, or the crown, or the gold, or the girl) *before* they finally receive their just deserts.

The way the dramatist portrays the victim, or victims, of their villainy has a great deal to do with the differing responses elicited by the various villains in Elizabethan drama. In the cases of Iago and Cornwall, the sufferings of the victims, and the unjust nature of the tortures inflicted upon them, are most dramatically stressed. In cases of vice figures like Richard, Barabas, and Volpone, the author initially shows their victims, generally, to be almost as, if not just as, guilty or avaricious or treacherous as the villain (in *The Jew of Malta*, as in

Rochester's satire, the central subject-matter of debate is, from the outset, 'Who's a knave of the first rate?'). Subsequently, however, as it were
by established convention, the author will emphasize the *innocence* of
the victim currently being preyed upon (Volpone's attempted rape of
the innocent Celia; Barabas's murder of the innocent Abigail; and the
slaughter of the little princes in the Tower are cases in point). It is as if
the authors considered this mandatory in order to keep the Devil's
party from finally winning the election, so far as the audience's enjoyment and affection are concerned. Morally speaking, the system cannot
fail. We can use Celia and Bonario, or the little princes, or Abigail, to
score any number of moral points against Volpone and Mosca and
Richard and Barabas. But when contrasted to Jonson's vivid and vital
images of the fox and the parasite, his figures of virtue seem so lifeless
that there probably always will be someone who complains that the
indisputably just punishments meted out to Volpone and Mosca are too
harsh for the ending of a comedy. And it is, of course, Volpone who
asks for the audience's applause in the Epilogue as if to remind us that
the moral and dramatic scores remain at odds,

> *Volpone.*   The seasoning of a play, is the applause.
>   Now, though the Fox be punish'd by the laws,
>   He yet doth hope, there is no suffering due,
>   For any fact which he hath done 'gainst you;
>   If there be, censure him; here he doubtful stands:
>   If not, fare jovially, and clap your hands.

Yet another series of moral problems arises from the fact that, as
major poets (along with Plato and a host of neo-classical critics) have
observed, in practically any drama designed to show vice her own
image, that image itself, familiar grown, may please. Here is the series of
psychological reactions described by Sin herself in *Paradise Lost* (II.
759–62):

> back they recoil'd afraid
> At first, and call'd me *Sin*, and for a Sign
> Portentous held me; but familiar grown,
> I pleas'd.

Or, as Pope puts it in his *Essay on Man,*

> Vice is a monster of so frightful mien,
> As to be hated needs but to be seen;
> Yet seen too oft, familiar with her face,
> We first endure, then pity, then embrace.

These seem remarkably accurate descriptions of Beatrice-Joanna's series of responses to De Flores – and, for that matter, of my own: familiar grown, De Flores pleases me. Nothing could be easier than to write a critical essay cataloguing and deploring the vices manifested, from the outset, by De Flores, or Richard, or Volpone. Yet familiarity with these characters may make some people less and less – even as it makes others more and more – appalled, or shocked, or surprised by sin, or by the fact that they themselves have been imaginatively seduced and woefully led astray by the Vice Figure in a morality play. But, at least so far as criticism of Elizabethan drama is concerned, this could be a good thing. For if *no* spectators or readers ever responded to the vices portrayed in their plays in anything *but* an unexceptionally moralistic and judiciously censorious way, then something like ninety-five per cent of all critics of Shakespeare, and his contemporaries and successors, would have to be declared redundant – including those Romantic critics who defended creative energy and exuberance in all its forms.

Shakespeare, Coleridge observed (see *Coleridge's Shakespearian Criticism*, ed. T. M. Raysor (London, 1930), p. 58),

had read nature too heedfully not to know that courage, intellect, and strength of character were the most impressive forms of power, and that to power in itself, without reference to any moral end, an inevitable admiration and complacency appertains, whether it be displayed in the conquests of a Napoleon or Tamerlane, or in the foam and thunder of a cataract.

To see the most obvious reason why moral philosophers and critics have objected to the kind of admiration often, if not inevitably, appertaining 'to power in itself, without reference to any moral ends', one need only insert the name 'Hitler' after the name 'Napoleon' in Coleridge's commentary.

'What shocks the virtuous philosopher delights the camelion Poet' wrote Keats, who defends the 'poetical character', which can take as much delight in 'an Iago as an Imogen', on the grounds that 'It does no harm from its relish of the dark side of things any more than from its taste for the bright one, because they both end in speculation.' Keats's argument surely has its validity, in that one can indeed contemplate, and even relish, Shakespeare's portrayal of Iago without approving of the character, or aspiring to be like him. Yet it is not always as easy, in fact, to dissociate the psychological effects of art from life as, in theory, it might seem to be.

For instance, we could, if we wished, get around every one of the moral issues involved in Shakespearian drama and criticism, by arguing that all such considerations fade into nothingness when seen in the light of the single, most obvious fact about the drama, which is that (as Hamlet, with obvious irony, taunted Claudius) the very worst characters portrayed in any play ever written 'do but jest, poison in jest; no offence i' th' world', and that, in the last analysis, a play's only real relevance is to its sources, which we may find extant in 'very choice Italian' – or in Saxo Grammaticus, or Kyd. In this view, all plays and characters alike are but walking shadows of other walking shadows. Yet these conclusions, in turn, lead us straight back into the critical quicksand whereby, in claiming that poetry has no power to hurt, and can do no harm in the world, we make it almost impossible to explain how in the world it can do any good. And so the screw-guns of Plato turn on us both ways: to defend the drama against his charges of triviality (i.e. it has no serious value or claim to truth, and is of no benefit to society) on the grounds of its psychological realism, its accurate account of the way things are, is to leave it vulnerable to attack on the grounds of its immoral implications; and to defend it against charges of immorality on the grounds of its essential unreality, is to leave it defenceless against charges of triviality.

Yet it might, finally, prove as comforting as it is obvious that these problems have been of central concern to critics and poets ever since Plato raised them in *The Republic*. Indeed, given our distinguished ancestry, as well as our common problems, everyone currently concerned with the issues of dramatic mimesis and morality might (temporarily, anyway) call a halt to our internecine battles and rivalries, and join together to boast of a genealogical line that can be traced back through the twentieth century to the Romantic revolution, and then, by way of neo-classical criticism, to the *Poetics*, and, finally, to the mighty precursor of Aristotle himself.

In processes comparable to those whereby works of art tend to grow, by reaction and development, from other works of art, critical theories tend to grow, by extension from, or in reaction to, previous critical theories. It is impossible to number how many critical arguments and counter-arguments have derived either directly or indirectly, in reaction to, or by development from, the theories originally posited by Plato. But that is as far back as the historical record will take us. The fact is that you can, with some historical accuracy, describe all subsequent discussions of poetic mimesis and morality as a series of 'footnotes to Plato'.[24] But you cannot, with any certainty, describe Plato's conclusions as 'footnotes' to any previous critic. Plato may be positively identified as the first of our (Western European) kind, by virtue of the fact that the most important of all his arguments were neither dependent upon, nor directed against, previous *critical* commentaries — they were derived from and directed against dramatic poetry itself. The precursors constantly quoted by Plato are those Titans of Greek poetry and drama whose 'terrible power' he had personally experienced, and had never ceased to feel, and about whose influence on society he was, himself, most anxious. It is, as it were, in Plato's *Republic* that one can watch poetry and drama give birth to literary criticism, even as the child determines to depose its parents. Moreover, in one or another of the arguments made in *The Republic*, our mutual parent hurled down the gauntlet to every critic who has subsequently been concerned with (1) the kinds of reality poetry reflects and (2) with the effect that poetry and drama have had, do have, ought to have, or ought not to have, on the very best of (and on what is best in) all of us, or on the very worst of (and what is worst in) all of us.

Critics may never finally finish discussing the issues Plato raised for the obvious reason that so many of his observations about Homer and the Greek playwrights are so demonstrably, as to be well-nigh irrefutably, true of dramatic poetry in general, and of Shakespeare's plays in particular. How we should respond to Plato's conclusions about poetic mimesis and morality are matters of continuing dispute, but the fact remains that every one of the following generalizations about what poetry does, but that Plato (and his succession of disciples) most emphatically insist it ought *not* to do, is dramatically confirmed in one or more of Shakespeare's plays.

1. The drama may, simultaneously, elicit contradictory moral, aesthetic, and emotional responses towards a single character (X. 433) — just as Shakespeare does in the cases of Falstaff, Richard III, etc.

2. Dramatic prose and poetry can be outrageously insolent and impudent to those in authority (III. 145) — as Shakespeare's prose and poetry is (whether we approve of the characters or not) in certain lines given to Falstaff and Lucio.

3. Drama may encourage us to relish, on the stage, behaviour that, in real life, we would certainly deplore (X. 436); even as I, personally, have relished the seduction of Lady Anne, and other nefarious goings-on in *Richard III*, including Queen Margaret's gloriously malicious exit-speeches ('These English woes shall make me smile in France', etc. (IV. iv. 115)). I know I am by no means the first nor the last to do so,

but cite myself here because the Platonic case is proved if only one person so relishes such manifest villainy, such triumphant vindictiveness.

4. The emphasis of the drama is, far more often than not, on the
worst aspects of human nature, on sensational, spectacular vices (X.
438). Where, commercially speaking, would *Othello* be without Iago?
Where would *Titus Andronicus* be without violence, sex, mutilation,
etc.? Indeed, given the history of the drama it is hard to deny that
theatrical representations of the seven deadly sins are more likely to
bring cash into the box-office than depictions of the seven cardinal
virtues, or to get round the obvious fact that commercially successful
plays that deal exclusively with rational and virtuous characters are still
as rare as Plato said they were (X. 435).

5. The greatest poets often hint, or imply, or come right out and
say, that the gods themselves are sometimes cruelly or arbitrarily unjust
to men and women — that good people are sometimes wretched, and
wrong-doing sometimes pays (III. 149) — or, as Shakespeare puts it,
'As flies to wanton boys are we to the gods'; and those who act 'with
best meaning' have sometimes 'incurr'd the worst'. Thus Shakespeare's
plays often suggest that what is, and what morally ought to be true are
not, or certainly not always, one and the same thing: rhetorically
speaking, ''tis true 'tis pity/And pity 'tis, 'tis true'; or, put in the context of tragedy wrought to its uttermost, 'I might have sav'd her; now
she's gone for ever.' 'Why should a dog, a horse, a rat have life,/ And
thou no breath at all?'

Nothing could be easier than to cite examples from Shakespeare's
plays wherein he does one or more of the various things that Plato
banished poets from the Republic for doing. Conversely, nothing could
be harder than to prove that the same plays *never* do any of these
things, or that individuals, or audiences generally, have never responded
to Shakespeare's characters in the ways that Plato said the best and the
worst of us alike were virtually bound to respond to the drama — that
is, in ways at odds with moral and rational judgements. Needless to say,
Shakespeare does not always do the things that Plato condemned Greek
poets for doing: but, then, neither did the poets he condemned. What
worried Plato was that they occasionally did them. And what is once
done or said with great dramatic impact may not be undone, unsaid;
what an audience has once seen cannot be unseen. To have even the
most reprehensible character posit, with great anguish, or wit, or
eloquence, ideas that are morally deplorable or socially disruptive —
Plato cites views that are critical of the ways of the gods themselves,

or are irreverent to those in temporal authority (III. 132–45) — is to implant those views in the memory of the audience, to allow the possibility of supposing that the Devil himself might speak true. The reasons for Plato's fear of the uncontrollable power of art might well be described through a Shakespearian metaphor. Very like Isabella, who, without intending to, but simply by being herself, aroused a lust that would raze the sanctuary and pitch its evils there, poetry may arouse, and finally bring out, what Plato described as the 'monstrous, multiform creature' that lurks in the subconscious of the best of us (IX. 392–3, 417). In a confrontation with poetic art that plays with reason and discourse, Plato concluded that we are all as helpless as an Angelo, who could no more control his own reactions to Isabella than she could control her effect on him.

In this sense at least, Plato — of *all* people — is far more democratic than many twentieth-century critics. In yet another series of arguments that I have never seen successfully refuted, the Philosopher King concluded that virtually no one — not he himself, not 'even the best of us', not 'even the most respectable of us' can finally control their personal (psychological, emotional, or subconscious) responses to the drama — much less control the reactions of all those yahoos in the pit. 'My point', Plato insists, 'is this —'

that even in the outwardly most respectable of us there is a terribly bestial and immoral type of desire, which manifests itself particularly in dreams. . . . when the reasonable and humane part of us is asleep and its control relaxed, and our fierce bestial nature, full of food and drink, rouses itself and has its fling and tries to secure its own kind of satisfaction. As you know, there's nothing too bad for it and it's completely lost to all sense and shame. It doesn't shrink from attempting intercourse (as it supposes) with a mother or anyone else, man, beast or god, or from murder or eating forbidden food. There is, in fact, no folly nor shamelessness it will not commit.

(IX. 392–3)

As well as supplying the greatest Greek dramatists with their raw materials for tragic and comic representation, it is to this element — to Mr Hyde, not Dr Jekyll, to the Yahoo, not the Houyhnhnm side of human nature — that the drama may finally appeal. Conversely, the 'reasonable element and its unvarying calm are difficult to represent and difficult to understand if represented', particularly by the 'motley audience gathered in a theatre, to whose experience it is quite foreign'. The dramatic poet 'will not therefore naturally turn to this element, nor will his skill be directed to please it, if he wants to win a popular reputation'. 'We are therefore', Plato concluded, 'quite right' to refuse to admit the poet to a properly run state, because 'his works have a low degree of truth and also because he deals with a low element in the mind' and 'wakens and encourages and strengthens the lower elements in the mind to the detriment of reason' (X. 435).

And so, in a series of arguments with which all dictatorships, as well as moralistic majorities and minorities down through the ages, have clearly agreed, Plato finally concluded that it is much easier to censor art, or to ban art altogether, than to control, or to censor, any given individual's, much less a whole audience's, emotional or imaginative responses to it:

> It is not only to the poets therefore that we must issue orders requiring them to portray good character in their poems or not to write at all; we must issue similar orders to all artists and craftsmen, and prevent them portraying bad character, ill-discipline, meanness . . . in sculpture, architecture or any work of art, and if they are unable to comply they must be forbidden to practise their art among us. We shall thus prevent our guardians being brought up among representations of what is evil, and so day by day and little by little, by grazing widely as it were in an unhealthy pasture, insensibly doing themselves a cumulative psychological damage that is very serious.
>
> (III. 162–3)

It would be comparatively easy to cope with Plato's most repressive contentions if he had concluded, along with many modern critics of Shakespeare, that whereas injudicious groundlings might let themselves get carried away, the wiser sort of spectators would never allow their rational or moral judgements to be swayed by dramatic and poetic appeals to their emotions. But without admitting that one has not responded to the poetry at all, it is almost impossible to counter Plato's assertion that, at the actual moment of impact, 'you know how even the best of us enjoy it and let ourselves be carried away by our feelings; and we are full of praises for the merits of the poet who can most powerfully affect us in this way' (X. 436). If this point is granted, and *if* it is also granted that certain passions and feelings are so bad for us that they should constantly be suppressed, then it is equally hard to refute Plato's contention that

> Poetry has the same effect on us when it represents sex and anger, and the other desires and feelings of pleasure and pain which accompany all our actions. It waters them when they ought to be left to wither, and

makes them control us when we ought, in the interests of our own greater welfare and happiness, to control them.

(X. 437)

It would still be difficult, but nothing like as difficult, to counter Plato's charges against poetry if he had concluded that only bad art appeals to, or arouses, passions that, rationally or morally speaking, should be left to wither. But Plato argues, as it were virtually by definition, that this is what the *best* poetry does. What Plato saw as terrible, Blake saw as good, but they are at one in concluding that true poets, whether they know it or not, always have been of the Devil's party. Plato cites the works of Homer and the very greatest of all Greek playwrights as manifest evidence of their 'terrible power to corrupt even the best characters, with very few exceptions.' (X. 436).

This is why he argued that poetry should not be used for the purposes of education:

When you meet people who admire Homer as the educator of Greece, and who say that in the administration of human affairs and education we should study him ... you must feel kindly towards them as good men within their limits, and you may agree with them that Homer is the best of poets and first of tragedians. But you will know that the only poetry that should be allowed in a state is hymns to the gods and paeans in praise of good men; once you go beyond that and admit the sweet lyric or epic muse, pleasure and pain become your rulers instead of law and the rational principles commonly accepted as best.

(X. 437-8)

Query: Has anyone proved — can anyone prove — that last statement false?

Assuming that we cannot but acknowledge the validity of some of Plato's observations, but do not want to see imaginative literature banished from the face of the earth, then we face yet another series of critical questions. Practically every critic, major or minor, ancient or modern, from Aristotle onwards, has had, either directly or indirectly, to concede some points to Plato, even while arguing against his final solution to the problems posed. And the cumulative critical result is a series of mutually and utterly contradictory counter-arguments, some of which seem true of certain works of art — or of several plays by Shakespeare — but none of which holds true in all cases. Here, for instance, are paraphrases of some of the most famous and influential of these arguments, followed by the Platonic objections that might be directed back against them:

1. As Aristotle, Milton, and their countless successors have argued, poetry does arouse our emotions, and is by nature sensual and passionate, but it does not leave the passions aroused. Indeed, it encourages us to get them out of our system, so that in the end they are purged and we are dismissed with calm of mind, all passion spent.

Here is an obvious Platonic objection to these arguments: Doesn't some poetry, and don't some plays, arouse passions and tensions and leave them aroused? For that matter, if you temporarily arouse certain passions in certain individuals, how can you make certain that they will not remain aroused — let Mr Hyde out once . . .? And precisely where do you draw the line between what may be imaginatively enjoyed or experienced and what may subsequently be enjoyed or experienced in fact?

2. According to numerous twentieth-century commentators on Shakespeare, Milton, and Spenser, poetry does arouse our passions, but it does so in order to surprise us and shame us and appal us with our own susceptibility to sin.[25]

The obvious Platonic objection to these arguments is that, far from being surprised by it, all too many people clearly relish their own susceptibilities to sin, and indeed pay at the box office to taste, vicariously, of the foods forbidden them in everyday life. How else can you account for the box-office appeal of villainy, sex, violence? And how can we ever be certain that dramatic representations of them do not make hungry where most they satisfy?

3. Any number of twentieth-century commentators have argued that injudicious readers and audiences may well get carried away by their passions, but the wiser sort of readers, for whom the poetry was originally intended, would never have let themselves get carried away in the first place, and modern critics and students who are sufficiently informed and judicious will critically analyse the responses involved and thus keep things in the proper perspective.[26]

But these conclusions could be countered by the following Platonic queries: aren't critics who make these assertions deceiving themselves and their readers? If the poetry is good enough, their own emotions will be aroused in ways beyond all critical control. In books and essays, critics and their students may write what they think ought to be said about the literary characters and conflicts involved; but that is not the same thing as saying what they really feel, or what they originally felt, about them. For that matter, you can analyse emotional responses forever, but you cannot control the subconscious forces that may be influencing your analysis of them. We may never consciously know precisely which of the seeds that drifted from the stage may have taken root in us — much less in anyone else. Indeed, the intellectual energies of critical analysis are feeble in comparison to the emotional energies and impact of art, in that the best moral argument ever propounded, by the best critic who ever lived, cannot stop another individual from admiring a monster of vice like Richard III, much less prevent him or her from sympathizing with and admiring Juliet, Cleopatra, and Hamlet. That is why poetry should be banned.

4. In my own favourite defences of poetry, Shelley, Blake, Hazlitt, Keats, and other Romantic critics argued that artists do sometimes treat their passionate sinners as if they loved them, but that this is a profoundly moral thing for them to do. It is thus that literature enlarges and deepens our sympathies and expands our vision and apprehension and comprehension of the world. And its spectacles of evil end in harmless speculation.

Yet here is the obvious Platonic objection to this defence of poetry: would you deem it a good thing to have the audience's admiration aroused for something that you, personally, consider most evil? Where, if ever, are you going to draw the line? And what if what doesn't distress, or inspire emulation, in you, does in fact cause genuine distress, or actually inspire emulation in others? To give some modern examples of the actual distress and emulation caused by art, the reason why American blacks protested against the screening of D. W. Griffiths's masterpiece, *The Birth of a Nation*, was that they feared it might encourage a revival of the Ku Klux Klan. Which was, of course, exactly what it did.

By the same token, it was out of fear that it would encourage anti-Semitism that the New York School Board banned *The Merchant of Venice* from all schools under its jurisdiction.[27] And the fact is that Shakespeare's play was exploited as a vehicle for anti-Semitic propaganda in productions mounted in Berlin and Vienna during the Third Reich, in one of which the star of the Nazi film *Jud Süss* (1940) played Shylock. I am indebted to Professor Werner Habicht for this information: there was a notorious Viennese production in 1943 with Werner Krauss as Shylock, and a Berlin production in 1942 where professional actors were distributed among the audience to boo at Shylock (played by Georg August Koch). In the earlier Nazi years, *Merchant* was put on quite often; there were about fifty German productions between 1933 and 1939, according to the known statistics.[28]

These Nazi presentations would make it seem extremely dangerous to argue that Shakespeare's plays are 'only to be known aright' in actual productions. In any case, the questions Plato raised about the social and moral and mimetic ramifications of certain works by the best, as well as the worst, of artists are anything but dead. To give another example: there is no argument against 'video nasties' that could not be levelled against *Titus Andronicus*, and it is hard to see how you could defend the latter without defending the former.

It could go without saying that some of the best literary criticism ever written is contained in major efforts to contend with various questions raised by Plato. What is equally obvious is that no critic — ancient or modern, traditionalist or revisionist, not Sidney, not Shelley, not Aristotle, nor anyone since — has solved *all* of the philosophical, psychological, educational, moral, and literary problems originally posited in *The Republic*. The consistently negative results of our best efforts may, however, be proof positive — or at least may be the best evidence we have — that certain matters of concern to critics nowadays are not just academic questions, not just the problems of our own age, or of any age or any school of criticism, and, therefore, that they are not only matters of vested, or tribal, or passing interest, but matters of enduring, as well as historical, importance to the human race itself in so far as art has affected, and constantly does affect our vision of human nature, of society, of vice, of virtue, and so on — just as certain plays and films, poems and novels, that we have personally seen or read may affect the way we see things around us, including the way we see other works of art, from childhood on. Sometimes it is hard *not* to see the world through the lenses of art, even as a landscape may look exactly as an artist has painted it. How does a sunflower look, if not like a Van Gogh?

Given the major issues at stake, one can predict, with well-nigh as much certainty as one can predict that the sun will rise again tomorrow (or that tomorrow's critical arguments will rise to counter today's) that, whatever answers may yet be given to them, certain questions posed in *The Republic* are going to remain central concerns of literary criticism in general, and of Shakespeare's critics in particular; for so long as drama and poetry have had, do have, or will have, anything whatsoever to do with education, with psychology, with morality, or with our vision of reality, or with actual behaviour, or with any questions of censorship (whether of art or of psychological responses to it), or with any other human and dramatic realities and illusions that

Plato was concerned with, or that you care to name. I have stressed the dialectical relationship between Platonic, Romantic, and modern counter-interpretations of Shakespearian drama, not just because of their historical importance, but because the issues involved seem so intrinsic, fundamental, essential to our apprehension of the nature and impact of art, and, by extension, to our apprehension of the nature and importance of criticism.

It seems, for instance, indisputably true that (as Plato observed), because the essence of drama is conflict, it is, therefore, virtually bound to arouse 'contrary opinions about the same objects in the realm of vision' (X. 433). Thus, the compound answer to the question we began with, 'How does a Shakespearian play, or character, look?' is that the same 'object in the realm of vision' may not only look different to different people at the same time, and may seem entirely different to the same person at different times, but may also appear in different ways to the same individual at one and the same time. The hedging around involved in these inconclusive conclusions creates many of the critical problems that are outlined in the next chapter.

Notes

1. See Plato, *The Republic*, translated by Desmond Lee (Harmondsworth, 1974 – the quotations are from Part II, p. 149, and Part X, pp. 438–9) – specific references to the arguments paraphrased here are subsequently cited, parenthetically, in the text. In this chapter, as elsewhere, my arguments concerning the problems posed in Parts III, IX, and X of *The Republic* are particularly indebted to Eric A. Havelock, *Preface to Plato* (New York, 1971); Iris Murdoch, *The Fire and the Sun: Why Plato Banished the Artists* (Oxford, 1977); and K. R. Popper, *The Open Society and Its Enemies*, Vol. 1 (London, 1966). I should add that certain neo-classical and modern counter-arguments outlined in this chapter are discussed in more detail (with chapter-and-verse references) later on.

2. Sir Philip Sidney, *An Apology for Poetry*, in *Criticism: The Major Texts*, ed. Walter Jackson Bate (New York, 1970), p. 97; and see also F. M. Krouse, 'Plato and Sidney's *Defence of Poesie*', in *Comparative Literature*, VI (1954), 138–47.

3. Jeremy Collier directed the same Platonic arguments against Restoration drama in his succession of attacks on the 'immorality and profaneness' of the stage; and countless modern discussions of the morality of Shakespearian drama can be seen as an effort to solve the problems that Plato originally posed.

4. In his *Apology for Poetry* Sidney insisted that Plato (whom he immensely admired) was himself the 'most poetical' of all philosophers, and that some of Plato's own fictions could be attacked on the grounds that they 'authorize

abominable filthiness'. And indeed, the morality of *The Republic* itself is open to critical dispute – see Desmond Lee's 'Translator's Introduction', pp. 50–6. The most formidable attack on *The Republic* is Popper's account of 'The Spell of Plato' in *The Open Society and its Enemies*.

5. See the cognate account of the suspension of disbelief by I.M.S., 'On Worthy Master Shakespeare and his Poems' (prefixed to the Second Folio, 1632), in *Shakespeare Criticism: A Selection, 1623-1840*, ed. D. Nichol Smith (London, 1916), p. 8 – hereafter cited as *Shakespeare Criticism*. While watching Shakespeare's plays, we are

> abus'd and glad
> To be abus'd, affected with that truth
> Which we perceive is false. . . . Now to move
> A chilling pitty, then a rigorous love:
> To strike up, and stroake down, both joy and ire;
> To steere th' affections; and by heavenly fire
> Mould us anew. Stolne from our selves –
>   This and much more which cannot bee exprest,
> But by himselfe, his tongue and his own brest,
> Was *Shakespeares* freehold.

As Evert Sprinchorn has observed, what can happen in a 'perfect performance' of a Shakespearian play is 'best illustrated by the apocryphal story of the Chicago actor on tour in the West who played Iago so splendidly that one of the cowboys in the house, unable to endure the triumph of evil, pulled out his pistol and shot the bastard. There was nothing for the townspeople to do but hang the cowboy and bury him and the actor under one tombstone inscribed: THE PERFECT ACTOR AND THE PERFECT SPECTATOR' (see Sprinchorn, 'The Handkerchief Trick in *Othello*', in *The Columbia University Forum Anthology*, ed. Peter Spackman and Lee Ambrose (New York, 1968), pp. 201–10). The modern vogue whereby any suspension of disbelief is discouraged, rather than evoked, in performance, is alien to Shakespeare's art. His own lines wherein dramatic illusion is fractured, and the audience is reminded that the play is only a play, are dependent for their impact on the fact that the illusion seems real; there is no way to fracture an illusion of reality that does not exist.

6. On the dangers involved in interpreting Shakespeare's works as purely 'self-reflexive' artefacts, see Norman Rabkin, *Shakespeare and the Problem of Meaning* (Chicago, 1981), p. 119. Apart from seeming a let-down – e.g. 'the unity of conception and its diversity within that unity' in *The Winter's Tale* 'is the reflection of its nature as a scrupulously constructed verbal artifact' (see A. F. Bellette, 'Truth and Utterance in *The Winter's Tale*', *Shakespeare Survey*, 31 (1978), 65–75) – purely literary, or systematically 'metadramatic', accounts of Shakespeare's plays tend to deny his mysterious capacity to provide an experience that goes beyond the literary, and is indeed extra-dramatic.

7. See Randall Jarrell, 'The Age of Criticism', in *Poetry and the Age* (London, 1979), pp. 73, 79, 80. This book was originally published in 1955, but these (and other) arguments in it are by no means out of date. Indeed, Jarrell's old-fashioned defence of the best criticism, on the grounds that it serves to enhance an appreciation of a work of art by encouraging the public, or another artist, to see better what is already there, still has its validity. Perhaps the best description of this process occurs in one of Jarrell's primary sources of insight – Proust's account of the death of the novelist, Bergotte, in *Remembrance of Things Past* (see *The Captive*, trans. C. K. Scott Moncrieff (New York, 1932), p. 509):

The circumstances of his death were as follows. An attack of uraemia, by no means serious, had led to his being ordered to rest. But one of the critics having written somewhere that in Vermeer's *Street in Delft* (lent by the Gallery at The Hague for an exhibition of Dutch painting), a picture which he adored and imagined that he knew by heart, a little patch of yellow wall (which he could not remember) was so well painted that it was, if one looked at it by itself, like some priceless specimen of Chinese art, of a beauty that was sufficient in itself, Bergotte ate a few potatoes, left the house, and went to the exhibition. At the first few steps that he had to climb he was overcome by giddiness. . . . At last he came to the Vermeer which he remembered as more striking, more different from anything else that he knew, but in which, thanks to the critic's article, he remarked for the first time some small figures in blue, that the ground was pink, and finally the precious substance of the tiny patch of yellow wall. His giddiness increased; he fixed his eyes, like a child upon a yellow butterfly which it is trying to catch, upon the precious little patch of wall. 'That is how I ought to have written', he said. 'My last books are too dry, I ought to have gone over them with several coats of paint, . . . like this little patch of yellow wall.' Meanwhile he was not unconscious of the gravity of his condition. In a celestial balance there appeared to him, upon one of its scales, his own life, while the other contained the little patch of wall so beautifully painted in yellow.

8. The first quotation is from Andrew Fichter's '*Antony and Cleopatra*: "The Time of Universal Peace"', *Shakespeare Survey*, 33 (1980), 103–4; the others are quoted by Richard Levin in *New Readings vs. Old Plays: Recent Trends in the Reinterpretation of English Renaissance Drama* (Chicago, 1979), pp. 80–3 (hereafter cited as *New Readings vs. Old Plays*). The assumptions governing the conclusions about Shakespeare's heroines posited in the first three quotations deserve, and will get, further discussion later on.

9. See Helen Gardner, 'Milton's "Satan" and the Theme of Damnation in Elizabethan Tragedy', *Essays and Studies*, 1 (1948), 46–66; reprinted in *Elizabethan Drama: Modern Essays in Criticism*, ed. Ralph J. Kaufmann (New York, 1961), pp. 320–41 – the following arguments are posited on pp. 333–6. Romantic criticism was often remarkably subtle and penetrating, but often lost a sense of the play in its discussion of the characters, even as it tended to 'minimize in the tragic heroes the very thing that made them tragic and not pathetic, the evil in them'. In the criticism of this period, 'Hamlet's savagery and Lear's appalling rages are overlooked'. Conversely, modern critics of tragic figures insist that because they have their tragic flaws they are not to be pitied or admired, but to be critically castigated and despised. Thus, C. S. Lewis's view of Milton's Satan seems 'like an inversion of Shelley's'.

10. Quotations are from L. G. Salingar, '*The Revenger's Tragedy* and the Morality Tradition', *Scrutiny* 6 (1938), 402–3; W. L. Godshalk, *The Marlovian World Picture* (The Hague, 1974), pp. 7–8; Mark Stavig, *John Ford and the Traditional Moral Order* (Madison, Wisconsin, 1968), p. xv; and Roy Battenhouse, *Marlowe's Tamburlaine: A Study in Renaissance Moral Philosophy* (Nashville, Tennessee, 1941), pp. 12, 16. These quotations are representative of the tip, not of a critical iceberg, but of a critical glacier. The whole body of Elizabethan and Restoration drama was reinterpreted in these terms. When he challenged these assumptions, in *The Moral Vision of Jacobean Tragedy* (Madison, Wisconsin, 1960), Robert Ornstein sounded like a voice crying out in the wilderness. There is, by the way, one basic (Platonic) question that *all* interpretations of Elizabethan drama in terms of their morality-play structures, and their affirmations of the

'traditional moral order', have tended to beg. Which advertisement is likely to bring more people into the theatre and more cash into the box-office? 'Let Marlowe force you to perceive the evils resulting from human pride!' or 'Come see Marlowe blaspheme the gods out of heaven with that atheist Tamburlaine, and watch a low-born shepherd rise to conquer Asia!'

11. See Shelley, 'On the Devil, and Devils' and 'A Defence of Poetry', in *The Complete Works of Percy Bysshe Shelley,* ed. Roger Ingpen and Walter Peck (London, 1930), vii. 101, 118.

12. See John Dennis, 'On the Genius and Writings of Shakespear', in *The Critical Works of John Dennis,* ed. Edward Niles Hooker (Baltimore, 1943), II. 7.

13. See C. T. Watts, 'Shakespearian Themes: The Dying God and the Universal Wolf', in *Critical Dimensions: English, German and Comparative Literature Essays in Honour of Aurelio Zanco,* ed. Mario Curreli and Alberto Martino (Saste: Cuneo, 1978), pp. 129–30, and Robert Ornstein, *The Moral Vision of Jacobean Drama* (Madison, 1960), p. 13.

14. See Kenneth Burke, 'Literature as Equipment for Living', in *Perspectives by Incongruity,* ed. Stanley Edgar Hyman (Bloomington, Indiana, 1964), pp. 100–9. The categories are listed on pp. 100–2. See also Burke's note to 'Psychology and Form', p. 24; 'In Shakespeare we have the union of extrinsic and intrinsic epigram, the epigram growing out of its context and yet valuable independent of its context'.

15. See Shylock's catalogue of grievances and grudges:

> He hath disgrac'd me and hind'red me half a million; laugh'd at my losses, mock'd at my gains, scorned my nation, thwarted my bargains, cooled my friends, heated mine enemies. And what's his reason? I am a Jew.
>
> (III. i. 46–9)

It would seem, Erich Auerbach concludes, that Shakespeare had no ideological axes to grind —

> Yet when one of his characters expresses [revolutionary] ideas out of his own situation it is done with an immediacy, a dramatic force, which gives the ideas something arresting and incisive: Let your slaves live as you live; give them the same food and quarters; marry them to your children! You say your slaves are your property? Very well, just so do I answer you: this pound of flesh is mine, I bought it.

'The pariah Shylock', Auerbach observes, 'does not appeal to natural rights but to customary wrong' (see Auerbach, *Mimesis,* tr. Willard Trask (New York, 1953), p. 286). Moreover, there is no better depiction of the ways that ancient, tribal, ancestral grudges can be 'fed fat' until somebody is likely to bleed.

16. You could read Shakespeare for the same reason that Bacon recommended Machiavelli's *The Prince* — because he set forth 'openly and sincerely' what men and women are 'wont to do'. For that matter, 'there's such a difference between the way we really live and the way we ought to live that the man who neglects the real to study the ideal will learn how to accomplish his ruin, not his salvation'. See *The Prince,* trans. Robert M. Adams (New York, 1977), Chapter XV, p. 44.

17. See George, Lord Lyttelton (the quotation is from his 'Dialogue of the Dead' (1765)) in *Shakespeare Criticism,* ed. D. Nichol Smith, p. 73.

18. See Brendan Gill, *Tallulah* (London, 1972), p. 21: 'Perhaps in despair of keeping his girls in school', Will Bankhead 'took to telling them that if they knew Shakespeare and the Bible and could shoot craps, that was all the education they would ever need'. The wisest man I ever knew had the Bible and Shakespeare by heart, and that was pretty much all the education he needed to have.

19. E. H. Gombrich, 'Focus on the Arts and Humanities', *Bulletin of the American Academy of Arts and Sciences* (1981), pp. 20–1, reprinted in Gombrich's *Tributes*, Oxford, 1984 (pp. 11–27).

20. See P. B. Medawar, *Advice to a Young Scientist* (New York, 1979), p. 13.

21. See Levin, *New Readings vs. Old Plays*, pp. 82–3.

22. See A. L. French, *Shakespeare and the Critics* (Cambridge, 1972), p. 225.

23. See Lily Bess Campbell, *Shakespeare's Tragic Heroes: Slaves of Passion* (New York, 1963), p. 287.

24. See Walter Jackson Bate, *Criticism: The Major Texts* (New York, 1970), p. 42.

Besides concentrating attention more strongly on the theory of art as 'imitation', Plato also gave a further prominence, not, as is sometimes thought, to the importance of the social influence of art – that importance was taken for granted by the Greeks – but to the philosophical questioning about the *desirability* of that influence. And this question Plato illuminated in so thoroughgoing a way that it has remained ever since an imposing challenge to apologists for the arts. In this particular respect, as in so many others, the situation illustrates the justice of Alfred North Whitehead's remark that the history of European philosophy is 'a series of footnotes to Plato'.

Even so, the usual view is that the importance of *The Republic* to the history of literary criticism rests on its having been countered by Aristotle in *The Poetics*. But looked at in terms of the history of critical discussions of dramatic and poetic mimesis and morality, the attack Plato levelled at poetry and drama in *The Republic* has had an influence equivalent to – not superseded by – Aristotle's *Poetics*. See Jonas Barish's important discussion of 'The Platonic Foundation' in *The Antitheatrical Prejudice*, Berkeley and Los Angeles (1981), pp. 5–37.

25. Examples of this line of reasoning are legion. See, for instance, the critic of Cleopatra cited by Levin in *New Readings vs. Old Plays*, p. 138:

If under the spell of the moment we allow ourselves to be caught [by 'her magic'], our second reflections should awake us to the realization of what salt fish we are. Perhaps the art of tragedy consists in this very temptation to confusion – for the sake of our subsequent recognition of our folly. That is, a tragedy's beguiling heroisms serve to prompt mistaken judgements, so that then we can confess and evaluate our proneness to illusion.

See also Stanley Fish, *Surprised by Sin: The Reader in 'Paradise Lost'* (London, 1967) – Fish is the most influential of all exponents of this approach; Arlene N. Okerlund, 'Spenser's Wanton Maidens: Reader Psychology in the Bower of Bliss', *PMLA* 88 (1973), 62–8); and Ralph Berry, *'Twelfth Night*: The Experience of the Audience', *Shakespeare Survey*, 34 (1981), 118–19:

[When Malvolio says] 'I'll be reveng'd on the whole pack of you' . . . at *pack* the subliminal metaphor discloses itself. It is a bear-baiting. The audience becomes spectators, Malvolio the bear. . . . Imagine a Malvolio in the centre of the platform stage, addressing others downstage: he is surrounded on three (or all) sides by tiers of spectators, who are still perhaps jeering at him, and turns on his heel through at least 180 degrees to take in 'the whole pack of you'. That way the house, not merely the stage company, is identified with the 'pack'. It is theatre as blood sport, theatre that celebrates its own dark origins. That, too, is 'festive' comedy. What the audience makes of its emotions is its own affair. I surmise that the ultimate effect of *Twelfth Night* is to make the audience ashamed of itself.

The problem with the argument that tragedy, epic, romance, and comedy alike are designed to make the audience, or reader, feel guilty is that there is no artistic portrayal of vice, or passion, or folly, or cruelty (including the works of the Marquis de Sade) to which it could *not* be applied – or reversed.

26. See Richard Levin, 'The Ironic Reading of *The Rape of Lucrece* and the Problem of External Evidence', *Shakespeare Survey*, 34 (1981), 90, and *New Readings vs. Old Plays* (Chicago, 1979), Chapters 3 and 4. The problems involved in this approach get fuller discussion below.

27. See Kenneth Muir, *Shakespeare's Comic Sequence* (Liverpool, 1979), p. 54. See also David Smidman's letter to the editor of the *Guardian* (7 Sept. 1981): 'Having recently played Shylock myself in what I believe was a most thoughtful and sensitive production and, I admit, having enjoyed the experience – because theatrically Shylock is a spellbinder – I am now convinced that he . . . embodies all the preconceptions of prejudiced non-Jews.'

28. Professor Habicht found a concise four pages on Nazi productions of *The Merchant of Venice* in Josef Wulf's documentary volume, *Theater und Film im Dritten Reich* (Berlin and Vienna, 1966, reprinted 1983), pp. 280–3, which has excerpts from contemporary reviews of three productions, along with further bibliographical data. It would be interesting to know what cuts, if any, were made to Shakespeare's text to satisfy the Nazi censors.

Chapter 2

The 'Books' and 'Counterbooks' of Shakespearian Drama and Criticism

What esthetic effect is produced when the Apollonian and Dionysiac forces of art, usually separate, are made to work alongside each other?

Nietzsche, *The Birth of Tragedy*

Where's that palace whereinto foul things
Sometimes intrude not? Who has that breast so pure
But some uncleanly apprehensions
Keep leets and law-days, and in sessions sit
With meditations lawful?

Iago

This thing of darkness I acknowledge mine.

Prospero

Where God hath a temple, the devil will have a chapel.

Robert Burton, *The Anatomy of Melancholy*

There can be no contentment but in proceeding.

Thomas Hobbes, *Leviathan*

Part i.
'The Art of the Insoluble': Some Open Questions in *Measure for Measure* and *Hamlet*

In Borges's 'Tlön' (a third world created by poets and scientists, artists and philosophers), books 'of a philosophical nature' invariably include 'both the thesis and the antithesis, the rigorous pro and con of a doctrine'. 'A book which does not contain its counterbook is considered incomplete.'[1]

This description of the 'books' and 'counterbooks' of 'Tlön' can serve to raise, even as it answers, some fundamental questions about literature and criticism alike. It certainly provides us with a remarkably accurate and critically useful account of many plays, poems, and novels. For instance, the images of 'loathed Melancholy' and 'heart-easing Mirth' in Milton's 'L'Allegro' are countered by the vain, deluding joys of 'idle Mirth' and the sage and holy visage of 'divinest Melancholy' in 'Il Penseroso'. Even the *Paradise Lost* that aspires to justify the ways of God to men would seem to contain a 'counterbook' that justifies the ways of the Devil as well. For Blake, certain 'contrarieties are equally true', and therefore his *Songs of Innocence* summon forth the *Songs of Experience* wherein the tiger, burning bright, forever confronts his image of the gentle little lamb. Likewise, Marvell challenges impressive arguments in favour of the Soul, and against the Body, with comparably valid arguments in favour of the Body, and against the Soul. And with all his sympathy for Aeneas, Virgil gives a fair share of pity, and a very good case, to Dido. Their own Sancho Panzas travel alongside many of the Don Quixotes of art. And many artists have been eloquent advocates for their very own devils. Whose are those things of darkness, if not theirs?

The theory that many works represent the confrontation of opposed forces or ideas between which even the author may be torn (or give the appearance of being torn) would explain why intelligent readers have interpreted the identical texts in diametrically opposite ways. The explanation, in terms of Borges's parable, would be that one interpretation emphasizes the 'book' at the expense of the 'counterbook', while the opposite interpretation emphasizes the 'counterbook' at the expense of the 'book'. Thus, one group of readers can insist (with Marvell) that, in *Paradise Lost*, Milton 'draw [s] the devout, deterring the profane', while another group may argue (with Blake) that Milton was 'of the Devil's party' whether he knew it or not. Likewise, critical counter-interpretations have been imposed upon Elizabethan tragedies: 'The plays justify the values of society, showing the hero to be deeply flawed . . . they justify the hero, showing society to be wrong; the hero is wrong, but the playwright had such sympathy for him that he is willing to be of the devil's party.'[2]

Of all the other works and authors to which they could be applied, Borges's observations about 'books' being — and being considered — 'incomplete' without their 'counterbooks' are most strikingly relevant to the plays of Shakespeare, and, by extension, to critical books about them, which, in turn, are bound to seem incomplete without *their* counterbooks. It is perhaps because Shakespeare generally tends to confront the strongest case in favour of something with the strongest possible case against it (and vice versa) that his plays often appear to confront us with the very 'books' and 'counterbooks' of life itself. This, of course, has provided his admirers and detractors alike with countless subjects for further speculation about art and life, and the manifold affinities and discrepancies between the two. Yet the internal dialectic (whereby differing dramatic questions and arguments summon forth altogether different counter-questions and counter-arguments) poses obvious difficulties, not only for those critics who attempt to explain the various works in terms of some single-faceted thesis, or one-sided theory (or psychological doctrine, or ideological perspective), but for any critic, student, or director who tries to interpret or analyse them, in so far as all of us are liable, often without realizing it, to mistake our own favourite 'counterbook' for the Shakespearian 'book' itself. For that matter, the conflicting and contradictory answers given to the diverse questions raised within the plays themselves sometimes make it very difficult to decide which — if any one of them — is right. Take, for instance, certain questions about sexual morality, society, psychology, and law that are raised by the characters and action in *Measure for Measure*.

How important — or unimportant — is Isabella's chastity? And what (if anything) constitutes a fate that is worse than death?

Claudio. Death is a fearful thing.
Isabella   And shamed life a hateful.
(*Measure for Measure*, III. i. 117-8)

And precisely what constitutes rape? How heinous a violation is it to be blackmailed, or tricked, into bed with somebody you would not choose to have intercourse with? Given a conflict between Christian virtues — like chastity and charity — which of them should take precedence? Should a brother allow his sister to prostitute herself for his sake? Should a young novice sacrifice her chastity, and thereby jeopardize what she believes to be her immortal soul, in order to save her brother's life? And if she, personally, considers it a deadly sin to do so, should she encourage another woman to do it for her?

And what about the rule of law? Does the scriptural dictum, 'Judge not that ye be not judged', extend to magistrates, who are professionally obliged to enforce the criminal laws of the land? For that matter, what should magistrates do when certain laws (set down in heaven or on earth) clash with the biological and psychological laws of human

nature? How socially acceptable, or socially disruptive, *is* pre-marital
sex or organized prostitution? And what about shot-gun weddings?
Isn't the free consent of both parties just as important in marriage as it
is in sex?[3] How binding is a legal certificate if there is not a marriage of
true minds?

Throughout this tragicomedy, differing characters give us contradictory answers to such questions, even as Isabella, Angelo, and Claudio
dramatically give each other measure for measure concerning the major
moral conundrum debated in their great confrontation scenes: *would* it
be a sin, or an act of virtue, for Isabella to save Claudio by yielding to
Angelo?

Isabella, of course, believes that it would be a mortal sin:

Isabella. Better it were a brother died at once,
    Than that a sister, by redeeming him,
    Should die for ever.

(II. iv. 106-8)

Conversely, Angelo argues that there would be a 'charity' in sinning to
save a brother's life, and, at the last judgement, our 'compell'd sins/
Stand more for number than for accompt' (II. iv. 57-8, 63-4). Claudio
himself goes even further, and tells Isabella that

What sin you do to save a brother's life,
Nature dispenses with the deed so far
That it becomes a virtue.

(III. i. 135-7)

Isabella, in turn, insists that if her brother had any virtue, then 'had
he twenty heads',

he'd yield them up
Before his sister should her body stoop
To such abhorr'd pollution.

(II. iv. 181-3)

'Wilt thou be made a man out of my vice?', she asks Claudio:

Is't not a kind of incest to take life
From thine own sister's shame?

(III. i. 140-1)

Which (if any) of these characters, or arguments, is right? Given
their differing personal, and moral, priorities and premises, as well as
their different vested interests and desires, are all of them, in one way

or another, right? Or, given the clash between differing values and virtues, like chastity and charity, aren't there certain cases where no single option or argument can possibly be deemed right or acceptable to all of the individuals concerned? When confronted with dramatic situations of this kind, we in Shakespeare's audience occupy a position comparable to that of the characters themselves, in so far as our personal situations, as well as our historically or theologically based opinions about the issues may, in turn, determine which of their arguments we ourselves finally concur with, or reject. This explains why differing, and equally distinguished, critics have well-nigh inevitably arrived at diametrically opposite conclusions about the characters and situations here portrayed, and why there has been a continuing controversy — as opposed to an historical or moral or critical consensus — concerning the correct answers to the sexual and ethical questions Shakespeare raises in this play.

So complex are the issues, so powerful are the contradictory arguments, that it would seem quite impossible to prove which, if any, of the arguments he gave to Isabella, Claudio, or Angelo was deemed to be right by Shakespeare himself. In the great confrontation scenes, the various characters — very like their critical counterparts — contradict each other with passionate and persuasive arguments. In other instances, which are even more difficult to come to terms with, certain characters contradict themselves.

For instance, in Act II, Scene iii, the Duke sanctimoniously arraigns Julietta's conscience for her 'sin' in having voluntarily had sexual intercourse with Claudio, whom she dearly loves, and to whom she had been pre-contracted, but whom she had not yet married in church.[4]

Duke. Love you the man that wrong'd you?
Juliet. Yes, as I love the woman that wrong'd him.
Duke. So then, it seems your *most offenceful act*
   Was mutually committed.
Juliet.   *Mutually.*
Duke. Then was your sin of heavier kind than his.
                              (II. iii. 24–8, my italics)

Julietta's sexual complicity is thus held morally against her. Yet the same action that, in the case of Julietta and Claudio, is described by the Duke as a wrong, a sin, a 'most offenceful act', is, in the case of Mariana and Angelo, proclaimed to be 'no sin' at all. 'Fear you not at all', the Duke tells Mariana,

> [Angelo] is your husband on a pre-contract,
> To bring you thus together *'tis no sin,*
> Sith that the justice of your title to him
> Doth flourish the deceit.
>
> (IV. i. 70–3, my italics)

Given the seemingly arbitrary and *ad hoc* judgements involved in the
Duke's moral about-turn, it is hard to see what common principle of
morality, or equity, or justice, or mercy governs either of them. 'Sin',
the Duke seems to imply, is – or is not – whatever he says it is – or
isn't.

A comparable inconsistency involving criteria of justice and judgement occurs in the fifth act, when Isabella argues that Angelo should
not be subject to the death penalty, on the grounds that, unlike
Claudio, who did the sexual deed for which she thought he had died,
Angelo was guilty only in intent:

Isabella.   . . . My brother had but justice,
In that he did the thing for which he died;
For Angelo,
His act did not o'ertake his bad intent,
And must be buried but as an intent
That perish'd by the way.

(V. i. 446–51)

Isabella is certainly correct so far as Angelo's intentions to force her
into sexual intercourse (and, for that matter, his subsequent intention
to have Claudio killed) are concerned. Yet judged by the standards of
her own argument concerning Claudio, Angelo was technically subject
to the death-penalty, under the identical statute by which he had
condemned her brother, since, as a result of the bed-trick, Angelo also
'did the thing' for which Claudio appeared to have died (having, likewise,
had sexual intercourse with a woman to whom he was pre-contracted,
but whom he had not finally married in church). 'When I that censure
[Claudio] , do so offend', Angelo had pointedly – and most ironically –
insisted earlier on,

> Let mine own judgement pattern out my death,
> And nothing come in partial.
>
> (II. i. 30–1)

Indeed, when seen in terms of the obvious dramatic ironies here
involved, the wheels of the play appear to have turned full circle, as
it were in order to assure that Angelo would, finally, offend against

the law of Vienna in *exactly* the same way that Claudio did.[5] To get Angelo off, and so allow for a comic resolution, requires Isabella's casuistical pleas concerning action and intent in order to persuade the audience that Angelo should be spared the death-penalty. Yet the fact remains that the truly significant differences between the act of sex for which Claudio was sentenced to death, and the act of sex between Angelo and Mariana, are that Claudio did intend to marry as well as to sleep with his fiancée, while Angelo (who had intended to have sexual intercourse with the unwilling Isabella) was tricked into having sexual intercourse with Mariana, whom he then had no intention of either sleeping with or marrying. This kind of legal and moral nit-picking would seem critically absurd with reference to a different kind of play; but since its characters constantly engage in it, this particular play positively encourages it. And whether looked at morally or legally, whether in terms of justice or mercy, the inconsistencies involved both in the Duke's and in Isabella's legal and moral judgements are very difficult to resolve. But what, finally, seems the oddest thing of all throughout this play is the fact that the act of sex between Claudio and Julietta, which (perhaps paradoxically) is the one that is most emphatically, consistently, and severely judged as sinful, is the *only* sexual act in *Measure for Measure* that was undertaken with mutual consent, prompted by mutual desire, and dignified by mutual love. By contrast, every other act of sexual intercourse that is contemplated or consummated in it involves coercion, prostitution, force, or trickery. What, finally, is the relationship between sex and sin in *Measure for Measure*? Which of its characters are we supposed to judge as sinners, or to see as sinned against?

It is as if, throughout this strange tragicomedy, Shakespeare set out to develop those photo-negative reversals between virtue and vice that he had earlier described in *Romeo and Juliet* (see p. 39). He certainly confronts us with specific situations wherein 'virtue itself turns vice, being misapplied', even as 'vice sometime's by action dignified'. Perhaps significantly, a state of complete bewilderment concerning virtue and villainy is comically encapsulated in poor Elbow's speech confusing 'benefactors' with 'malefactors':

Elbow. ... I know not well what they are; but precise villains they are,
that I am sure of, and void of all profanation in the world that
good Christians ought to have.

(II. i. 52–5)

Can its historical context help us resolve the play's contradictions, or does *Measure for Measure* itself reflect a profound historical — and enduring — *uncertainty* concerning the degree of 'profanation in the world that good Christians ought to have', or ought to tolerate in others? On a number of the sexual and moral issues involved in the play, differing Christian denominations, rather like the differing characters, then held (just as they still hold) conflicting views. For instance: if, as St Paul observed, 'it is better to marry than to burn', then, Catholics argued, it is obviously better still to live chastely, to take Holy Orders, or enter a convent or a monastery. Conversely, Protestants generally extolled marriage, as opposed to monasticism. For that matter, there were, as there always are, some downright irreligious people around in seventeenth-century England, and Shakespeare's audience itself may well have contained (at least) a few irreverent libertines like Lucio, or like one Thomas Webbe, who is cited by Christopher Hill as having concluded that 'There's no heaven but women, nor no hell save marriage'.[6]

Given the course of action in *Measure for Measure* it does seem indisputably true that to attempt to expunge all profanation from the world is to invite disaster — which is precisely what the Duke of Vienna does when he summons Angelo, 'a man of stricture, and firm abstinence', to bring back the birch of law.[7] Indeed, even as Angelo crosses it, Shakespeare dramatically erases the fine line between legal severity and sadism: '[I hope] you'll find good cause to whip them all', Angelo tells Escalus (II. i. 131). 'Punish them unto your height of pleasure', says the Duke, later on, when Angelo asks to have his 'way' with Isabella and Mariana (V. i. 236–7) — thus implying that the bed-trick failed to effect a miraculous reformation so far as Angelo's pleasure in punishing people was concerned.[8] For that matter, what was (and still is) commonly deemed a form of sexual vice that should be punishable by law — commercial prostitution, with all the diseases it entails — here seems relatively innocuous when compared to Angelo's 'sharp appetite' and 'salt imagination'; that is, when compared to the diseases of the soul.

Thus the play confronts us with a tragicomic state of affairs wherein benefactors and malefactors are confused, where prayers themselves may cross (II. ii. 159), and where the extremes of asceticism and sensuality are seen, in turn, to repel, attract, change places with, embrace, or defy each other. In their central confrontations, Isabella's virtue is what enkindles Angelo's vice:

Angelo.   Can it be
   That modesty may more betray our sense
   Than woman's lightness? Having waste ground enough,
   Shall we desire to raze the sanctuary
   And pitch our evils there? O, fie, fie, fie!
   What doest thou, or what art thou, Angelo?
   Dost thou desire her foully for those things
   That make her good? . . .
   . . . .
   O cunning enemy, that, to catch a saint,
   With saints dost bait thy hook!
                                        (II. ii. 168–81)

There is a vicious circle here, since the saintlier Isabella is, the more
Angelo will desire her. Moreover, Isabella's fiery refusal to yield to him
is charged with an erotic power of its own:

         . . . were I under the terms of death,
         Th' *impression of keen whips I'd wear as rubies,*
         And *strip myself* to death *as to a bed*
         That longing have been sick for, ere I'd *yield*
         My body up to shame.
                                        (II. iv. 100–4, my italics)

Although everything here is associated with death, Isabella's references
to stripping herself, to whips, and rubies of blood, would seem dramatically designed by Shakespeare to further enflame a saint-turned-
sensualist like Angelo. And so, of course, they do.

Angelo. And now I give my sensual race the rein:
   Fit thy consent to my *sharp* appetite;
   Lay by all nicety and prolixious blushes
   That banish what they sue for; redeem thy brother
   By *yielding up thy body* to my will;
   Or else he must not only die the death,
   But thy unkindness shall his death draw out
   To ling'ring sufferance.
                                        (II. iv. 160–7, my italics)

Angelo here seems to be recalling, and either deliberately or unconsciously echoing Isabella's passionate lines. She must fit her consent to
his 'sharp appetite' (his sexual equivalent of 'keen whips'?). She must
'lay by' (strip herself of) all blushes 'That banish what they sue for'.
In short, she must come to *his* bed 'as to a bed/That longing have been
sick for'. Otherwise, he will have Claudio subjected to prolonged

torture before he has him killed. Angelo's lines are far more explicitly sexual, his threats more sadistic, than earlier propositions urging Isabella to ransom her brother with the treasure of her body: they are also far more demanding. He insists upon a completely uninhibited response *however* unwilling Isabella is to give it. He will allow her no modesty, no blushes. Seeing sadism and criminal sexuality in him, it was impossible for Coleridge to accept 'the pardon and marriage of Angelo': 'For cruelty, with lust and damnable baseness, cannot be forgiven, because we cannot conceive of them as being morally repented of'.[9]

Looking at their confrontations from another angle, one might infer that Angelo sees in Isabella the feminine counterpart of himself. As 'black masks/Proclaim an enshielded beauty' (II. iv. 79–80), so the saintly asceticism of her life, precisely like his own, may mask a keen appetite that could give full and fit consent to his desire. As he will give the 'sensual race the rein', so must she. He will have a response equivalent to his own sexual passion. Do their confrontations establish strange affinities between Shakespeare's fallen angel and his fiery saint? Does Isabella's initial desire for 'more severe restraints' within the convent suggest that there is something to restrain? Why her emphasis on woman's frailty? Why does she embrace martyrdom in such explicitly and passionately sexual terms — unless Shakespeare here wished to suggest that the line between martyr and masochist, between extreme asceticism and sensuality is indeed a narrow one, and all too easy to cross?[10] Why, finally, does Isabella's last speech thus refer to Angelo's desire for her? 'I partly think/A due sincerity govern'd his deeds/Till he did look on me'?

As J. C. Maxwell has observed, it is easy to see the germs of twentieth-century psychological theories in *Measure for Measure*: 'I have even been told of untutored playgoers who thought that it was Jonathan Miller and not Shakespeare who conceived the notion of setting it in Vienna'.[11] For that matter, the fact that sexual repression could result in neurosis, in a diseased imagination, in sexual aberrations, seems to have been as obvious to Freud's seventeenth-century predecessor, Robert Burton, as it was to Shakespeare — or to Freud himself. Indeed, Burton's compendium of Renaissance psychological theories, *The Anatomy of Melancholy*, can provide us with external evidence — if any is needed — that certain issues involved in *Measure for Measure* seemed just as complicated and problematical in Shakespeare's time as they do today.

In his discussion of sex and religion Burton (very like Shakespeare in *Measure for Measure*) brings together 'Great precisians' and 'fiery-spirited zealots' as well as certain types that may well have composed a part of Shakespeare's audience: there are the 'good, bad, indifferent, true, false, zealous, ambidexters, neutralists, lukewarm, libertines, atheists, etc.'.[12] In Burton, as in Shakespeare, virtue itself may turn to vice: 'Howsoever they may seem to be discreet', the 'preposterous zeal' of great precisians [like Angelo] may result in actions that go 'beyond measure' (iii. 372). In sexual matters, 'Venus omitted' may do just as much damage as 'intemperate Venus' – it may cause 'priapismus, satyriasis, etc.' and 'send up poisonous vapours to the brain and heart'. If the 'natural seed be over-long kept (in some parties) it turns to poison' (i. 234-5). To Burton, the tyranny of religious 'superstition' seemed as terrible as the tyranny of princes: 'What power of prince or penal law, be it never so strict', could enforce men and women (rather like Isabella) to do that which they will voluntarily undergo for religion's sake 'As to fast from all flesh, abstain from marriage, . . . whip themselves . . . abandon the world?' (iii. 332). Zealots of this kind will endure any misery, 'suffer and do that which the sunbeams will not endure to see, *religionis acti furiis*', endure 'all extremeties', 'vow chastity', 'take any pains', 'die a thousand deaths' (iii. 350).

According to Burton, organized religion itself may provide dispensations that are spurious, ways out that are too easy. As a Protestant, Burton deplored the 'general pardons' issued by Catholics, and complained that their 'ghostly fathers' all too easily 'apply remedies . . . cunningly string and unstring, wind and unwind their devotions, play upon their consciences with plausible speeches and terrible threats, . . . settle and remove, erect with such facility and deject, let in and out' (iii. 403-4). I have never seen anywhere what appears to be a better gloss on the dubious contrivances of Shakespeare's Duke-disguised-as-a-friar, as he plays upon the consciences of other characters; sets up, and then removes, the rod of law; arbitrarily orders people into, and out of, death-row; and finally issues general pardons for all offences. One could, using Burton's arguments, write an essay concluding that Shakespeare intended us to be comparably critical of the Duke. But it is just as easy to argue the opposite case: given the structure of the play, Shakespeare himself appears to be on the side of the Duke, whose compromises, contrivances, improvisations, and intrigues may be necessary in order to maintain any stability or order, or justice, or mercy, in a fallen world. Yet the poetry of the play loses power from the moment the Duke takes over.[13] And even in the second half of the play, Shakespeare still allows his characters a degree of recalcitrance. Lucio goes, protesting, to marry his whore. Angelo asks only for death (never for Mariana), while Isabella's response to the Duke's proposal is silence; so that in the end, as in their confrontation scenes, they still seem, oddly, to be two of a kind. Thus even in the Fifth Act, when the organization of the play seems to reinforce it, the characterization seems to challenge the assumption that human nature can be made to perform according to a scenario of the Duke's — or of Shakespeare's, or of anyone else's — contriving.

Moreover, by way of Julietta, Claudio, Lucio, and Barnardine, Shakespeare treats certain sinners with genuine sympathy and tolerance. Markedly unlike the Duke, the play itself does not (my terms are again from Burton) 'repel a fornicator, reject a drunkard, resist a proud fellow, turn away an idolator, but entertains all, communicates itself to all' (iii. 413). It is in this spacious humanity, and, perhaps, only in this, that Shakespeare might be said to reflect the ultimate grace of God. Yet he also gives the Devil his due. In the fall of Angelo, as Coleridge observed, he confronts us with things that are 'horrible'. He crosses the boundary between the angelic and the demonic to remind us that God's temple itself may contain the Devil's chapel.

In *Measure for Measure*, Shakespeare presents us with an imaginary landscape inhabited by spiders and flies, burrs that stick, the basest of weeds, and lilies that fester. In this wild terrain, and not in the ending which appears to have tidied it up, may lie the source of the play's vitality, of its enduring relevance. To my mind, anyway, what seems least significant about it are the ducal solutions offered us, whereby 'all difficulties are but easy when they are known' (IV. ii. 192–3), and all the moral, sexual, psychological, and legal problems can be solved by substitutions, bed-tricks, and marriage certificates. What seem most significant are the open questions posed along the way.

Yet why should any admirer of Shakespeare object to the ending of a tragicomic masterpiece because it offers dramatic solutions to the problems posed within it? I believe the reason for this critical reaction is that the kinds of solutions offered us by the Duke — whether Shakespeare intended them to or not — seem hopelessly inadequate in the face of the psychological, sexual, and moral conflicts they are supposed to have resolved. By contrast, it seems just fine when, in the end of *The Comedy of Errors*, some basic problems are solved when twin finally meets twin, and Aegeon is spared. For the death-threat to Aegeon was, from the outset, amenable to a practical solution (i.e. the payment of 1,000 marks), even as all the dramatic complications arising from the mistaking of one twin for another can, instantaneously, be unravelled when both twins finally appear together on the stage.

Count Otto von Bismarck described politics as 'the art of the possible', and Sir Peter Medawar has described science as 'the art of the soluble'.[14] And both these descriptions could be applied to a certain kind of dramatic art, in which (as in, say, Roman comedy, or *The Comedy of Errors*) the playwright poses dramatic problems (however complicated they may appear to be) that are finally amenable to a dramatic resolution. On the other hand, a very different kind of dramatic art operates in certain scenes in *Measure for Measure*. That is the artistic method involved both in classical and in Shakespearian tragedy, and which might most accurately be described as 'The Art of the *Insoluble*', in so far as it confronts the audience, as well as its characters, with certain problems inherent in the human condition, that are no more amenable to dramatic resolution – or, for that matter, to critical resolution – than they are amenable to any final solution in real life.

For instance: discussing the problem of justice in Greek tragedy, Hugh Lloyd-Jones has observed that Aeschylus' revenger, Orestes, is confronted with a dilemma as perplexing as the paradoxes of Zeno. If Orestes 'had failed to avenge his father', the Furies would have pursued him for his failure to see that justice was done. Since he does avenge his father, the Furies 'pursue him for the killing of his mother'.[15] In *Hamlet*, Shakespeare confronts us with a no less perplexing dilemma. Hamlet is prompted to his revenge by every claim of justice that there is. Yet his efforts to avenge his father's 'foul, and most unnatural murder' finally lead, not only to the death of the murderer, Claudius, but also to Hamlet's own untimely death, as well as the deaths of Gertrude, Ophelia, Laertes, Polonius, Rosencrantz, and Guildenstern; and the final result is the loss of the state of Denmark to the son of Hamlet's father's old enemy, Fortinbras of Norway. Should Hamlet, therefore, be critically judged as having made a considerable mess of things?

Hamlet's tragedy, of course, takes place in a Christian context, and Christian theology dictated against revenge. 'Vengeance is mine', said the Lord in the Bible, 'I shall repay'. Should Hamlet, therefore, have left vengeance to God, left Claudius to Heaven, let bygones be bygones, and let the murderer of his father wear the crown of Denmark? If that is the case, then what about the claims of justice itself? Not only Hamlet, but the soldiers on the parapet, were keenly aware that something was rotten in Denmark and that something seemed to bode a strange eruption to the state. From its first act to its last, when it is looked at, not in terms of the hero's behaviour, but in terms of the tragic sequence of events involved in it, the play itself constantly insists that the ultimate source of all the suffering in the play, the reason for the need for revenge, for justice, is the 'murder most foul' that was committed by Claudius, who is, therefore, pursued by dramatic Furies of his own making.

'My offence is rank', Claudius confesses to Shakespeare's audience,

> it smells to heaven;
> It hath the primal eldest curse upon't —
> A brother's murder!

> (III. iii. 36–8)

Yet Claudius cannot finally repent.[16] He will not give up his crown, or his queen, albeit by his own admission he is just as guilty as Cain. The murder of Hamlet's father, that took place before the opening scene of Hamlet's own tragedy, can thus be seen as what precipitated everything that followed from it, and Claudius can be seen as what's rotten in Denmark, as the serpent in the garden, who is to blame for his own suffering and damnation, as well as for the deaths of Hamlet, Gertrude, Laertes, Ophelia, Polonius, Rosencrantz, and Guildenstern. This view of the play is posited in one of the earliest published interpretations of *Hamlet*. In a book on *The Antient and Modern Stages Survey'd* (published in 1699), James Drake concluded that the crime and punishment of Claudius are crucial to the moral, as well as the dramatic, effect of Shakespeare's tragedy. '*Hamlet*', Drake observed, is an account of 'Murther privately committed, strangely discover'd, and wonderfully punish'd'.[17]

Down through subsequent centuries, however, the hero, Hamlet, not the villain, Claudius, has been the one pursued by critical commentators who, rather like the Greek Furies, have condemned the Prince of Denmark, on the one hand for not having avenged his father quickly enough, or on the other hand for not having left vengeance to God, as any good Christian would have done. In recent years, critics and directors alike (a good example occurred on television in *Shakespeare Lives*, where a whole programme was devoted to Michael Bogdanov's directorial debunking of Hamlet) have insisted that

Hamlet's deplorable obtuseness, or sheer ineptitude, or uncharitable vindictiveness towards his father's murderer, are what we ought to see as blameworthy. Thus the Prince of Denmark emerges, from many modern productions and critical essays alike, not as the play's hero-victim, but as the anti-hero of an anti-revenge, anti-Hamlet play.

To give only one critical example of this interpretative vogue, in a recent article,[18] John F. Andrews morally deplores Hamlet's vision of a *bella vendetta* in the crucial scene where he decides not to kill Claudius at prayer, because he wants the murderer of his father to face Judgement, *just as his father did*, with all his sins upon him. Here is the speech that Andrews finds especially objectionable; even as Dr Johnson had found it shocking:

Hamlet. Now might I do it pat, now 'a is a-praying;
And now I'll do't − and so 'a goes to heaven,
And so am I reveng'd. That would be scann'd:
A villain kills my father; and for that,
I, his sole son, do this same villain send
To heaven.
Why, this is hire and salary, not revenge.
'A took my father grossly, full of bread,
With all his crimes broad blown, as flush as May;
. . . .
. . . and am I then reveng'd
To take him in the purging of his soul,
When he is fit and season'd for his passage?
No. . . .
When he is drunk asleep, or in his rage;
Or in th' incestuous pleasure of his bed;
At game, a-swearing, or about some act
That has no relish of salvation in't −
Then trip him, that his heels may kick at heaven,
And that his soul may be as damn'd and black
As hell, whereto it goes.
(III. iii. 73−95)

'Ought we', John Andrews asks us, to identify with any cause, however just, that requires us to desire the eternal damnation of a soul, like that of Claudius, who prays 'for grace to help in time of need'? Doesn't the Christian context of the tragedy implicitly remind us that vengeance should be left to the Lord, and that Hamlet's determination to send Claudius to judgement, without shriving time allowed, is most un-Christian and itself 'potentially damnable'? Given Hamlet's vindictiveness, his cruelty to Ophelia, his indifference to the fates of

Rosencrantz and Guildenstern, Andrews complains that far too many of us still seem intent on viewing Horatio's final benediction — 'Now cracks a noble heart. Good night, sweet prince,/And flights of angels sing thee to thy rest!' — as if this were Shakespeare's way of assuring us that, however many 'purposes mistook' lay along his way, Hamlet did the best that he — or anyone else — could have done under the circumstances, and thus was 'proved most royal'. Andrews himself is convinced that Shakespeare would have expected the more 'judicious' members of his audience to take a far more detached and critical view of Hamlet than Horatio did, and he therefore concludes his essay by urging the rest of us to 'Be judicious', and to keep our sympathetic responses to Hamlet under critical control.

Yet Andrews's interpretation of Hamlet (like other critical and directorial interpretations of Shakespeare's tragedies that sound very much like it) raises a major Aristotelian question. Without feelings of great sympathy, or admiration, for its protagonist — that is, in the absence of pity and terror — how can there be any tragic effect to a play at all? The answer to this question may well be, 'There can't'. Although Aristotle would be the first to acknowledge that tragic heroes obviously have their tragic flaws, in seemingly conflicting arguments elsewhere in the *Poetics,* he concluded that tragic heroes should be neither better nor worse than we are, but 'like ourselves' — yet also seem, in some way, superior to us. All three of these apparently contradictory requirements seem to me to be dramatically fulfilled in the case of Hamlet, who may be infinitely superior to us in his wit and intelligence, albeit neither better, nor worse, but very 'like ourselves' *in having flaws* and being, likewise, subject to 'The heart-ache and the thousand natural shocks/That flesh is heir to'. This is why I am not persuaded that even the most judicious modern critic's, or director's (or Elizabethan spectator's) moral superiority to Hamlet ought to be taken for granted. Andrews, for instance, assumes that because he wants revenge, Hamlet is manifestly worse than we judicious critics are. But is he?

The fact is that the central question raised by Andrews, 'Ought people to desire the damnation of anyone, however great their sins?' is one thing. 'Do they?' is an entirely different question. 'To Hell with Him!' was the title of a commentary on the death of Hitler's henchman, Albert Speer — even though, like Claudius, Speer had made an effort to repent. 'Go thou and fill another room in hell'; 'Villain, thy own hand yields thy death's instrument' — thus expressing a grim

satisfaction, Richard II dispatches two of Exton's hit-men (V.v. 106-7).
'It is a poison tempered by himself', observes Laertes, contemplating
the death of Claudius with comparable satisfaction: 'He is justly serv'd'
(V. ii. 319-20). Perhaps because life all too often lets the wicked
flourish like the green bay tree, there is a certain satisfaction in seeing
a playwright, by way of his revenger, give wicked characters exactly
what they have coming to them, and thus, in one sense anyway, 'When
the bad bleeds, then is the tragedy good'. Or so – whether one accepts
Andrews's arguments or not – it once was. The poet, Sir Philip Sidney
observed, may invent 'new punishments in Hell for tyrants'. Looked
at from this angle, the theological premiss that the wicked will finally
be punished in Hell is very much like a dramatist's emphasis on retribu-
tive justice, in that both may serve to satisfy a desire for justice that
often goes unsatisfied in this our life. So far as punishments in Hell are
concerned, one does wonder why, if revenge is so awful, the Almighty
saw fit to claim it for His own – that is, unless the claims of justice
would, otherwise, remain eternally unsatisfied.

The very theology of Hell, as well as the popularity of revenge in
Greek drama, and in Elizabethan drama (and in the modern cinema),
would seem to confirm the conclusions posited by Eric Bentley, who
observes that 'Life itself is everywhere pervaded by the fact, or the
imagination of revenge.' 'Getting one's own back', taking real, or
imagined revenge, for all too real, as well as imaginary wrongs, 'has
good title to be considered one of the principal activities of Homo
Sapiens'. So much (Bentley argues) may be obvious. Somewhat less
obvious is the fact that the idea of revenge is not nearly as welcome as
the reality. 'Revenge', Bentley concludes, appeals to dramatists because
they are 'masters of reality', not ideologues.[19]

Paradoxically enough, Eric Bentley's conclusions would seem to
have been confirmed, rather than refuted, by John Andrews's own line
of critical reasoning whereby (1) Hamlet's desire to damn Claudius for
damning his father is itself 'potentially damnable', and (2) therefore
the 'judicious' spectator ought, potentially anyway, to damn Hamlet
for determining to damn Claudius for having damned his father.
Couldn't this be described as a form of critical revenge on Hamlet
himself? And does it not follow that an 'ultra-judicious' critic might, in
turn, write an article damning 'judicious' critics like Andrews for
wanting to damn Hamlet for wanting to damn Claudius, and so on?
When they are seen from this perspective, there could be a valid moral,
as well as dramatic case for the defence of Shakespeare's lines that

finally break the chain of vindictiveness, and summon flights of angels
to sing Hamlet to his rest.

Assuming, however, that Andrews is right, and we really ought to
adopt a detached, judicious, and morally censorious attitude towards
Hamlet, then whose fault is it that Hamlet has dramatically and historically evoked precisely the kind of injudiciously sympathetic and
admiring responses that critics and directors have to urge us to suppress? Is not Shakespeare himself the one to blame for having so
unwittingly, or, worse still, deliberately misdirected the injudicious
spectator's, or reader's, sympathies towards, rather than away from
Hamlet? Far from scoring moral points for doing so, doesn't Shakespeare
deserve to be charged with the rankest hypocrisy, if on one level he
produced a morally orthodox, anti-revenge play for the delectation of a
judicious minority, and, simultaneously, pandered to popular taste by
arousing and finally satisfying not only Hamlet's, but the audience's
desire (a desire that does not preclude some pity for him, as well as
terror at his fate) to see Claudius dispatched, even as he sent his own
brother to the infernal regions, with all his sins upon him?[20]

These questions are wide open, in the sense that there is no scholarly, directorial, or critical certainty concerning the right answers to
them. But would *Hamlet* be dramatically better if it did consistently
put down the hero, and thus conformed to certain modern critical
and directorial theories about it? Would it be truer to human experience if Shakespeare had, emphatically, insisted that a Christian decision
to leave vengeance to God would solve *all* of the problems in the
play? Given this standard of judgement, Tourneur's *The Atheist's
Tragedy* would be a far greater play than *Hamlet*. Conversely, would
Shakespeare's tragedy be any better if the author had implied that the
problems would have been readily solved if Hamlet had only diverted
his energies by fighting over an eggshell (like Fortinbras), or if he had
rushed to his revenge, like Laertes? For that matter, given a script, and
a long record of actual responses to it indicating that Shakespeare did
not do so, is it really the duty of modern critics and directors to insist
that the hero (and not the author) of the tragedy should be morally
castigated for having failed to see the final solution that would be
obvious to any judicious and right-minded critic, or director, or
spectator, or reader of the play?

'You are', wrote Chekhov, 'confusing two concepts: *The solution of
a problem* and *the correct posing of a question*. Only the second is
obligatory for an artist.' 'Not a single problem', he added, 'is solved

in *Anna Karenina* and in *Eugène Onegin*, but you will find these works quite satisfactory because all the questions in them are correctly posed.'[21] I believe that Chekhov is right in insisting that what accounts for the survival of certain works of art is that the questions in them are so 'correctly posed'. This, I believe, also explains why, as Maynard Mack has observed, the world of *Hamlet* is pre-eminently conceived of in 'the interrogative mood'. Shakespeare's play itself, Mack reminds us, 'reverberates with questions, anguished, meditative, alarmed'. From the opening line ('Who's there?'), through the most famous of questions, 'To be or not to be', the interrogations posited seem to point, not only beyond the context, but beyond the play, 'out of Hamlet's predicaments into everyone's'. Like all of us, also, Hamlet is confronted with the immediate problem of interpreting what is going on around him: 'His mother — how could she "on this fair mountain leave to feed, And batten on this moor?" The ghost — which may be a devil, for "the de'il hath power T' assume a pleasing shape". Ophelia — what does her behaviour to him mean? . . . Even the king at his prayers is a riddle. Will a revenge that takes him in the purging of his soul be vengeance, or hire and salary? As for himself, Hamlet realizes, he is the greatest riddle of all — a mystery, he warns Rosencrantz and Guildenstern — from which he will not have the heart plucked out'. Thus, Mack concludes, the 'mysteriousness of Hamlet's world is of a piece'.[22] It is not simply a matter of supplying missing motivations, nor is it a puzzle that can be solved by critics, or directors, if only they can find the perfect clue. The questions are 'built-in', they are an important part of whatever the play has to communicate to us, from the moment that Bernardo asks Francisco 'Who's there?' Hamlet, of course, raises the same question with reference to the ghost. Who and what was the intimate, yet unidentifiable spectre that summoned Hamlet to the parapet at Elsinore?

Ought Hamlet to have known, since everyone in Shakespeare's audience would have known, that the ghost must have been a 'goblin damned' because, in defiance of the divine edict, it cries out for vengeance? This view has been posited by Eleanor Prosser,[23] as well as in the Royal Court production of *Hamlet* in London a few years ago wherein the relationship between Hamlet and the ghost was interpreted as one of demonic possession, and the ghost spoke from Hamlet's own belly. Yet dramatically speaking, the most obvious function of the ghost is, arguably anyway (see below, pp. 134-6) to ensure that the major problems in this play are, from the very outset, 'correctly posed'. And the fact is that the most fundamental of all these problems has nothing whatsoever to do with demonic possession. Had Hamlet learned about the murder of his father from another source — from, say, the sworn testimony of an unimpeachably honest eye-witness — he would still have had to make up his mind what to do about Claudius, and when and how to do it. Moreover, in Shakespeare's play itself there would seem to be more evidence that the ghost was an 'honest ghost' than evidence that it was a devil with the power to assume a pleasing shape. Whichever it was, its testimony concerning Claudius was proved true. And Hamlet was obliged to act upon that truth — that the murderer of his father wore his crown. And one cannot but wonder if any audience, Elizabethan or modern, would have preferred it if Hamlet *had* forgone revenge, and gone back to Wittenberg, or chosen exile in England.

Moralistic arguments that Hamlet obviously should have left vengeance to the Lord tend to run aground against the realities of theatrical experience. For there are certain times in the course of dramatic events when most members of any audience — whether they are judicious or injudicious, Elizabethan, Jacobean, modern, or ancient Greek, will be virtually forced to join the Devil's party. For instance: given the choice, 'You can watch Marlowe's Faustus go forward; or you can watch him repent and be saved', how many spectators would actually choose the latter? Throughout *Doctor Faustus*, Marlowe confronts his audience, as well as his hero, with precisely this choice:

Bad Angel. Go forward Faustus, in that famous art.
. . . .
Good Angel. Sweet Faustus, leave that execrable art.

(I. i. 74, I. v. 15)

Indeed, at crucial moments in many tragedies (be they classical, Elizabethan, or modern) wherein the protagonist has decided to pursue a course of action known to his audience to be dangerous, or evil, or in any case inevitably tragic (or potentially damnable) in its consequences, he will be offered at least one chance to desist or to turn back. He may then decide (in the words of Macbeth) to 'proceed no further in this business'. 'Ask me no more', pleads Teiresias to Oedipus: 'I mean to spare you, and myself"; and later on Jocasta herself implores Oedipus to abandon his tragic quest. Yet who, in the audience, wants Oedipus to leave the terrible truth unknown? At the very last minute before that final encounter with the White Whale, the virtuous Starbuck begs, and, momentarily at least, almost persuades Captain Ahab to return to

Nantucket. But after hundreds of pages of pursuit, after incident after incident leading up to the final confrontation, does any reader really want Ahab to reverse course and head for home? Having come this far, would we not feel emotionally and aesthetically let down if, at this point, Ahab decided to abandon all thoughts of revenge, forget Moby Dick, and return to his dear wife and children? Similarly, had Marlowe's Faustus heeded the Old Man and managed an eleventh-hour repentance, many members of the audience might feel dramatically let down. Thus an author's, or a character's, satisfaction of an audience's desire for an ultimately tragic confrontation or catastrophe may be objectionable in ethical terms – but an ideally moral and ethically satisfying conclusion to certain works might seem objectionable on emotional or on aesthetic grounds.

In certain tragedies, as in *Hamlet*, the author creates a powerful appetite on the part of his audience for climax, not anti-climax. Even on subsequent readings, even with the certain knowledge that the Old Man offers Faustus his last chance for salvation, do we not join forces with Lucifer and Mephistophilis to urge Marlowe's hero on into the very heart of darkness? And even on subsequent viewings, is there not a satisfaction in seeing the murderer of Hamlet's father so 'wonderfully punished'? For the audience, as for many tragic heroes and heroines, there can be 'no contentment but in proceeding'. A tragic hero or heroine may thus serve as a kind of surrogate for one's own desires to 'try the utmost', to go all the way. And it is perhaps partly because we ourselves join with whatever forces – good or evil – that urge them on towards the tragic catastrophe, that we can so profoundly pity those heroes and heroines, villains and villainesses, who must face the consequences of their (and our) desires for ultimate knowledge, or justice, or revenge, or power, or passion – or whatever outer limits of human experience there are. These tragic heroes and heroines may be superior to us in their intellect, their sensitivity, their glamour, or their courage, yet they are our comrades in so far as they, too, suffer from the slings and arrows of outrageous fortune, the oppressor's wrong, the pangs of sexual jealousy, and other ills that our own flesh is heir to: 'By the image of my cause I see/The portraiture of his'. Moreover,

When we our betters see bearing our woes,
We scarcely think our miseries our foes.
Who alone suffers suffers most i' th' mind,
Leaving free things and happy shows behind;
But then the mind much sufferance doth o'erskip

When grief hath mates, and bearing fellowship.
How light and portable my pain seems now,
When that which makes me bend makes the King bow —

(*King Lear*, III. vi. 102–9)

Looked at from this point of view, tragedy allows us to see 'our betters' as our co-mates and brothers and sisters in passion and guilt, or in exile and suffering, and thus tragedy may make our own pain seem comparatively 'light and portable'.

What, if any, final conclusions we might arrive at concerning the behaviour and the fates of Shakespeare's tragic protagonists (e.g. 'Would we have, or could we have, done any better?' 'Would the alternative courses of action offered them have been equally bad?') are left entirely to us. 'The court', says Chekhov, 'is obliged to pose the questions correctly, but it's up to the jurors to answer them, each juror according to his own taste' (*Letters*, p. 88). It goes without saying that different jurors, upon viewing the same evidence, may come back with altogether different verdicts:

For though the nature of that we conceive, be the same; yet the diversity of our reception of it, in respect of different constitutions of body, and prejudices of opinion, gives everything a tincture of our different passions.... For one man calleth *Wisdome*, what another calleth *feare*; and one *cruelty*, what another *justice*; one *prodigality*, what another *magnanimity*. . . . From the same it proceedeth, that men give different names, to one and the same thing, from the difference of their own passions: As they that approve a private opinion, call it Opinion; but they that mislike it, Hærisie.[24]

By the same token, an art that contains its own contradictions may actively encourage us to size up the same situation from differing points of view, and thus to realize how very close to the way the artist seems to want us to see his characters and actions are other ways of seeing them. Where do we draw the line between Hamlet's 'cruelty' and his frustrated desire for 'justice'? Shakespeare's tendencies to stack the deck, then shuffle it, to deal the cards, then leave the game, to let his witnesses plead their own cases, and let the evidence speak for itself, obviously help to account for the richness, as well as the enduring relevance of his plays. Yet the manifest technical difficulties involved in writing about plays that contain their own counterplays may explain why certain modern theories and techniques of criticism have proved inapplicable to Shakespeare's plays.

Part ii.
'On the Other Hand':
The 'Counterbooks' of Criticism

It is (for instance) very difficult to see how a modern critic could possibly 'deconstruct' a play like *Measure for Measure* (or *Hamlet*, or *Antony and Cleopatra*), when all the most crucial of deconstructions – and reconstructions – have already been built into the script by Shakespeare himself. So far as semiotics are concerned, how can a critic cope with a drama where, as Terence Hawkes has observed, absolutely everything counts – where all the signals and significations of language, gesture, facial expression, setting, costume, groupings, silences, etc. may act upon and interact with or against each other in differing ways, and with differing effects, from moment to moment, from scene to scene, from beginning to end, from production to production?[25] Moreover, as Harold Bloom has noted, Shakespeare himself manifests no discernible anxieties in the course of assimilating, reacting to, and transcending the accomplishments of any number of poetic and dramatic precursors, or, for that matter, in the process of transcending his own apprentice efforts. Indeed, Shakespeare seems to have felt about his various sources of knowledge, information, know-how, inspiration, and insight in much the same way Drake felt about Spanish treasure-ships – that any valuables in them were his for the taking.[26]

Thus, assuming that anyone actually could write a critical study examining all the influences that Shakespeare might, conceivably, have assimilated, and discussing all of the signals and countersignals, texts and sub-texts, and constructions and deconstructions and reconstructions that interact on, and beneath, the surface of a single play, the resulting book might be so long, convoluted, and self-contradictory that its own author (to say nothing of its readers) might finally quail at the sheer volume of verbiage required to spell out what Shakespeare does, with immeasurably more eloquence and impact, in a sixty-page script. Worse yet, when stripped of rhetorical flourishes, the critical conclusions finally arrived at might not amount to very much more than an interminable sequence of counter-arguments like these:

On the one hand, we must realize that Cleopatra (or Antony, or Octavius, or Egypt, or Rome) is flawed, in that . . . But, on the other hand, we must also remember that she (or he, or it) is admirable in that . . . And whereas the poetry implies that certain characters are semi-divine, the action suggests that they are all too human . . .

And so on and on, like a 'vagabond flag upon the stream', going to and back, 'lackeying the varying tide, to rot itself with motion.' (*Antony and Cleopatra*, I. iv. 45-7).

Yet the 'on the one hand, this', and 'on the other hand, that' kind of rhetoric which occurs quite literally all over the place, and which has served as the deep structure for countless critical discussions of Shakespeare's plays (including this one),[27] may itself be as metaphorically significant as it is scientifically interesting:

Right hand, left hand; that was the deep clue that Pasteur followed in his study of life. The world is full of things whose right-hand version is different from the left-hand version . . . they can be mirrored one in the other, but they cannot be turned in such a way that the right hand and the left hand become interchangeable.[28]

Like the 'books' and 'counterbooks' interacting in a given play, our 'on the one hand' and 'on the other hand', or 'yes, but' or 'no, but' responses to them would seem to be essentially different, yet 'incomplete' without each other. Very like the rational and moral, and passionate and irrational facets of the human mind, our differing responses to a play may complement, as well as compete with or confound each other:[29] but they are not interchangeable. Indeed, Shakespeare's dramatic worlds could be accurately said to mirror the great globe itself in that they, too, are full of things 'whose right-hand version is different from the left-hand version'. And neither the things themselves, nor our emotional and intellectual responses to them, are capable of being altered so that they will be identical.

Obviously, in certain cases, moral and emotional judgements of individual characters and situations may mirror one another — just as hands may come together to applaud, or to pray, or to fire a revolver. Thus, in watching *King Lear*, emotional and moral judgements may cohere against, say, Cornwall, and in favour of the stand taken by that servant who risked, and lost, his life defying Cornwall. Yet there are countless other cases where emotional and moral responses — to, for instance, characters like Richard III, Falstaff, and Shylock — do not cohere. Nor do they cancel each other out. They simply coexist. For although we often experience them simultaneously in art as in life, the counter-claims of pity, admiration, moral disapproval, and imaginative enjoyment are not, or certainly not always, mutually exclusive. But while it is psychologically easy to experience what Plato called the 'simultaneous' presence of 'opposite impulses' and responses, it is impossible to analyse several different emotions or impulses at one and the same time. Thus the critical dialectic often tends to impose a sequential, alternating, or hierarchical order on responses that occur simultaneously, and so tends to falsify (at least in a temporal sense) the very complex of effects that the critic is attempting to describe.

We may feel this way, that way, and several other ways, about Shylock at one moment; or that way, this way, and an entirely different way about him at another moment, but it is impossible to write about such reactions without either explicitly or implicitly drawing temporal, or hierarchical, lines of demarcation between (on the one hand) the sympathies elicited by his suffering, and (on the other hand) a moral concern with his terrifying vindictiveness; or with his conformity to anti-Semitic stereotypes; or with any number of other responses that may crowd in upon each other all at once.

To make things even more difficult, there are certain dramatic cases where differing 'rights by rights falter, strengths by strengths do fail' (*Coriolanus*, IV. vii. 55), and where a character's very virtues may contribute at least as much to his suffering, or to his destruction, as any of his flaws. 'Why are you virtuous?' Adam asks Orlando, 'And wherefore are you gentle, strong, and valiant?'

> Know you not, master, to some kind of men
> Their graces serve them but as enemies?
> No more do yours. Your virtues, gentle master,
> Are sanctified and holy traitors to you.
> O, what a world is this, when what is comely
> Envenoms him that bears it!
>   (*As You Like It*, II. iii. 10-15)

Hamlet, Claudius correctly concludes, 'will not peruse the foils', because he is 'Most generous, and free from all contriving' (IV. vii. 135-6). 'The Moor', Iago gloats, 'will as tenderly be led by th' nose/As asses are', because he is 'of a free and open nature'. And it is out of Desdemona's 'own goodness' that will be made 'the net/That shall enmesh them all' (*Othello*, I. iii. 393-6; II. iii. 350-1). Thus, in Shakespearian drama, if not in all great drama (?), there are tragic virtues as well as tragic flaws. Moreover, in certain other instances, moral vices may manifest themselves as dramatic virtues. There is something dramatically compelling about a character, however evil, who is absolutely firm of purpose, and who behaves with utter resolution — whatever that character may be resolved to do.[30] There is also something almost irresistibly appealing about villains who treat us, in the audience, as their gossips, confidantes, and co-conspirators. However hypocritically he behaves towards the characters on the stage, Iago *is* honest with us. And sometimes the theatrical appeal of certain vices will win at the odds against less appealing portrayals of moral virtues. What actor would choose to play the Lord Chief Justice if he were offered the part of Falstaff; and who, if offered the part of Richard III, would really prefer to play Richmond? To which of these characters is an audience likely to give its most heartfelt applause?

In the preface to his edition of Shakespeare (1709), Nicholas Rowe observed that the dramatic pleasure afforded by Shakespeare's portrayal of Falstaff may finally outweigh a moral concern with even his most egregious vices. 'Falstaff', Rowe concluded, 'is allow'd by every body to be a Master-piece'. Yet one cannot but wonder whether this holds true *because* of, rather than in spite of, the fact that

if there be any fault in the Draught [Shakespeare] has made of this lewd old Fellow, it is, that tho' he has made him a Thief, Lying, Cowardly, Vainglorious, and in short every way Vicious, yet he has given him so much Wit as to make him almost too agreeable; and I don't know whether some People have not, in remembrance of the Diversion he had formerly afforded 'em, been sorry to see his Friend *Hal* use him so scurvily, when he comes to the Crown in the end of the Second Part of *Henry* the Fourth.[31]

Depending on whether one looks at Falstaff morally, or looks at him dramatically, the 'wit' involved in Shakespeare's portrayal of the lewd old fellow could be condemned as a moral 'fault', or extolled as a paramount theatrical virtue. Would Falstaff have been 'allow'd by every body to be a Master-piece' if Shakespeare had underscored his moral vices at the cost of eliminating, or playing down, the diversions afforded us that, in effect, make the old reprobate 'almost too agreeable' to an audience? And since Shakespeare didn't do it in the script, should the wit of the part be subordinated to a moral preoccupation with Falstaff's manifest vices in critical essays, or in production itself?

Discussing a production designed to emphasize the obvious moral vices of Richard III at the expense of his (equally obvious) dramatic virtues, Charles Lamb observed that

Not one of the spectators who have witnessed Mr. C.'s exertions in that part, but has come away with a proper conviction that Richard is a very wicked man, and kills little children in their beds, with something like the pleasure which the giants and ogres in children's books are represented to have taken in that practice; moreover, that he is very close and shrewd and devilish cunning, for you could see that by his eye.

But is in fact this the impression we have in reading the Richard of Shakespeare? Do we feel any thing like disgust, as we do at that butcher-like representation of him that passes for him on the stage? A horror at his crimes blends with the effect which we feel, but how is it qualified, how is it carried off, by the rich intellect which he displays, his resources, his wit, his buoyant spirits, his vast knowledge and insight into characters, the poetry of his part, — not an atom of which is made perceivable in Mr. C.'s way of acting it. Nothing but his crimes, his actions, is visible; they are prominent and staring; the murderer stands out, but where is the lofty genius, the man of vast capacity, — the profound, the witty, accomplished Richard?

The truth is, . . . that while we are reading any of his great criminal characters, — Macbeth, Richard, even Iago, — we think not so much of the crimes which they commit, as of the ambition, the aspiring spirit, the intellectual activity, which prompts them to overleap those moral fences.[32]

Query: doesn't Lamb's point also hold true of the greatest performances of Shakespeare's most villainous parts?

In any event, if Lamb and Rowe are right, or even partly right (as both of them surely are), then it is easy to see why the clash between moral and dramatic values and virtues has posed such serious problems for moral philosophers and critics from Plato's time to ours. So far as the moral conundrums posed by the 'books' and 'counterbooks' of poetry and drama are concerned, Plato (yet again) was the critic who got there first. Indeed, the moral and dramatic conflicts and contra-dictory opinions evoked by Greek literature were what he found especially objectionable, and what have seemed equally objectionable to moralistic critics of the drama ever since. None the less, the very greatest poets and playwrights down through the ages (like Homer or Shakespeare, or like the authors in Borges's 'Tlön') seem to have considered themselves professionally obliged to include 'both the thesis and the antithesis, the rigorous pro and con of a doctrine', and in the process of doing so, they often have had to give some confusions, or inner conflicts, or weaknesses, or vices, or irrational passions and errors of judgement to even their most admirable characters, and, conversely, to give at least some valid arguments and admirable characteristics (courage, wit, imagination, intelligence, etc.) to their most reprehensible villains. Therefore, so long as their art is judged, solely or primarily, in terms of the moral idealisms that are, or are not, embodied in their individual characters, Shakespeare and the Greek poets alike could be morally condemned for (on the one hand) having given far too many admirable, attractive, or sympathetic qualities or arguments to some of their least virtuous characters (like Falstaff and Richard III), and (on the other hand) for having given too many moral defects, passions, vices, follies, and frailties, to some of their most sympathetically and glamorously portrayed heroes and heroines (like Hamlet and Cleopatra). It was because of the state of total confusion between moral and emotional, pejorative and favourable judgements of their characters that Plato finally ordered poets to portray unexceptionally virtuous characters, or not to write at all. 'We cannot', he argued,

> have our citizens believe that Achilles, whose mother was a goddess . . . and who had in Chiron the wisest of schoolmasters, was in such a state of inner confusion that he combined in himself the two contrary maladies of ungenerous meanness about money and excessive arrogance to gods and men. . . . . We must therefore neither believe nor allow . . . any of the other lies now told about the terrible and wicked things which other sons of gods and heroes are said to have dared to do. We must compel our poets to say either that they never did these things or that they are not the sons of gods; we cannot allow them to assert both. . . . We must therefore put a stop to stories of this kind before they breed in our young men an undue tolerance of wickedness.
>
> (*The Republic*, III. 147–8)

This is the original version of the 'example' theory of the drama; and the effect of watching attractive sinners on the stage has been a subject of critical controversy from Plato's time to the present.[33] Vice, familiar grown, and embodied in appealing characters, may please; and as Plato observed (and as anyone in advertising knows), both consistently and frequently to associate certain kinds of behaviour with especially amusing, attractive, or glamorous models on the stage (or on screen, or on television, or in imaginative literature of any kind) is to make those forms of behaviour seem, by association, attractive, or at least acceptable, fashionable, tolerable, customary.

Moreover, given a conflict between morally unfavourable and emotionally favourable or sympathetic responses to the drama's erring characters, Plato may well have been right in concluding that the passionate, irrational responses would almost inevitably win out. In evidence of this fact, he cites specific cases in Greek tragedy wherein playwrights — very like Shakespeare in *King Lear* — so powerfully portray the 'sufferings of a hero, and have him bewail them at length' that the audience is bound to share the hero's grief (even as it is extremely difficult to conceive of an audience so flinty-hearted that it would *not* share King Lear's grief at the death of Cordelia). Yet in real life, Plato insisted, we ought to, and do rightly, pride ourselves on the ability to bear our personal bereavements in silence. Thus tragic poetry gratifies and indulges the instinctive desires of a part of us, which we forcibly restrain in our private misfortunes, with its hunger for tears and for an uninhibited indulgence in grief. Our better nature . . . relaxes its control over those feelings, on the grounds that it is someone else's sufferings it is watching and that there's nothing to be ashamed of in praising and pitying another man with some claim to goodness who shows excessive grief; besides, it reckons the pleasure it gets as sheer gain, and would certainly not consent to be deprived of it by condemning the whole poem. For very few people are capable of realizing that what we feel for other people must infect what we feel for ourselves, and that if we let our pity for the misfortunes of others grow too strong it will be difficult to restrain our feelings in our own.

Moreover, the identical point holds true of comedy ('Does not the same argument apply to laughter as to pity?'):

For the effect is similar when you enjoy on the stage . . . jokes that you would be ashamed to make yourself, instead of detesting their vulgarity. You are giving rein to your comic instinct, which your reason has restrained for fear you may seem to be playing the fool, and bad taste in the theatre may insensibly lead you into becoming a buffoon at home.

Indeed, 'the same argument' is equally applicable to imaginative portrayals of 'sex and anger, and the other desires and feelings of pleasure and pain which accompany all our actions'. Art waters passions that should be left to wither, and 'makes them control us when we ought, in the interest of our own greater welfare and happiness, to control them'. Should we not, therefore, condemn rather than applaud a poet who 'wakens and encourages and strengthens' the passions to the detriment of reason? (*The Republic*, X. 435-7.)

Plato's line of reasoning is, of course, countered in the *Poetics* by Aristotle's theory that, through arousing pity and fear, tragedy effects the proper purgation of these emotions. Yet Saint Augustine was (and is) obviously not the only human being who ever lived, whose personal experience of the drama would seem to have confirmed Plato's — as opposed to Aristotle's — conclusions about its actual impact and aftereffects. Augustine thus describes those days back in Corinth, when he himself was 'in love' and 'lashed with the cruel, fiery rods of jealousy and suspicion' (and therefore would seem to have particularly enjoyed watching Corinthian equivalents of *Romeo and Juliet, Othello*, and *Antony and Cleopatra*):

I was much attracted to the theatre, because the plays reflected my own unhappy plight and were tinder to my fire. . . . I used to share the joy of stage lovers and their sinful pleasure in each other even though it was all done in make-believe for the sake of entertainment; and when they were parted, pity of a sort led me to share their grief. I enjoyed both these emotions equally. . . . I always looked for things to wring my heart and the more tears an actor caused me to shed by his performance on the stage, even though he was portraying the imaginary distress of others, the more delightful and attractive I found it. Was it any wonder that I, the unhappy sheep who strayed from your flock, impatient of your shepherding, became infected with a loathsome mange? . . . I had no wish to endure the sufferings which I saw on the stage; but I enjoyed fables and fictions, which could only graze the skin. But where the fingers scratch, the skin becomes inflamed. It swells and festers with hideous pus. And the same happened to me. Could the life I led be called true life, my God?

'What a miserable delirium is this!', Augustine exclaimed: People go to see tragedies because 'they hope to be made to feel sad, and the feeling of sorrow is what they enjoy':

But what sort of pity can we really feel for an imaginary scene on the stage? The audience is not called upon to offer help, but only to feel sorrow, and the more they are pained the more they applaud the author. Whether this human agony is based on fact or is simply imaginary, if it is acted so badly that the audience is not moved to sorrow, they leave the theatre in a disgruntled and critical mood; whereas, if they are made to feel pain they stay to the end watching happily.[34]

The aesthetic and emotional and moral conundrums that Augustine describes in his *Confessions* are markedly similar to some of the ones that Plato posited in *The Republic*: while watching the sufferings of a tragic hero or heroine, 'you know how even the best of us enjoy it', and 'let ourselves be carried away by our feelings', and are 'full of praises for the merits of the poet who can most powerfully affect us in this way' (X. 436). Thus, despite the force of Aristotle's conclusions about catharsis, the major moral, psychological, dramatic, and critical paradoxes posed by Plato and Augustine have never been satisfactorily resolved.

It is, for instance, virtually impossible to refute their arguments whereby the passionate and irrational responses elicited by dramatic poetry are inextricably associated with its excellence: the better the poetry is, the more moved by it even 'the best of us', even the 'most respectable' of us, will be, and the more we will applaud the author or the production. Conversely, if the play is bad, or badly acted, the spectator will leave the theatre in a critical and disgruntled mood. Thus, it is in cases of *unsuccessful* art that the critical, rational faculties of the audience take precedence over emotional responses. The less successful the play, or performance, the more likely the audience will be to adopt a detached, judgemental, condescending, and critical attitude towards the characters, action, and script. In certain instances, this can itself be an amusing thing to do. As the author of 'Pyramus and Thisbe' obviously knew, it can be great fun to watch an ostensibly serious performance elicit responses that are diametrically opposed to the ones it was ostensibly designed to arouse — so that we laugh when we are supposed to cry, or feel frightened, or whatever. Thus the pain of watching a great tragedy can, paradoxically, be pleasurable, and a ludicrously bad tragedy (or love story, or horror film) can be enjoyed as comic. There is, however, no pleasure to be derived from watching a comedy, or a comedian, fail in the effort to amuse an audience. If there is any emotion felt at a bad comedy, it will be pity for the performers, or embarrassment or disgust at the whole thing. Conversely, even the most respectable and judicious spectators at a great comedy will be carried away by laughter and enjoyment to the point where they may relish things that, in ordinary life, would seem deplorable — irreverence, outrageous behaviour, slapstick, and so on.

The fact that *unsuccessful* efforts to arouse emotions are what result in detached, critical, judicious, and moralistic reactions from the audience would seem to hold true for audiences generally, and for show-business generally. The impact of any successful art is — given show-business criteria — analogous to the effect a star-stripper or erotic dancer will have on an audience. If the act is good enough, even the most puritanical or inhibited members of the audience will respond in the way the performer is in business to make them respond. By contrast, in the case of an unsuccessful, or feeble strip-act (or comedy, or tragedy) the audience will be critical in so far as it is bored or disgusted or condescendingly amused by the ludicrous failure to elicit the intended response.

In any case — and this seems applicable to all audiences and all forms of show-business — the most lethal response that any performance can evoke is boredom. For boredom not only precludes any emotional involvement, it also overrides any critical interest in what is going on. What people may ultimately pay their hard-earned money for, at any theatre, in any age, is not to be bored.[35] In this sense, comedy and tragedy alike may indeed have a cathartic effect. By satisfying an audience's desire and need to escape from boredom, through imaginatively experiencing catastrophe, terror, the outer limits of passion, or, in the case of comedy, through vicariously experiencing carnival, misrule, social inversions, levelling, explosive laughter, irreverence, etc., drama may enable people to endure the tedium of their everyday lives without themselves going berserk, or indulging in anti-social or criminal behaviour just to break the general monotony. Conversely, however, it could also be argued that such art affords an escape from real life, a substitute for action. Yet in either case, it would seem obviously true that the primary reality people pay to escape from is boredom. The perennial popularity at the box office of sex, violence, revenge, disaster, foolishness, strokes of good or bad luck, the infinite number of ways that things can go wrong, irreverence, ribaldry, mixed-up-ness, etc. would seem to suggest that these are not the kinds of realities people seek to escape from, but the realities they find it most enjoyable to experience, or imaginatively face up to, in the safety of a theatre (or in a library). Thus poetry, drama, films, and novels alike can, on the one hand, be condemned as unreal substitutes for experience, and can also be condemned as incitements to experience, to act out fantasies in real life — indeed, Flaubert encapsulated practically every one of the problems posed here, in and through his *Madame Bovary*. And so again, today as yesterday, for modern critics as for Plato, it seems virtually impossible to separate a critical concern with the ways that art does (or does not) imitate life, from a cognate concern with the ways that life itself imitates (or does not imitate) art. Moreover, in any number of plays, Shakespeare himself would seem to have been artistically concerned with both. This is why the relationship between what is acted on the stage, and various actions in real life — or between reality and dramatic illusion — in, say, *Antony and Cleopatra, Hamlet, A Midsummer-Night's Dream, The Tempest* (or whatever play you will) is perhaps the most popular of all the themes in Shakespearian criticism.

Yet the moral criteria involved in many critical considerations of the relationship — or lack of it — between imaginative fiction and reality were (and, as often as not, still are) determined by Plato and his neo-classical successors, or dialectically determined by the need to counter their attacks on art's unreality and immorality alike. As we have seen, when one is confronted with Platonic arguments that imaginative literature imitates all the wrong kinds of realities (or unrealities); provides us with the very worst possible kinds of role-models; creates

an undue tolerance of wickedness; and encourages us to enjoy, or —
worse still — to emulate, forms of behaviour that ought, both morally
and rationally, to be condemned, the most obvious defensive ploy
would seem to be the counter-assertion that imaginative literature
provides us with minatory examples, and moral lessons concerning how
we ought *not* to behave. This is the 'negative example' theory of art
which, over the centuries, was used to counter Platonic attack after
Platonic attack, in defence after defence of poetry and drama throughout the English Renaissance and Restoration (and which is still being
posited in critical discussions of Shakespeare's plays).[36] It is worth
taking a more detailed look at some of the major arguments involved
in the neo-classical case for the defence, as well as for the prosecution,
of English drama, since they serve to raise a major question concerning
critical methodology in general — i.e. can a body of critical theory
which turns out to be of next to no use in explaining what Shakespeare
actually does do, finally prove of genuine use in telling us precisely
what he does not do?

Part iii.
In Particular: What Neo-Classical Criticism Has to Tell Us About What Shakespeare Does Not Do

Many scientific theories have, for very long periods of time,
stood the test of experience until they had to be discarded owing
to man's decision, not merely to make other experiments, but to
have different experiences.

                                                        Erich Heller

And one wild Shakespeare, following Nature's lights,
Is worth whole planets, filled with Stagirites.

                                                        Thomas Moore

'Now what, I beseech you,' asked Dryden, could be 'more easy than
to write a regular French play', or 'more difficult than to write an
irregular English one', like those of Fletcher — or of Shakespeare?
In their manifest 'irregularity', Shakespeare's plays were (and still are)
impossible to imitate ('Shakespeare's Magick could not copy'd be,/
Within that Circle none durst walk but he').[37] And they also defied
analysis in terms of the only body of critical theory available to
Dryden. Classical poetry and drama, along with theoretical principles
derived from Aristotle's *Poetics*, Horace's *Art of Poetry*, and other

ancient sources had provided Renaissance and seventeenth-century critics and playwrights alike with the formal rules (e.g. the unities of time, place, and action; protasis, epitasis, catastasis, catastrophe, etc.) by which comedy and tragedy could be constructed, analysed, and critically judged. Some of the best minds in Western Europe had articulated and affirmed those critical and dramatic principles that could be deduced from the art and criticism of classical antiquity. And many great playwrights had conformed to the consequent tradition amenable to analysis in terms of those rules. Shakespeare, of course, did not. Thus the transcendent greatness of the 'man who, of all modern, and perhaps ancient poets, had the largest and most comprehensive soul' seemed a wonder of nature – an object of reverence not subject to critical examination. Dryden, therefore, chose one of Ben Jonson's comic masterpieces, not one of Shakespeare's, for the most detailed analysis given to a single play in his *Essay of Dramatic Poesy*.

Like all critical theories, neo-classical theories of the drama can be compared to prescription lenses that may obscure what lies outside their focus even if they clarify things within it. Thus the same theories that provided major playwrights and critics (like Dryden and Jonson) with practical rules for application, as well as topics for critical inquiry, effectively impaired critical consideration of Shakespeare's plays. This is why reading, say, Rymer's discussion of *Othello* seems rather like reading a dog's criticism of the behaviour of a cat, or – to echo Isaiah Berlin's distinction – following a blinkered hedgehog through wild fox country. In the case of Shakespeare in particular, the example of neo-classical criticism would seem to suggest that our vision of the very greatest literature may very well be distorted – as well as restricted – by the lenses of critical theory. Conversely, one could argue that the idea that critical theory does, in fact, promote observation and discovery carries more (not less) weight if it can be shown that under certain circumstances it has impeded both. In any case, the circumstances whereby far the most long-lived, widely held, and internationally influential of all critical theories at first impeded, but subsequently promoted, a critical understanding and appreciation of Shakespeare's unique accomplishment are what remain of methodological, as well as historical importance, still today. What needs accounting for, first, is the way in which, by a kind of emergent, if not miraculous novelty, Shakespeare's masterpieces finally brought about the most radical reversal of values in the history of literary criticism.

Finding it impossible either to explain, to judge, or to justify the works of Shakespeare in terms of neo-classical theory, Dr Johnson used Shakespeare's plays as criteria by which to criticize the theory itself. Given the usual intellectual tendency to analyse and judge literary practices in terms of theory (and not vice versa), and given the tendency of most of us to confuse our own criteria of analysis with criteria of value, one can only look back at the *Preface to Shakespeare* with astonishment. Dr Johnson puts a critical theory to its best possible use – and yet that use is paradoxical. By using the tenets of neo-classical criticism to show precisely what Shakespeare does *not* do, Dr Johnson opened up a new world of speculation as to how and why Shakespeare did what he does do. It is through Dr Johnson's application-of-it-in-reverse that neo-classical theory can truly be said to illuminate Shakespeare's dramatic practice.

Whether Shakespeare knew all the rules 'and rejected them by design, or deviated from them by happy ignorance' is, as Johnson observed, 'impossible to decide, and useless to enquire'. The ways in which he deviated from them, and the dramatic impact of those deviations, are what count. Shakespeare does not (for instance) present us with an intrigue 'regularly perplexed and regularly unravelled'; he does not endeavour 'to hide his design only to discover it'; to 'the unities of time and place' he shows little regard; he is 'so much more careful to please than to instruct' that 'he seems to write without any moral purpose'. He makes no 'just distribution of good or evil', nor is he always careful to 'shew in the virtuous a disapprobation of the wicked'; he carries his persons indifferently through right and wrong, 'and leaves their examples to operate by chance'. His plays are neither strict tragedies nor strict comedies, but compositions that purposely mingle hornpipes and funerals. His plots are often so loosely formed that 'a very slight consideration may improve them'. When he found himself near the end of his work, and in view of his reward, 'he shortened the labour, to snatch the profit'. He therefore remits his efforts where he should most vigorously exert them, and his catastrophe 'is improbably produced or imperfectly represented'.

Judged according to the neo-classical rules he violated, Shakespeare's plays must needs plead guilty as charged, defying justification on either aesthetic or on moral grounds. Dr Johnson, therefore, challenged the formal axioms of neo-classical criticism itself, treating them not as criteria of judgement, but as points of departure from whence to launch his appeal from criticism to 'nature', to the supreme court of human experience, to Pope's 'source and end and test of art'. Boldly judging plays and rules alike in terms of their conformity to the truths of human experience, Johnson concluded that it was Shakespeare's very adherence to 'general nature' that rendered him most vulnerable to critical attack: 'Dennis and Rymer think his Romans not sufficiently Roman; and Voltaire censures his kings as not completely royal.' But Shakespeare 'thinks only on men': 'He knew that Rome, like every other city, had men of all dispositions; and wanting a buffoon, he went into the senate-house for that which the senate-house would certainly have afforded him.' Likewise, Johnson observed that those plays that had incurred censure by mixing comic and tragic scenes do accurately exhibit 'the real state of sublunary nature, which partakes of good and evil, joy and sorrow, ... in which, at the same time, the reveller is hasting to his wine, and the mourner burying his friend; in which the malignity of one is sometimes defeated by the frolick of another; and many mischiefs and many benefits are done and hindered without design.'

Thanks to Johnson's *Preface to Shakespeare*, it seems too obvious to need saying that an individual play's conformity to, or deviations from, the dicta of neo-classical theory have nothing whatsoever to do with its merit or lack of merit. Significantly, however, very much the same thing may be said of *any* critical criteria – including one's own. Like any other criticism, the criticism of our own time inevitably tends to confuse its own criteria for analysis with criteria of merit. Thus, for a critic to have proved that a play by Shakespeare has iterative imagery, thematic and structural unity, a metadramatic sub-structure, Christian overtones – or Freudian undertones – would, at various times in the second half of the twentieth century, appear to have demonstrated that it was, therefore, more profound or interesting or admirable than it had appeared to be before this-or-that-facet of it was acknowledged. Yet a play might have all the components favoured by the criticism of our own age, and still be deadly dull, while another play that lacks them may blaze with light. What critical theory did not dictate, that theory cannot fully explain, and it goes without saying that Shakespeare's plays were all, without exception, written to be experienced by an audience, not to be analysed by critics. Moreover, as Johnson's *Preface* also demonstrates, no theory, however distinguished its proponents, is itself above suspicion or beyond criticism. Are critical theories truly conducive to an understanding of literature? As the minatory example of neo-classical theory indicates, only when they serve it by showing precisely what goes on in individual works (as in

Dryden's 'Examen' of *The Silent Woman*), and only when the critic remains free to say how and why they do not, and need not, apply to others. Conversely, criticism becomes formulaic, sterile, and boring when it is simply a matter of applying some reigning theory to works of radically different kinds, and when its arguments are directed against, and dictated by, each other, to such a degree that they have next to nothing to do with the human and literary problems posed by the various works of art ostensibly being discussed. Here are two such arguments:

Comedies make men see and shame at their own faults.
(Thomas Heywood, *An Apology for Actors* (1612))

Comedy . . . corrupts the mores of men and makes them effeminate and drives them towards lust and dissipation . . . and the habit of seeing them affords the spectator the licence of changing for the worse.
(I.G., *A Refutation of the Apology for Actors* (1615))

Neither Heywood's defence of comedy, nor I.G.'s Platonic attack on it, is concerned with any particular play. Neither has anything whatsoever to do with (for instance) *The Comedy of Errors* or *As You Like It*, or *The Old Wive's Tale*, or with any number of other contemporary comedies that might serve to prove both generalizations suspect, if not false. Moreover, both these assertions about comedy are equally moralistic, equally one-sided, and (perhaps significantly) equally humourless.

Looking back at the long history of comic art (as opposed to the history of comic theory), one might decide that it reflects a determination, on the part of various artists, not merely to make new experiments in comic form, but to create new forms of comic experience. Thus, while (almost?) everyone would agree that *The Frogs, The Menæchmi, The Miller's Tale, A Midsummer-Night's Dream, Twelfth Night, Bartholomew Fair, Love for Love, She Stoops to Conquer, The Importance of Being Earnest, My Little Chickadee, Some Like It Hot,* and *The Producers*, all serve what Dr Johnson described as the 'great end of comedy' — that is, 'to make the audience merry' — their individual shares in the total glory of comic art could more readily be explained in terms of their differences — in subject, frame of reference, vocabulary, characterization, and so on — than by any (whether or not there are any is another question) generic features that are common to them all. On the other hand, when reading through neo-classical discussions of the genre, one might well conclude that, somewhere over the rainbow, there is the perfectly realized Ideal of Comic Form, to which all earthly efforts aspire, and by which they all may be judged. And that ideal is severely judgemental, and morally didactic. Recurring over and over again is the same refrain, according to which, as Sidney insisted in his *Apology for Poetry*, 'Comedy is', as it were by Aristotelian definition, an 'imitation of the common errors of our life', in the 'most ridiculous and scornful sort that may be, so as it is impossible that any beholder can be content to be such a one'.

Here, chosen from any number of other critics who reiterate the identical theory, is Minturno's account of what comedy is and ought to do: 'Now comic poets imitate the life of private persons so as to induce everyone to correct the manners which he sees criticized in others and to imitate those which he sees approved' (*The Art of Poetry*, 1563). And here is Thomas Shadwell, saying the same thing well over a century later: the comic playwright should 'adorn his images of *Vertue* so delightfully to affect people with . . . an emulation to practice it in themselves: And to render their Figures of *Vice* and *Folly* so ugly and detestable, to make People hate and despise them, not only in others, but (if it be possible) in their dear selves' (*Preface* to *The Humorists*, 1671). Even when confronted with comedies (like some of Shakespeare's) that wildly diverged from its dicta, this particular theory of comedy held sway.

And so did the equally irrelevant counter-theory. By the same token, and at the same time, a whole chorus of commentators insisted, along with I.G., Stephen Gosson, and Jeremy Collier, that the examples of comic characters are bound to corrupt our morals. One reason for the tenacity of these theories is that, however individual comedies may differ from each other in intent or in effect, critical discussions of 'Comedy' have, over the centuries, served essentially the same purposes, and, therefore, followed similar patterns. Seeking to define comedy in terms of its generic characteristics, they trace its origins, name its parts, and finally either denounce or defend the genre in terms of the moral effect that it has, or ought to have, or ought not to have, upon its audience. What is odd, however, is that Platonic and neo-classical attacks on its explosive, excessive, undignified, irreverent, contagious, and irrepressible energies seem to pay a far higher tribute to the actual impact of comic art than do the countless critical defences of it that serve to bring those energies, as well as the audience's responses to them, under the control of a sober didacticism.

Yet the major weakness in the 'example' theory of comedy, whether it is used by witnesses for the prosecution, or for the defence, is what, at first glance, might well appear to be its major strength. It is all-purpose. The effect of any comic — or tragic — drama ever written may be either deplored or commended, depending on which way the critic wants to moralize it, or on which critic is doing the moralizing. Ever since Plato, the 'example' theory has served as an easy weapon in the hands of moralists who attack comic writers for creating characters attractive enough to seduce the audience itself. On the other hand, defenders of the drama could cite exactly the same theory, and claim that the affectations, follies, and vices of those characters are condemned rather than recommended. So, to the charge that, say, Falstaff is so engaging as to drive us towards dissipation, one need only argue that he is the incarnate figure of the vices we should banish. And ditto for any other character you choose to defend. The problem is that this particular defence of the drama may be based on assumptions that are false. To argue that characters with obvious vices, like Falstaff or Richard III (or Dorimant — or J. R. Ewing) provide us with examples of the kind of behaviour we should morally deplore is to discount, rather than account for, the obvious pleasure audiences actually have derived from watching them, and the obvious relish with which they have watched them, indulge in just such behaviour. Moreover, one longs to know exactly how many people, over the centuries, have, in fact, reformed their ways as a result of having seen them ridiculed on the comic stage (the exact number might well turn out to be very much the same as the number of Yahoo follies and vices that have been reformed since Gulliver published his *Travels*). It would also be interesting to have some statistics indicating how many people have bought tickets to any comedy because of the moral instruction there. Do we actually — or ought we to — read and watch comedies as if we were so many Malvolios, solemnly classifying their characters as idle, shallow, rude things who are not of our element? And having contemplated their noxious examples, do we sinners in the audience determine, hence-forth, to confine ourselves within the modest limits of order? If this is the case, then precisely which of our own follies and vices are we encouraged to eschew whilst watching *As You Like It*? And what characters in *The Comedy of Errors*, or *Measure for Measure*, are we encouraged, or inspired, to emulate? I, personally, cannot think of one, but the answers to these questions would seem to be left entirely to the individual. Dr Johnson therefore seems right in con-cluding that Shakespeare often appears to write without any direct moral design upon us, and so leaves the examples of his characters 'to operate by chance'.

Yet there is no denying that life occasionally does imitate art, and that impressionable members of an audience might well be inspired to emulate the more glamorous characters portrayed on the stage or screen. Nowadays, young people try to look like rock-stars, even as young girls in the first half of the twentieth century tried, in turn, to 'talk tough' like Harlow, look world-weary like Garbo, walk like Monroe, and pout like Bardot (none of whom were notable for portraying paragons of traditional female virtue). In the wake of Brando and James Dean, a lot of young men looked smoulderingly rebellious. And so did numerous young actors. The kind of identification, or emulation involved often has less to do with the question, 'Is character X like me?' than with the questions, 'What kind of character (or star) would I like to be like?', 'What kind of role would I prefer to play (on the stage or in life)?', and 'How would I most like to play that part?' It is thus that characters and performers inspire emulation from members of the audience and from other performers as well. And what aspiring actress, or real (or potential) 'dark lady', would, having observed Cleopatra's tragic fate, subsequently choose to play, or to be, like Octavia?

It is most profoundly true (as Plato knew and the Kremlin knows) that the energies of art may well be subversive of the moral, political, and sexual codes of conduct upheld by the state. It is also true that, given the freedom to do so, life may imitate art. Moreover, given its freedom to do so, art will — occasionally at least — set out to imitate life. This fact allows for a whole range of drama (a range that includes a number of plays by Shakespeare) wherein playwrights set out to exhibit, rather than to moralize about, the varieties of human behaviour, and thus fly in the face of the 'example' theory whereby dramatic characters must, necessarily, inc•ɔ us either to emulate, or to eschew, their vices. Certain plays by Shakespeare prove that theory false, since they provide us with any number of characters and situations where no mimetic responses are called for one way or the other.

Here again, the generalizations of neo-classical theory can serve to underscore what Shakespeare does not do. For instance: Shakespeare's comedies do not (or at least not very often) represent the errors of his characters in the most 'scornful way that may be'. Nor does he render his figures of folly and vice 'so ugly and detestable' as to make us 'hate and despise them'. Quite the contrary. We cannot but respond with pleasure and appreciation to any number of unsavoury individuals, like Falstaff and Lucio, and Barnardine and Autolycus. Even his villains, like Shylock and Caliban, claim their fair share of understanding and sympathy. Shakespeare himself does not appear to hate and despise those of his characters who misbehave (like Sir Toby), misapprehend (like Olivia), or make fools of themselves (like Sir Andrew). Nor does he encourage us to do so. Indeed, the cardinal sin in Shakespearian comedy may be the vice of contempt for others. To scorn those who are doing their best to entertain us, however determined they may be to make asses of themselves, is, so far as Shakespeare seems concerned, 'not generous, not gentle, not humble' (*Love's Labour's Lost*, V. ii. 621). It is, moreover, to make silly asses of ourselves by failing to recognize that we, too, are players in the human comedy. Thus it is, surely, the praise of − not a critical condemnation of − folly that resounds throughout Shakespeare's merriest plays. And rightly so. For the frailties, follies, and vices portrayed in them − and these include even the incorrigible pomposity and self-righteousness of Malvolio, which it might well seem the use of the comic action to correct − have to be amusing and interesting enough to hold an audience in the theatre for several hours and, finally, to command its applause. And to be engaging enough to do that is to be, in a dramatic sense at least, altogether praiseworthy.

One might conclude that, as opposed to making us 'see and shame at our own faults', Shakespeare allows us to accept and to relish the human weaknesses manifested by his comic characters with the same generous measure of tolerance with which we accept our own frailties. Does he not encourage us to share the attitude of amused acceptance directed towards themselves and each other by Rosalind and Touchstone, and to relish (even as we recognize) the faults of Jaques, Sir Andrew, and a host of other characters as well? Even his 'much-abused' Malvolio gets summoned back in the end. It could, therefore, be argued that the primary message of Shakespeare's merriest comedies was most succintly reiterated in the immortal end-line of *Some Like It Hot*:

Osgood. Nobody's perfect.

If we must have a moral, perhaps this is the main one conveyed, as Shakespeare transforms us from spectators to participants in the comic recognition.[38]

This was, of course, precisely the point of the drama to which Plato and his successors have most strongly objected: it creates an 'undue tolerance' of human folly, frailty, and vice. The defence of the drama designed to argue that it should not, or does not, do anything of the sort, serves only to beg, rather than to answer, the great question so often raised by Shakespeare's comedies themselves: 'What's so terrible about tolerance?' Indeed, the ultimate purpose of Shakespearian comedy and tragedy alike may be not to turn us into judges, but to make the spectators *understanders* of the differing comic and tragic persons, passions, perspectives, conundrums, and complexities involved in a given course of human and dramatic events. And this, surely, is exactly the same purpose that the best criticism of Shakespearian drama has served. Yet if one accepts the central premiss of much recent critical commentary on the plays, Shakespeare and his previous critics have been as one in their failure to achieve that purpose. As we shall see in the next chapter, the central argument of many recent commentators is that previous performers, critics, and audiences alike have completely *misunderstood* the tragic and comic characters and situations that Shakespeare intended them to understand.

Notes

1. See Jorge Luis Borges, 'Tlön, Uqbar, Orbis Tertius', in *Labyrinths,* ed. Donald A. Yates and James E. Irby (Harmondsworth, 1974), p. 37.
2. See Eugene Waith, *The Herculean Hero* (London, 1962), p. 12. See also Robert M. Adams, *Strains of Discord* (Ithaca, New York, 1959), for a pioneering discussion of 'open form' in Shakespeare, Keats, Cervantes, Molière, and Flaubert, as well as John Bayley's *The Uses of Division: Unity and Disharmony in Literature* (London, 1976). In *Shakespeare and Tragedy* (London, 1981), p. 1, John Bayley gives us a major reason why certain modern techniques of criticism have 'not so far been much used' with reference to Shakespeare's plays: something 'very like' the 'conscious tenets of structuralism and semiotics have long been unconscious assumptions where Shakespearean criticism is concerned'. See also Robertson Davies, *The World of Wonders* (in *The Deptford Trilogy*), Harmondsworth, 1983, p. 568: 'Shakespeare usually brought the subtext up to the surface and gave it to the audience directly'.
3. In the following catalogue of all the things that cause serious difficulties for love and marriage alike, the most important is the lack of 'sympathy in choice':

Hermia. O cross! too high to be enthrall'd to low.
Lysander. Or else misgraffed in respect of years —
Hermia. O spite! too old to be engag'd to young.
Lysander. Or else it stood upon the choice of friends —
Hermia. O hell! to choose love by another's eyes.

Lysander. Or, if there were a sympathy in choice,
War, death, or sickness, did lay siege to it,
(*A Midsummer-Night's Dream*, I. i. 136–42)

4. See *Measure for Measure*, I. ii. 138–43:

Claudio.   . . . upon a true contract
I got possession of Julietta's bed.
You know the lady; she is fast my wife,
Save that we do the denunciation lack
Of outward order; this we came not to,
Only for propagation of a dow'r

5. See the Duke's account of the contract between Angelo and Mariana (III. i. 207–17): 'She should this Angelo have married: was affianced to her by oath, and the nuptial appointed; between which time of the contract and limit of the solemnity her brother Frederick was wreck'd at sea, having in that perished vessel the dowry of his sister.' The sexual and legal situations are so similar, that Claudio's words could be put into Mariana's mouth after the bed-trick, thus: 'Upon a true contract, I got possession of Lord Angelo's bed. You know the man; he is fast my husband, save that we do the denunciation lack of outward order; this we came not to, only for propagation of a dow'r.' For further discussion of the moral and legal problems involved, see Arthur H. Scouten, 'An Historical Approach to *Measure for Measure*', *Philological Quarterly*, 54 (1975), 68–84; Muriel Bradbrook, 'The Balance and the Sword in *Measure for Measure*', in *Artist and Society in Shakespeare's England*, Vol. 1 (London, 1982), pp. 144–54; and my article, 'What Kind of Pre-contract had Angelo?', *College English*, 36 (1974), 173–9.

6. See Christopher Hill, *Irreligion in the 'Puritan' Revolution* (London, 1974), p. 9.

7. *Duke.* We have strict statutes and most biting laws,
The needful bits and curbs to headstrong steeds,
Which for this fourteen years we have let slip;
Even like an o'ergrown lion in a cave,
That goes not out to prey. Now, as fond fathers,
Having bound up the threat'ning twigs of birch,
Only to stick it in their children's sight
For terror, not to use, in time the rod
Becomes more mock'd than fear'd; so our decrees,
Dead to infliction, to themselves are dead;
And liberty plucks justice by the nose;
(I. iii. 19–29)

8. For the theory that Angelo's 'libidinousness' was miraculously transformed by the bed-trick, see Arthur C. Kirsch, 'The Integrity of *Measure for Measure*', *Shakespeare Survey*, 28 (1975), 89–106. There is not, and perhaps never will be, a critical agreement on the major issues involved in *Measure for Measure*. See the 'Preface' to *Aspects of Shakespeare's 'Problem Plays'*, ed. Kenneth Muir and Stanley Wells (Cambridge, 1982), p. ix: 'With *Measure for Measure* the controversy has sometimes been acrimonious between those who regard it as Shakespeare's most Christian play, and those who think it cynical. The difficulty here has been that each article on the play published in *Shakespeare Survey* has been followed by an indignant rejoinder. The opening pages of a number of recent articles have been devoted to a summary of the damnable errors they seek to confute.'

It could – but perhaps should not – go without saying that I, too, transported by the mode, have, at one time or another, committed every one of the critical sins of omission and commission catalogued in this book, and (in this chapter as elsewhere) I preach to others as a fellow-castaway.

9. See *Coleridge's Shakespearean Criticism*, ed. T. M. Raysor, 1 (1930), p. 131. One may deplore, or relish, the reverberations of the confrontations between Angelo and Isabella, but who would not be fascinated by them? 'Where's that palace whereinto foul things sometimes intrude not?' The falling, fallen, Angelo (like the Isabella of the first half of *Measure for Measure*) is among the most brilliantly portrayed characters in Shakespearian drama.

10. Other characters (like Claudio and Antony) associate death with sex; and other threatened heroines of the time (like Whetstone's Cassandra and Jonson's Celia) would prefer torture or death to dishonour. But none of their speeches combines the extremes of sensuality and asceticism in the way that Isabella's does. Contrast, for instance, the altogether different pleas that the heroine makes to the villain before the rape in Shakespeare's *Lucrece*.

11. See J. C. Maxwell, '*Measure for Measure*: The Play and the Themes', *Proceedings of the British Academy*, 60 (1974), 3.

12. See Burton's *The Anatomy of Melancholy*, ed. Holbrook Jackson (London, 1932), Vol. iii, 386. Subsequent page references are cited in the text.

13. For a good summary of the poetic and dramatic differences between the two parts, see E. M. W. Tillyard, *Shakespeare's Problem Plays* (Harmondsworth, 1970), pp. 118–37.

14. See P. B. Medawar, *The Art of the Soluble* (London, 1967), and see also his discussion of 'Science and Literature', reprinted in *Pluto's Republic* (Oxford, 1981).

15. See Hugh Lloyd-Jones, *The Justice of Zeus* (Berkeley, Los Angeles, and London, 1971), p. 91.

16. See Alan Sinfield's discussion of the 'prayer scene' in 'Hamlet's Special Providence', *Shakespeare Survey*, 33 (1980), 89–97: 'Is it fair that God refuses to allow a man like Claudius (or Dr Faustus) to repent?' Is it not 'at variance with the divine mercy' to deny the *capacity* to repent to those who beseech it? Calvin disposed of this problem by arguing, 'It is not said that pardon will be refused if they turn to the Lord, but it is altogether denied that they can turn to [full] repentance, inasmuch as for their ingratitude they are struck by the just judgment of God with eternal blindness.' Looked at from this angle, Hamlet seems no harder on Claudius than God is. In the prayer scene, Claudius himself describes the 'wretched state' of one who 'can not repent'.

17. See James Drake, *The Antient and Modern Stages Survey'd* (1699), pp. 204–6.

18. See John F. Andrews, '"The Purpose of Playing": Catharsis in *Hamlet*', in *Poetry and Drama in the English Renaissance*, ed. Koshi Nakanori and Yasuo Tamaizumi (Tokyo, 1980), pp. 1–19.

19. See Eric Bentley, *The Life of the Drama* (New York, 1967), pp. 320, 321, 328. See also Richard Brucher, 'Fantasies of Violence: *Hamlet* and *The Revenger's Tragedy*', *Studies in English Literature*, 21 (1981), 257–70: 'although the idea of revenge may offend our moral sensibilities, it may also appeal to our fantasies about power, control, and poetic justice in a corrupt world.' See also Paul A. Cantor's article on 'Shakespeare's *The Tempest*: The Wise Man as Hero', *Shakespeare Quarterly*, 31 (1980), 64–75: Prospero's statement, 'The rarer action is/In virtue than in vengeance' is 'no doubt sound philosophy', but it is 'an inversion of the normal principle of drama' whereby 'audiences prefer to see a character who is swept away by the passion of a vendetta'. Occasionally, however, they like to have both at once, and enjoy fantasies of power so great that the

renunciation of vindictiveness is the ultimate exercise of that power – as in the cases of Prospero and Edmond Dantès. It seems to me that Dumas created a paradigmatic wish-fulfilment fantasy in *The Count of Monte Cristo*, wherein the victim of a cruel conspiracy achieves unlimited wealth and knowledge, and, having brought his old enemies to utter destruction, finally denounces vindictiveness and sails off into the sunset with Haydée, his beautiful child/mistress/wife. But the Count of Monte Cristo, very like the right Duke of Milan, had brought the villains to their knees. The immediate problems confronting Hamlet are altogether different.

20. The 'double audience' theory, whereby Shakespeare preached pious messages to the wisest Elizabethans in his audience (the refined and judicious sort of spectators who would already have been converted anyway), even as he pandered to the worst instincts of the groundlings, gets him into, not out of, moral difficulty. See, for instance, René Girard's 'Reading of *The Merchant of Venice*', wherein it is argued that Shakespeare managed to satisfy the 'most refined' as well as the 'most vulgar' members of his audience by countering the play's overtly anti-Semitic meanings with ironic perspectives on the Christian characters. If that is in fact what Shakespeare did do, he should not be commended for directing his moral message exclusively to the 'most refined', and sending 'the vulgar' just the kind of vulgar messages that would most satisfy them. This is not the whole point of Girard's essay – see '"To Entrap the Wisest"': A Reading of *The Merchant of Venice*', *Selected Papers from the English Institute* (1978), pp. 110-19 – but the unsavoury ramifications of the élitist premiss whereby Shakespeare made his moral points for the edification of the few, and, simultaneously, appealed to the basest instincts of the common herd, need more consideration than they tend to get in the many essays wherein that premiss is used as evidence of the 'morality' of Shakespearian drama.

21. See the *Letters of Anton Chekhov*, ed. Avrahm Yarmolinsky (London, 1974), p. 86 – hereafter cited as *Letters*.

22. See Maynard Mack, 'The World of *Hamlet*', in *Shakespeare: Modern Essays in Criticism*, ed. Leonard F. Dean (New York, 1967), pp. 242-62.

23. See Eleanor Prosser's influential book on *Hamlet and Revenge* (Stanford, California, 1967; revised and reprinted in 1971).

24. Thomas Hobbes, *Leviathan*, ed. C. D. Macpherson (Harmondsworth, 1968), pp. 109, 165.

25. See Terence Hawkes, *The Review of English Studies*, 32 (1981), 322: 'On stage, *everything* signifies. Speech, costume, make-up, hair-style, scenery, props, all form part of a vast communicative complex in which the primacy of any specific feature is unlikely to be constant.' See also Hawkes's article, 'Opening Closure', *Modern Drama*, 24 (1981), 353-6: 'It has been clear since Vetrusky's conclusion "All that is on stage is a sign" that any performance of any play can make anything signify. Is there, in short, any event, no matter how gratuitous or unsought for, that might occur no matter how haphazardly before or during any performance of *Hamlet* that a modern audience would be *unable* to close with?' (pp. 355-6).

26. See Harold Bloom, *The Anxiety of Influence: A Theory of Poetry* (New York, 1973), p. 11: 'The greatest poet in our language is excluded from the argument of this book for several reasons. ... The main cause, though, is that Shakespeare's prime precursor was Marlowe, a poet very much smaller than his inheritor. ... Shakespeare is the largest instance in the language of a phenomenon that stands outside the concern of this book: the absolute absorption of the precursor.' Bloom seems to me a liberating critic in having opened up new ways in which art can be critically used to illuminate art. As will be obvious, I personally

believe that his theories concerning influences, reactions, and anxieties have (at least) as much relevance to critical theories and processes as they do to artistic ones.

27. See, for instance, Louise Schleiner, 'Providential Improvisation in *Measure for Measure*', *PMLA* 97 (1982), 227-36, who argues that (on the one hand) the Duke 'is fallible, meddling, and laughable', but (on the other hand) he is 'also beneficent, inventive, and in large measure successful in helping his subjects'; and whereas the 'humor in *Measure for Measure*' is, on the one hand, 'very funny', there is — on the other hand — a kind of 'black humor', reinforcing 'the themes of hollow justice and tyrannous authority'. See also Nancy S. Leonard's discussion of the Duke in her interesting essay on 'Substitutions in Shakespeare's Problem Comedies', *English Literary Renaissance*, 9 (1979), 281-301. On the one hand, the Duke's behaviour as Friar Ludowick is 'surely charming enough in his half-studied, half improvised plans for reunion and ransom'. 'Yet shiftingly he does appear in dark corners' — falsely preparing Claudio for death, and falsely reporting that death to Isabella.

28. J. Bronowski, *The Ascent of Man* (London, 1973), p. 313.

29. On 'complementarity' in Shakespearian drama, see Norman Rabkin, *Shakespeare and the Common Understanding* (New York, 1967). And for altogether different perspectives on oppositions in Shakespearian drama and criticism, see also Robert Grudin, *Mighty Opposites: Shakespeare and Renaissance Contrariety* (Berkeley, California, 1979), and Michael McCanles, *Dialectical Criticism and Renaissance Literature* (Berkeley and Los Angeles, California, 1975). From his consideration of Shakespeare's plays, McCanles concludes that

> The third moment of dialectic is the schema for a work's dianoia. The dianoia is the total information delivered to reader or audience which, when reduced to propositional, thematic form, states the dialectical logic that causes, controls, and carries out the actions of the work's mythos. We behold in the mythos the agents' attempts to impose some sort of nonconflictual model on the world around them: the first moment. We behold the conflicts and re-achievements of partial resolutions that this attempt generates: the second moment. But when we grasp the interrelation between attempted denial of conflict and resultant conflict, between the ideal of a non-dialectical world and the dialectic that attends the attempt to enforce that ideal, we grasp the work's total meaning, its dianoia. (p. 227.)

30. The one constant in a world of change is (in my experience, anyway) the student paper arguing that Lady Macbeth is 'stronger' than Macbeth in the opening scenes of the play, and that Macbeth gets 'stronger', even as Lady Macbeth gets 'weaker', later on. Yet by any moral standard — and these students were not immoral — Macbeth gets worse, not 'stronger', as he hardens into evil. The students were using the word 'strong' in a dramatic, rather than a moral, sense. For a character in a play to want something, and be irresolute about getting it, makes that character seem 'weak' (Hamlet is often condemned as 'weak' because he does not rush to his revenge). To appear utterly resolute is to create, as it were, the dramatic illusion of strength — a fact not lost on certain politicians.

31. See Rowe, *Some Account of the Life of Mr. William Shakespear*, in *Shakespeare Criticism*, ed. D. Nichol Smith, pp. 27-8.

32. See Lamb 'On the Tragedies of Shakespeare' in *Shakespeare Criticism*, ed. D. Nichol Smith, p. 203. It should be noted that Lamb is referring to a performance of Colley Cibber's version of *Richard III*. But the most brilliant portrayal of 'the profound, the witty, accomplished Richard' that I can remember was in Olivier's film version based, to some degree, on Cibber's adaptation.

33. Dr Johnson provides a good summary of the moral problems (and a major critical footnote to Plato) in *The Rambler*, 31 March 1750:

> ... if the power of example is so great, as to take possession of the memory by a kind of violence, and produce effects almost without the intervention of the will, care ought to be taken that, when the choice is unrestrained, the best examples only should be exhibited; and that which is likely to operate so strongly, should not be mischievous or uncertain in its effects.... Many writers for the sake of following nature, so mingle good and bad qualities in their principal personages, that they are both equally conspicuous; and as we accompany them through their adventures with delight ... we lose the abhorrence of their faults, because they do not hinder our pleasure, or, perhaps, regard them with some kindness for being united with so much merit.

34. See Saint Augustine, *Confessions,* trans. R. S. Pine-Coffin (Harmondsworth, 1964), pp. 55–7.

35. According to Lord Olivier (see Leslie Halliwell, *Halliwell's Filmgoers Book of 'Quotes'* (London, 1979), p. 20), 'The main problem of the actor is not to let the audience go to sleep, then wake up and go home feeling they've wasted their money.'

36. Throughout the Renaissance and Restoration, 'Attackers and defenders of the stage, literary sophisticates and philistines all argued from the same basic premises.... the whole [controversy] turned finally, from a critical point of view, on the interpretation of the moral "examples" in the plays' – see Andrew Bear, 'Restoration Comedy and the Provok'd Critic', in *Restoration Literature: Critical Approaches*, ed. Harold Love (London, 1972), pp. 1–26; and see also my article, 'The "Example Theory" and the Providentialist Approach to Restoration Drama: Some Questions of Validity and Applicability', in *The Eighteenth Century: Theory and Interpretation*, 24 (1983), 103–14.

37. See Dryden's *Essay of Dramatic Poesy*, in *Criticism: The Major Texts,* ed. W. J. Bate (New York, 1970). The couplet is from Dryden's 'Prologue' to *The Tempest, or The Enchanted Island* (1667, published 1670).

38. Although evoking a tolerance, even relish, for the frailties of others that is clearly comparable to the tolerance, or relish, with which we accept (or enjoy) our own, is precisely what the major critical tradition insists that playwrights should, or do, *not* do, there *is* a case for learning to live with the ways of our world, and with the frailties and follies of others, as well as to live at ease with ourselves. The same things Congreve's Mirabell says about his Millamant (see *The Way of the World*, I. iii) could be said about a host of Shakespearian characters as well – we 'like' Falstaff, Cleopatra, etc., with – nay, *for* – all their faults:

> *Mirabell* . . . I like her with all her Faults; nay, like her for her Faults. Her Follies are so natural, or so artful, that they become her; and those Affectations which in another woman wou'd be odious, serve but to make her more agreeable. ... she once used me with that Insolence that in Revenge I took her to pieces; sifted her, and separated her Failings; I study'd 'em, and got 'em by Rote. The Catalogue was so large that I was not without Hopes one Day or other to hate her heartily; To which end I so us'd my self to think of 'em, that at length, contrary to my Design and Expectation, they gave me ev'ry Hour less and less Disturbance; 'till in a few Days it became habitual to me, to remember 'em without being displeas'd. They are now grown as familiar to me as my own Frailties; and in all probability in a little time longer I shall like 'em as well.

We can critically sift, study, and catalogue the vices and failings of Falstaff,

Cleopatra, etc., until we've got 'em by rote, but the result may well be that they give us ever less and less disturbance, to the point where it becomes habitual for us to remember them 'without being displeased'. Its evocation of this kind of tolerance towards human vice and frailty — in others, and in ourselves — constitutes the major premiss of the case for the immoral impact of the drama. Yet it also involves a comprehension, understanding, and compassion ('to err is human, to forgive divine') that could be seen as most profoundly moral (see below, pp. 158-9). Art may, or may not, provide us with the best possible criticism of life, but it certainly does provide us with the best possible criticisms of literary criticism.

Chapter 3

'Conjectures and Refutations':
The Positive Uses of Negative Feedback
in Criticism and Performance

I wish to propose for the reader's favourable consideration a
doctrine which may, I fear, appear wildly paradoxical and subversive. The doctrine in question is this: that it is undesirable to
believe a proposition when there is no ground whatever for
supposing it true. I must, of course, admit that if such an opinion
became common it would completely transform our social life
and our political system . . . In spite of these grave arguments, I
maintain that a case can be made out for my paradox.

Bertrand Russell

Repeated observations and experiments function in science as
tests of our conjectures or hypotheses, i.e. as attempted refutations. . . . It is easy to obtain confirmations, or verifications, for
nearly every theory — if we look for confirmations. Confirming
evidence should not count *except when it is the result of a genuine test of the theory*; and this means that it can be presented
as a serious but unsuccessful attempt to falsify the theory.

K. R. Popper

Part i.
The Burden of Disproof

Yet another series of methodological conundrums arises from the
fact that, if he were to be judged on the basis of certain critical and
directorial interpretations of his plays, then Shakespeare, as a professional man of the theatre, would have to be accounted a failure.
For instance: discussing the various kinds of information and insights
that Shakespeare shares with, or withholds from, his characters and his
audience, Bertrand Evans has arrived at what appear (to him) to be the
'inescapable' conclusions that Antony never loved Cleopatra, he

deliberately feigned a passion for her in order to conceal his real reason for staying out of Rome (his terror of Caesar), and intended to betray her, 'in the worst way possible', through that final, misdirected warning, 'None about Caesar trust but Proculeius.' According to Evans, this attempted betrayal was prompted by Antony's desire for revenge, as well as by the knowledge that, 'displayed in Rome', Cleopatra's charms 'would do more to verify the legend of his enslavement than any number of mere reports'.[1]

Now regardless of whether we credit or reject it, this radically new interpretation of *Antony and Cleopatra* raises some fundamental questions about Shakespeare's technical competence that (perhaps significantly) are neither posed nor answered by the critic who propounded it:

1. If Evans's conclusions are indeed valid, then why has the truth concerning Antony's motivation not only gone unnoticed, but been completely misinterpreted by so many performers, playgoers, and readers, for going on four hundred years?

2. So far as performance is concerned, in the absence of any soliloquies or series of asides so stating, how on earth is the actor portraying Antony supposed to inform everyone in the audience that he is only faking it and, simultaneously, convince everybody on the stage (including Cleopatra, who is 'cunning past man's thought'; and Octavius, who is nobody's fool; and Enobarbus, who sees the tragic consequences inherent in it) that his passion is real?

After all, the public nature of the drama requires that motivation be established, and necessary information got across to the audience with maximum impact, in the course of only two or three brief hours on the stage. That is the time-limit within which a popular dramatist must create a consensus of comprehension which (as Ben Jonson puts it) will 'make the spectators understanders' of the major tragic or comic ironies that are involved in the action and characterization of a play. For no matter what its other merits may be, in the absence of any such understanding, a play will inevitably fail.[2]

Except in so far as the professional pressures under which his plays were written may suggest some outer limits to the range, and kinds, of possibly valid interpretations that can be imposed upon them, it would seem too obvious to need saying that Shakespeare, who showed no interest in publishing the text, could not have taken it for granted that anyone in his audience would see *Antony and Cleopatra* more than once, much less study the script in advance of seeing it, or subsequently read – and re-read – it to ponder its subtleties. Nor could he have assumed that the truth about Antony's motivation would finally manifest itself unto generations yet unborn. To succeed as a playwright in the commercial theatre, he was obliged to write for the general public, and against the deadline set by a single performance; and both these contingencies suggest that, so far as his major meanings and effects are concerned, some credence may be given to the historical record of responses to his plays, including critical disagreements about their meanings and effects. And so far as the love affair between the 'brave Mark Antony' and his 'serpent of old Nile' is concerned, long-standing controversies about its moral and political implications, and whether their world was, or was not, 'well lost for love', ultimately serve (rather like the quarrels between the lovers themselves) to confirm the critical and theatrical verdict of centuries; which is that – for better or for worse, and whether one personally approves of or deplores it – the passionate affinity between Shakespeare's 'mutual pair', as opposed to any lack of it, is what has most powerfully manifested itself in their countless one-night stands.[3] It therefore follows that, if Evans is right in concluding that Antony's passion was feigned, then we must blame Shakespeare himself for a most grievous failure in communication, and summon him to critical account for having so inexplicably, or perversely, or unwittingly misled the rest of us about the emotional and sexual relationship between Cleopatra's 'man of men' and his 'lass unparallel'd'. And this would seem a specially sad thing for us to have to do to him, given Robert Benchley's immortal reminder of 'the hard work' that Shakespeare 'must have put in on his wording' while writing this poetic tragedy.[4]

Although it might appear to be an extreme example, Bertrand Evans's reinterpretation of *Antony and Cleopatra* is representative of numerous 'new readings' of Shakespeare's plays which, in effect, force us to make one of two decisions. If the critic's interpretation of the play is credited, then Shakespeare must be judged professionally incompetent (for having hitherto failed to communicate his *most important* meanings). Conversely, if one credits Shakespeare with technical competence, then the critic's reading of the play must be deemed suspect, or false. Yet in either event, the burden of disproof falls on the critic's readers, who must decide for themselves whether the new interpretation can stand up against whatever dramatic, or historical evidence would seem to, or could serve to, refute it, since those critics who posit them often tend to disregard even the most obvious arguments that might challenge their own conclusions, and thus present their readers with a case for the defence of a given interpretation in virtual isolation from the extant evidence against it.

In a markedly analogous fashion, certain directorial interpretations of Shakespeare's plays have required that any and all textual evidence against them must be disregarded by the audience. In the theatre, this can be most efficiently accomplished by cuts or augmentations to the play in performance. Therefore, in recent productions of *King Lear*, the servants joined in tormenting the blinded Gloucester, and the dying Edmund did not attempt to do his one good deed.[5]

Of course, when it is looked at in terms of one kind of dialectic, for critics or directors to present, or to emphasize, only those features of a script that confirm their own theories about it would seem a fair game for them to play. After all, the premisses on which many recent productions and essays are based are essentially conditional and conjectural. Nowadays, something like the following series of assumptions is tacitly taken for granted by many of Shakespeare's critics and directors alike:

The critical or theatrical justification for my new publication or production, is simply that *if*, or *when*, Play X is looked at in the light of this particular theory, then it can be read or performed in a new and exciting way. It can therefore go without saying that numerous alternative approaches might also serve to illuminate the text, and that it is up to the reader or the audience, to judge whether the interpretation here posited seems as fascinating and revelatory to them, as it appears to me to be.

But these assumptions are logically, critically, and dramatically valid only in so far as they are, in fact, understood, shared, and accepted by readers and audiences as well as by critics and directors. Serious trouble arises when they are not.

For just exactly where — a purist or sceptic might object — do such premisses place the author himself? And where does all this leave the *playwright's* plays? So far as consumer-relations and fair advertising practices are involved, what most infuriates many fans of Shakespeare's plays is not so much that the directorial or critical interpretations posited seem reductive, or distorted, or fallacious, or topsy-turvy, but the way in which some critic's, or director's, conjectures concerning Antony's motives towards Cleopatra, or the behaviour of the dying Edmund, or the nature of the ghost in *Hamlet*, are explicitly or implicitly presented to the reader, or to the audience, *as if they were*

Shakespeare's own conclusions about the characters and actions he portrayed.[6] Because recent criticism and productions have tended to emphasize the interpretative conjectures and insights of critics and directors, or of critically 'informed' and enlightened readers and audiences, it is immensely refreshing to have a popular playwright's perspective on the issues here involved. In a lecture with a title well worth pondering, 'Is It True What They Say About Shakespeare?', Tom Stoppard raises a most pertinent question concerning Peter Brook's 'truly revolutionary' — and by now very influential — production of *King Lear*:

The first-act curtain occurred after the scene of Gloucester's blinding and very moving it was, too, because there he was with blood pouring down his face . . . and the servants were rather callously ignoring him and, in fact, jostling him in a rather callous way. Many of you will know that the scene does not, in fact, end that way and Shakespeare wrote the servants as people who were distinctly sympathetic towards the blinded Gloucester, and one of them says he is going to apply some flax and whites of eggs to the bleeding face. Well, on whose face is the egg?[7]

Considering Shakespeare's claim to fame as the 'author of an event and not merely a text', Stoppard goes on to describe various other performances that have called into question Shakespeare's technical proficiency and, in interpretative effect, have usurped the prerogatives of the playwright himself. Here — quoted at length for the purposes of further discussion later on — is Stoppard's account of the Royal Court production of *Hamlet* which posited the following 'solution to the problem — not that it was a problem to Shakespeare, of course — of the Ghost':

In this Royal Court production . . . what happens is that, at the moment where he is brought to the pitch of confronting the Ghost of his father, and at the moment where Shakespeare was ready for the Ghost to utter, Hamlet sinks to his knees and appears about to be sick, and an awful retching noise starts coming from his stomach, and lo! the retching becomes the words 'Mark me!' The duologue takes place between the actor playing Hamlet and a voice, his own distorted voice, being wrenched out of his guts. . . . One might reasonably ask: if the Ghost of Hamlet's father is being wrenched up from Hamlet's stomach, what happens to the scene where the Ghost is first seen by Horatio, Marcellus, and Bernardo? The answer is perfectly simple in this case: the scene is simply cut and the production begins with the second scene of the play. But this needs to be looked at slightly more carefully. You all recall that first scene: there is a real theatrical excitement about the way the play just kicks off, it goes off like a motor-bike: 'Who's there?' – 'Nay, answer me! Stand, and unfold yourself!' – 'Long live the King!' – the whole thing is so fast ... 'What! Has this thing appeared again tonight?' – and, what thing?, we all say, what thing, what thing? But without that scene, we begin with a gathering-together of the court, and there is Claudius saying: 'Though yet of Hamlet our dear brother's death/The memory be green', and so on. The scene misses that retroactive glance at what we have been shown and ... I must say I was not surprised to read at least one commentator say that without that first scene the production gets off to a slightly tedious start. (pp. 5, 8–9)

Thus Brook's adaptation of *King Lear*, and the Royal Court's alter-ations to *Hamlet* serve to raise Stoppard's central questions concerning the relationship between the 'writer's art', which is 'to artfully convey certain information', and about the 'quality of the textual material' and the 'quality of the experience in the theatre': 'To what extent, if any, is the one necessary and contingent upon the other? How much is the one responsible for the other?' (p. 5.)

Stoppard's general queries, as well as his specific points about the pace, transitions, foreshadowings, and retrospective allusions involved in the opening scenes of *Hamlet*, are surely of equal significance to critics, actors, audiences, and directors alike. To have the ghost speak from Hamlet's belly not only alters the meaning of the Shakespearian confrontation; it also alters the over-all configuration and kinds of re-sponses evoked, in so far as dramatic form functions to arouse specific questions, concerns, emotions, and appetites in an audience. For these reasons, it is worth looking back at Kenneth Burke's pioneering dis-cussion of the fusions between various psychological, structural, and rhetorical effects that are involved in the dramatic crescendo which climaxes in Hamlet's confrontation with the ghost. As Burke observes,

It is not until the fourth scene of the first act that Hamlet confronts the ghost of his father. As soon as the situation has been made clear, the audience has been, consciously or unconsciously, waiting for this ghost to appear, while in the fourth scene this moment has been definitely promised. For earlier in the play Hamlet had arranged to come to the platform at night with Horatio to meet the ghost, and it is now night, he is with Horatio and Marcellus, and they are standing on the plat-form. Hamlet asks Horatio the hour.

> *Horatio.* I think it lacks of twelve.
> *Marcellus.* No, it is struck.
> *Horatio.* Indeed? I heard it not. It then draws near the season
>   Wherein the spirit held his wont to walk.

Promptly hereafter there is a sound off-stage. 'A flourish of trumpets, and ordnance shot off within.' Hamlet's friends have established the hour as twelve. It is time for the ghost. Sounds off-stage, and of course it is not the ghost. It is, rather, the sound of the king's carousal, for the king "keeps wassail". A tricky, and useful, detail. We have been waiting for a ghost, and get, startlingly, a blare of trumpets. And, once the trumpets are silent, we feel how desolate are these three men waiting for a ghost, on a bare 'platform', feel it by this sudden juxtaposition of an imagined scene of lights and merriment. But the trumpets announcing a carousal have suggested a subject of conversation. In the darkness Hamlet discusses the excessive drinking of his countrymen. He points out that it tends to harm their reputation abroad, since, he argues, this one showy vice makes their virtues 'in the general censure take corruption'. And for this reason, although he himself is a native of the place, he does not approve of the custom. Indeed, there in the gloom he is talking very intelligently on these matters, and Horatio answers, 'Look, my Lord, it comes'. All this time we had been waiting for a ghost, and it comes at the one moment which was not pointing towards it. This ghost, so assiduously prepared for, is yet a surprise. And now that the ghost has come, we are waiting for something further. Program: a speech from Hamlet. Hamlet must confront the ghost. Here again Shakespeare can feed well upon the use of contrast for his effects. Hamlet has just been talking in a sober, rather argumentative manner — but now the flood-gates are unloosed:

Angels and ministers of grace defend us!
Be thou a spirit of health or goblin damn'd,
Bring with thee airs from heaven or blasts from hell . . .

and the transition from the matter-of-fact to the grandiose, the full-throated and full-voweled, is a second burst of trumpets, perhaps even more effective than the first, since it is the rich fulfillment of a promise.[8]

To return to the alterations made to *Hamlet* at the Royal Court, the point here is that whatever consistency and power that version of the confrontation might have claimed in its own right, its impact on an audience had to be altogether different from the complex collocation of responses evoked by Shakespeare's significant juxtapositions and sequence of scenes, in that every one of the effects described by Burke and Stoppard would be lost. For there is no way that an audience could ask 'What thing, what thing?' during the opening scene, or that Horatio could announce that 'It draws near the season/Wherein the spirit held his wont to walk' immediately before the cannon fires and those trumpets sound in the fourth scene, if the only spirit involved in the performance is confined to Hamlet's belly. Therefore any members of the first-night audience at the Royal Court who were not well acquainted with

Shakespeare's play would have emerged from the theatre with an *auteur's* — as opposed to the author's own — account of what happens in *Hamlet*; while those who were familiar with the script, and with other productions of it, were left to judge for themselves whether whatever was gained by the cuts and alterations seemed adequate compensation for what was lost. Likewise, admirers of Shakespeare who subsequently read reviews stressing the radical alterations to the tragedy, had to decide if they wanted to buy tickets to a cut-and-tailored version of *Hamlet*, or if they would rather stay home and read the original play again. In the theatre, or in the library, the affirmative and negative answers that differing playgoers and readers of criticism might give to the questions, 'Is it true what they say about Shakespeare?' and 'Is it new what they say about Shakespeare?' may complement, or conflict with, each other in various ways. Some members of the original audience at the Royal Court may well have looked forward to seeing what new interpretation of *Hamlet* the director was going to come up with, even as others grumbled that they hadn't got what they thought they had paid to see — which was a production of Shakespeare's tragedy, not a director's revisions to it. Nowadays, anyway, there is no guarantee that radical revisions of Shakespeare's plays will bring any more cash into the box-office, or get better reviews, or have higher ratings on television, than productions designed to celebrate the writer rather than his interpreters. A lot has to do with the differing presuppositions and expectations of individual members of the audience.

Discussing the relationship between an audience's expectations and a film's commercial and artistic success, the Hollywood producer, David O. Selznick, warned against tampering with what he called the 'chemicals' of a well-known play or novel being adapted for the screen, on the principle that 'the same elements that drew people to a classic or a Broadway hit or a best-selling novel would attract them to the movie [version of it]'. He assumed that audiences knew the conventions of the cinema, and would accept the cuts and revisions necessary for an adaptation into film, but he consistently vetoed major alterations to the original structure or characterization, on the grounds that 'No one can certainly pick out the chemicals which contribute to the making of a classic. And there is always the danger that by tampering you may destroy the essential chemical.'[9]

Quite apart from any commercial considerations, Selznick's minatory dictum poses a profoundly humbling question to critics and directors alike. To put the case in Shakespeare's own terms: how can any of us be absolutely certain that the very scenes or poetic effects that we ignored, or discounted, in a critical essay, or which were cut — or undercut — in production did not involve what Hamlet, when speaking on behalf of the playwright, so pointedly describes as 'some necessary question of the play' then to be considered (perhaps like the question 'Who's there?').[10] Indeed, their author's well-known observations that, in 'Striving to better, oft we mar what's well', even as we may, in effect, 'Make something nothing by augmenting it', could help to account for the fact that those critical studies and productions of his plays which have generally received the most heartfelt acclaim and enduring approbation — no matter what pyrotechnical, incidental, or accidental effects they might otherwise involve — have not tampered with, to the point of destroying, the essential chemistry of the Shakespearian properties they were dealing with.[11]

This is why it seemed to me to be paradoxical, patronizing, and demonstrably erroneous when, at the World Congress devoted to Shakespeare *as* a 'Man of the Theatre' (held at Stratford in 1981), several directors and academics alike insisted, as if it were truth beyond controversy, that because audiences, nowadays, are far too sophisticated to believe in ghosts, witches, spirits, and fairies, modern productions must necessarily de-mystify or otherwise up-date Shakespeare's supernatural beings in order to make them palatable to modern theatregoers. Now it might be true to say that the modern theatre is not, technically, as good at portraying spooks and monsters as the modern cinema. But the idea that modern *audiences* are incapable of crediting, or enjoying, spectacular portrayals of witches, and ghosts, and demons and spirits and monsters can be proved false by a glance at any list of popular hits in the twentieth-century cinema — from the original *King Kong* and *Dracula* to *Rosemary's Baby*, *The Omen*, *Star-Wars* and *E.T.* — the box-office success of which would seem to suggest that far from being put off by them, modern audiences are starved for mystery, for magic, for the paranormal, for demonic, and benevolent, beings from elsewhere, and, today as yesterday, will willingly pay to watch supernatural beings not a whit less difficult to believe in than the ghost in *Hamlet*, the witches in *Macbeth*, or Oberon, or Ariel, or Caliban.

It therefore seems a pity that modern productions of plays that were obviously designed to do so, do *not* satisfy an audience's desire for theatrical magic and mystery. The audience at Stratford productions, for instance, always includes lots of American and British tourists (who may not be intimately acquainted with Shakespearian drama, but who may well have grown up watching *Star Trek* and *Dr Who* on television, and who especially enjoy going to see horror films). Yet tourists were by no means the only members of the audience who — if they did not leave at the interval — dozed off during the RSC production of *Macbeth* (directed by Howard Davies in 1982) wherein (1) the witches were not witches — they were three perfectly ordinary young women innocuously passing a piece of cloth back and forth; (2) Macbeth was costumed like a yobbo, and portrayed as a very stupid one at that; and (3) the poetry was delivered in a flat monotone and at a snail's pace. Strip *Macbeth* of its metaphysical ramifications; take away its most dramatic 'instruments of darkness'; hold the tragic hero in contempt; deprive the poetry of any emotional impact; and you will ensure that the audience spends a very boring three hours in the auditorium (if not a lot of cash at the theatre bar). Brechtian alienation is alien to the spirit of a drama designed to engage our emotions and sympathies by every means at its disposal (including supernatural effects, sensationalism and pathos). This is why, if one had only Davies's *Macbeth* and Bogdanov's National Theatre production of *The Spanish Tragedy* (with its eerie Ghost; its supernatural stage-management from Revenge; its sympathetic portrayal of Hieronimo; and its horrific effects) to judge by, Kyd would have seemed a far better 'man of the theatre' than Shakespeare. Divest any work of art — whether a Shakespearian tragedy or a classic horror film like *King Kong* — of the terror, the pity, the emotional engagement, the special effects, or whatever qualities made it popular to begin with, and it will turn out as boring as that RSC *Macbeth*. Likewise, the appeal and impact of a popular song by The Beatles would be destroyed if the lyrics were worried to death for new meanings in the same way Shakespeare's verse is often treated in current productions. A directorial determination to turn Shakespeare into some kind of non-popular, non-sentimental, anti-heroical, anti-romantic, anti-spectacular playwright may explain why so many of the BBC television productions of his plays have been so drab, so boring.

Be that as it may. What seems indisputably true is that, by now, any number of critical and directorial interpretations of Shakespeare's plays (perhaps precisely because there have been so many of them — see Chapter 4) have raised virtually identical queries concerning the quality, the quantity, the validity of, and the limits to, the kinds of interpretations which may be imposed upon a masterpiece without altering it for the worse. No one wants to see a deadeningly conservative, timid, passive, simplistic, and narrow set of restrictions imposed on directorial and critical interpretations of the drama, but that is not the danger we face here. Indeed, the identical points could be made about Shakespearian studies and productions that Margot Heinemann has made about current interpretations of Brecht's plays:

> The problem isn't of a 'rigid cult', but, rather, that the mass of commentary — moral, academic and political — will overwhelm the great plays altogether, so that even where Brecht's central meaning is clearly stated it's treated as irrelevant or unfashionable.

Like Shakespearian productions, new Brecht productions can 'present anything as anything' (i.e. *The Measure Taken* [has been] moved from China to the Committee on Un-American Activities'), and there are critical and theatrical interpretations of him as a 'Stalinist Brecht, a Trotskyist Brecht, and a Brecht so "ambivalent" that he can safely be regarded as timeless, non-political English'.[12]

By now, the 'anything goes' situation described by Heinemann is so widespread in the theatre and in criticism generally, that various parodies of it — like the fictional account of the trendy drama department which was staging 'a Marxist adaptation of *King Lear*', 'a capitalist adaptation of *The Good Woman of Setzuan*', and *The Importance of Being Earnest* in the nude,[13] or like the *Spectator* contest calling for radically unorthodox settings of Shakespeare's plays, which resulted in *A Midsummer-Night's Dream* set in the Third Reich; *King Lear* staged in Wembley Arena, where they hang Cordelia from the goal-posts; and *Othello* being portrayed as a poor white in a 'mixed, multi-racial community'[14] — in turn suggest such infinite possibilities for daringly revisionist interpretations and settings that the whole process becomes a joke that might well give us pause. How about portraying Shylock as a rich Palestinian Arab in Jerusalem? or setting *Titus Andronicus* in the Old South and thus revealing Shakespeare, in his treatment of rape, dismemberment, madness, interracial lust, etc., to have been the obvious precursor of both Tennessee Williams and William Faulkner? — or what you will? Precisely because anyone remotely familiar with any play can dream up any number of ingenious settings for it, or theories about it, there is no reason why anybody should be particularly impressed by the sheer ingenuity of, or for that matter, by the sheer number of, alternative interpretations that can be, or have been, imposed upon Shakespeare's plays in performance — or in critical discussions of them.

The unlimited number of interpretations that could, conceivably, be imposed upon *any* given script, together with the tendency to shift the burden of disproof on to the critic's readers, or the director's audience, would seem to place more, not less importance on the evidence *against* an interpretation that may occur within the text itself. For unless one has some co-ordinate (like a copy of the script) with which to gauge their relative importance or explanatory value, and which affords some basis for evaluation, criticism, or refutation, of one's own — or anyone else's — theories about it, then there is no way to see, or to say, why any one of countless interpretations should be deemed especially praiseworthy, or stageworthy, or publishable, or perishable, or worthy of further consideration and debate, or so utterly inane that it would be an equal waste of time to propound or to refute it. It is one thing to admit that one hundred per cent validity in interpretation is impossible to achieve, and that we can never be absolutely certain that the answer to the question, 'Is it true what they [or I, or we, or all of us] say about Shakespeare?' is 'Yes'. It is an altogether different thing to conclude that, therefore, no theory can be proved any *less* illuminating or informative than any other one, and that the answer to Tom Stoppard's question may not be 'No', as it were, in thunder.

For instance, as opposed to recent productions of *King Lear*, in neither the Quarto nor the Folio version of Shakespeare's tragedy does any servant ever behave callously or cruelly towards the blinded Gloucester. In the Quarto, as Stoppard reminds us, several servants come to his aid; and in the Folio, the only servant who appears is the one who protests to Cornwall at the cost of his life. Why did Shakespeare himself see fit to include some protest against the persecution of Gloucester in both versions? Surely the central point being made — whether by one or by several servants — is that some humane being is bound to protest against such cruelty. Arguably, anyway, Shakespeare's servants dramatically serve to express feelings of moral outrage and revulsion presumably shared by certain members of the audience, as well as to communicate their outrage to anyone in the audience who might not share it. And so the Shakespearian answer to the question, 'Do people enjoy tormenting, or watching others torture, those who are at their mercy?' is, yet again, that 'Some (like Cornwall and Regan) certainly do; but others (like Servant X, or Servants X, Y, and Z) do not.' This holds true however you look at the script of *King Lear*, and whichever script you are looking at. It also seems a historically accurate account of the way various human beings actually do respond to cruelty and suffering in the world the play reflects. To shift the balance, by turning the Quarto's sympathetic servants into sadists, is to crack one side of the mirror that Shakespeare here holds up to human nature, showing 'virtue her own feature', as well as showing vice its own image, and – in effect – to make its reflection of human nature seem less authentic (albeit currently more fashionable) than it originally was. The same points could be made about Nahum Tate's adaptation, which spared Cordelia to make the play conform to eighteenth-century theories about poetic and providential justice. By excising the dramatic evidence against them, both Tate and Brook have, in turn, forced Shakespeare's tragedy to conform with, and thus to confirm, the unrealistically idealistic, and just as unrealistically cynical, generalizations about human experience and behaviour that its action and characterization would otherwise appear to have challenged. By the same token, *King Lear* could just as easily be revised to confirm the theoretical orthodoxies reigning at any given time. Thus various productions of it tell us what different ages have believed that Shakespeare ought to have done, as opposed to what he actually did do. But, *mutatis mutandis*, there is no reason why the whole interpretative process cannot be reversed, even as Dr Johnson reversed it. Why shouldn't various critical and directorial interpretations be used to raise the question why Shakespeare himself did *not* do what successive critics and directors have done to his plays? As Stoppard's lecture demonstrates, the scripts afford us ways to see, and to say, why what's now being said about Shakespeare may not be true at all.

Can, for instance, the following sexual connotations be truly said to encompass, or in any sense to illuminate, these particular characters, lines, and situations?

[In *Romeo and Juliet* the horsehair which Queen Mab] so assiduously plaits is, of course, female pubic hair, a reading easily justified by recalling the Renaissance slang use of 'jade' for 'prostitute', not to mention the many *double-entendres* in Shakespeare where horse and woman are linked.

A marriage between Rosalind and Phebe would be biologically impossible, although never likely anyway, since denouement prevents it. But in *Twelfth Night* the situation is more complex. The possibility of an all-female marriage demands the substitution of a spouse. Faced with the all-to-be-avoided union of Olivia and Viola/Cesario, Shakespeare has Olivia marry Sebastian.

[In renouncing their] superiority to the rest of Adam's kindred, [Beatrice and Benedick] make just those renunciations which originate in the infant relinquishing the breast . . . . and which, when successfully renounced, provide substitutes and sublimations which enrich the personality. [Moreover,] in following the destinies [of those characters] we share also in Shakespeare's triumph over his own anxiety and depression.[15]

Of course, if one accepts the validity of all critical interpretations-by-free-association, then no refutation of these, or any other assertions like them, is possible. Who cares what Shakespeare's lines actually say, if it's what you think (or what Freud might have thought) they might have meant that counts? On the other hand, to a sceptical eye, a glance at the scripts themselves renders the above assertions wide open to critical refutation on the grounds that, in Shakespeare's *Twelfth Night*, there is never any possibility of an 'all-female marriage' ('Poor lady, she were better love a dream', etc.), and that there is no more evidence that Mercutio's line informing us that Queen Mab 'plaits the manes of horses in the night' actually refers to 'female pubic hair' than there is evidence that Richard III was calling for a woman when he offered his kingdom for a horse. By the same token, it is difficult to see why the above conclusions about them have any more portentous (or less puerile) relevance to Beatrice and Benedick than to, say, Berowne, Richard II, King Lear, or any other characters who renounce their superiority to the rest of Adam's kindred. Nor is it clear why the 'remaking' of Shakespeare's 'own moral and artistic self-hood' should manifest itself in *Much Ado About Nothing* more than in any other play. His own titles happily call attention to the fundamental incongruity of those interpretations which, by investing them with some over-the-counter profundity, have resulted in what Richard Levin calls the 'decomicalization' of Shakespeare's merriest plays.

Yet in so far as such interpretations are seriously credited (and if they are not deemed worth crediting, why should they be deemed worth publishing?), then they pose far graver problems than those faced by jaded readers or reviewers inclined to dismiss them with a shrug, a yawn, or a laugh. It might be argued that even the most severe Bowdlerization would leave Shakespeare's plays essentially intact, in that they would still make good sense, and remain good drama, even though his more explicitly sexual references and bawdy jokes had been deleted or toned down. Whether his comedies and tragedies can survive a modern Bowdlerization-in-reverse, whereby everything in them must be interpreted in sexual terms, is another matter. To deny Shakespeare the freedom to focus on sexual matters is one form of censorship; to deny him the freedom not to is another. It is for reasons like these that Bernard Beckerman would seem to have made a specially important – a kind of Miltonic – distinction between true liberty and sheer licence in the interpretation of Shakespearian drama, when he concluded that,

Feeling at liberty to interpret a role or scene in unlimited ways is not truly being free imaginatively. It is far more thrilling and emancipating to discover the limits within which a given work allows legitimate interpretation.[16]

On the other hand, it is also possible to argue that the easiest, if not the only, way to discover the outer-limits to legitimate interpretation is by examining specific instances – both in performance and in criticism, both in one's own work and that of others – where they appear to have been broken or violated. To posit this case in Blakean terms, it may not be the road of caution, but the road of excess that finally brings us to the palace of wisdom, since it is only by finding out what is too much that we can find out what's enough – or not enough. And, indeed, the various truths and half-truths involved in these, and other, arguments and counter-arguments that might be brought to bear upon these issues confront us with some of the most serious methodological problems faced by Shakespeare's critics today. How can we maintain the freedom of speculation and interpretation which is conducive to new and illuminating insights and ideas, and, simultaneously, impose *any* limits whatsoever on the kind and number of possible interpretations that we are supposed to take into account? By the same token, how can we avoid unacceptable censorship of critical and directorial interpretations, and also avoid what amounts, in interpretative effect, to critical and directorial censorship of the plays themselves? Whether morally or logically speaking, it seems manifestly hypocritical to oppose any limits, or censorship, on criticism and performances without, in all fairness, going on to criticize those interpretations which, by disregarding or discounting any extant evidence against them tend – at least in so far as they *are* accepted as valid by the interpreter's readers, audience, or students – to impose their own forms of censorship upon Shakespeare's plays.

Part ii.
The Popperian Alternative

For ... if we ourselves condemn not our own weak and frivolous teaching, and the people for an untaught and irreligious, gadding rout, what can be more fair than when a man ... of a conscience, for aught we know, as good as theirs that taught us what we know, shall not privily from house to house, which is more dangerous, but openly by writing, publish to the world what his opinion is, what his reasons, and wherefore that which is now thought cannot be sound? Christ urg'd it as wherewith to justifie himself, that he preacht in publick; yet writing is more publick than preaching; and more easie to refutation.

Milton, *Areopagitica*

Every source, every suggestion, is welcome; and every source, every suggestion, is open to critical examination. . . . Neither observation nor reason are authorities. Intellectual intuition and imagination are most important, but they are not reliable: they may show us things very clearly, and yet they may mislead us. They are indispensable as the main sources of our theories; but most of our theories are false anyway. The most important function of observation and reasoning, and even of intuition and imagination, is to help us in the critical examination of those bold conjectures which are the means by which we probe into the unknown.

K. R. Popper, 'On the Sources of Knowledge and of Ignorance'

A series of methodological questions strikingly comparable to those discussed above has already been raised about the relationship between theory and practice, and about the verification and falsification of, as well as about the freedom necessary to, and the need for critical evaluation of, scientific hypotheses about the ways of nature itself. And so far as the problems surveyed here are concerned, Sir Karl Popper's insistence on the vital importance and positive uses of negative evidence in scientific methodology would seem to have a most practical relevance to critical and directorial interpretations of Shakespeare's plays. In the book from which the title, epigraphs, and main lines of argument throughout this chapter were lifted, Popper has insisted that, although there are no absolute criteria by which a scientific theory can conclusively be proven true, we can, 'if we are lucky', find various ways by which it can be proved inconclusive, incomplete, or false.[17] Indeed, in Popper's view, scientific theories themselves may be described as 'conjectures boldly put forward for trial' to 'be eliminated' if they clash with observations of the evidence, or with the results of experiments that are, 'as a rule undertaken with the definite intention of testing a theory by obtaining, if possible, a decisive refutation' of it (p. 46).

The synergistic relationship between conjectures and refutations, and between defensive and sceptical attitudes towards its own tenets and practices is, Popper argues, essential to scientific progress, since so many theoretical, as well as practical advances result from critical modifications to previously existing theories or techniques. Indeed, the 'raw materials' for criticism, generally, are 'as it were, theories or beliefs which are held more or less dogmatically', since a 'critical attitude must be directed against existing and influential beliefs in need of revision'. For that matter, a measure of defensiveness, even dogmatism, is both natural and necessary — for if, as proponents of established views, we concede defeat too easily, 'we may prevent ourselves from finding that we were very nearly right' (p. 49). Thus there are *equally good grounds* for adopting a critical attitude towards reigning orthodoxies, and for adopting a critical attitude towards criticisms of those orthodoxies. What counts is the contrast between the unduly dogmatic attitude — which 'is clearly related to the tendency to *verify* our laws and schemata by seeking to apply them and confirm them, even to the point of neglecting refutations' — and the critical attitude, which is 'one of readiness to change them — to test them; to refute them; to *falsify* them, if possible' (p. 50). It is its open-mindedness towards refutations, and not the current, or historical, orthodoxy, or heterodoxy, of the theories being propounded or attacked, that allows Popper to 'identify the critical attitude with the scientific attitude' and to describe the dogmatic attitude — which will not take 'no' for an answer — as 'pre-scientific', or, in some of its modern manifestations, as 'pseudo-scientific' in so far as any evidence that might challenge or refute it tends to be reinterpreted in the light of the theory itself and thus is triumphantly alleged to confirm it (pp. 34-50).

Human nature being what it is, of course the tendency of most of us (regardless of whether we are critics or scientists, directors or students) is not to seek out the evidence against our own theories, hypotheses, or beliefs, but to seek ways to confirm or apply them (even Freud was not incapable of mistaking the order of his ideas for the order of nature). And, as anyone who has ever been so infatuated knows, no lover was ever so blind to the faults of his mistress than one

who has fallen in love with his own — or with somebody else's —
theories about Art, Nature, History, Psychology, etc. For that matter,
the notion that scientists are, by nature or inclination, any more
objective than other mortals is false.[18] When it is looked at in terms of
its methodological premiums and penalties, scientific objectivity is the
result of the 'friendly-hostile' co-operation between (and competition
amongst) scientists which tends to assure that if they do not publish
the extant evidence that could refute their own conclusions, then some
other scientist will, in all likelihood, be delighted to claim professional
credit, advancement, and prestige for doing just that. Given the absence
of any clear reward for presenting it, or any penalty for not doing so,
who *wouldn't* be inclined to overlook, or underestimate, or discount
the evidence against their own convictions, theories, or beliefs? This is
why scientific methodology places such a high premium on negative
feedback, on the confrontation that its theories must, finally, make
with a 'real world' which 'does provide the possibility of disproof'.[19]

If Shakespeare's plays are looked at from this particular angle, they
could, once more, be compared to the creations of nature itself, in that,
given their richness and complexity, it is easy to come up with some
evidence that would appear to confirm practically any theory about
them that any one of us might wish to publish — yet this holds true
only so long as all we look for are confirmations, since, again like the
'real world', the plays themselves do provide the possibility of disproof.
Indeed, there is no reason why, if we wanted to, we could not adopt
the methodology advocated by Popper, which is to seek out and
present the best possible arguments against our own theories as well as
those of our rivals, colleagues, and students. Even if this proved psychologically impossible, we could, at least, assume that the primary
purpose of publishing our conjectures is to expose them to criticism
and refutation by others. It would take some of the sting out of hostile
reviews of one's own best efforts if the following premises had
prompted their publication in the first place: 'If you are interested in
the problem which I tried to solve by my tentative assertion, you may
help me by criticizing it as severely as you can; and if you can design
some experimental test which you think might refute my assertion, I
shall gladly, and to the best of my powers, help you to refute it.' (p.
27).

There are, of course, altogether different ways of looking at the
methodological and dialectical processes involved in science and
critism alike (e.g. Thomas Kuhn's account of the ways in which

reigning paradigms are applied to the point where their explanatory value is exhausted, and in turn replaced by new paradigms, has its own obvious relevance to the ways that critical theories tend to change). Yet in the criticism and performance, as well as in the teaching, of Shakespeare's plays, there seems a virtually unlimited potential for the improvement and enrichment of interpretative conjectures and refutations alike in the methodological principle whereby negative evidence should be sought out rather than suppressed. So far as the quality and prestige of scholarly and critical commentaries are concerned, it is hard to see how putting a premium on the presentation of counter-evidence could do any more damage to Shakespearian studies than the opposite has done. As Norman Rabkin has observed, far too many discussions of Shakespeare's plays have already suffered from the 'premium placed on reductiveness'; suffered, as it were, from 'the assumption that what can be brought by self-contained arguments to a satisfactory conclusion is what is worth discussing and responses that don't work into the argument must, therefore, be discounted'.[20]

Although the premium placed on reductiveness has, by now, been critically challenged on several different fronts, the fact remains that in many publications and performances still, the governing theory or approach is obviously what has dictated the author's or director's interpretation of Shakespeare's plays — rather than vice versa, in which case (either prior to, or in the course of, the publication or the performance itself) the plays could be used to test, challenge, or refute (rather than be selectively adapted, or cited, in order to make them confirm) whatever theory about them is being posited. It would certainly open things up, and liberate authors of critical studies from the confines of an unduly restricted theory or approach, if they felt perfectly free to acknowledge, and to discuss the reasons why, a critical, or ideological, or historical perspective which genuinely seemed to illuminate Play X had proved of little or no use to them in coming to terms with Play Y.

The Popperian method also seems especially liberating because it does not rule out *any* method or source of insight. Quite the contrary. Any and all sources of knowledge concerning the plays — imagination, reason, personal experience, previous discussions or productions of the plays, other literature, ancient and modern criticism, Elizabethan documents, and so on, would be most welcome. But all interpretations, *whatever* their origins, and *however* distinguished their proponents, would be open to critical challenge. Indeed, to place a premium on the acknowledgment of counter-evidence might prove conducive to less refutable arguments, since it is precisely because they have been presented without regard to contradictory arguments, or evidence, that certain critical assertions are sitting targets for refutation in terms of the evidence against them that was ignored, in a critical counter-attack that may, in turn, be equally one-sided in its treatment of the evidence against it.

What Popper's method would discourage us from presenting (as anything other than conjectural speculations) are interpretations that are, in principle, unfalsifiable. A strong interpretation is one which could be proved false, but has not yet been shown to be wrong. If, contrariwise, no conceivable evidence against it could have any effect, and if the question, 'How would the play (or the world) be identifiably different if this interpretation were not correct?' cannot be answered concretely, that interpretation would seem vacuous (for an example of this kind of interpretation, see the Providentialist interpretation of the death of Cordelia cited on p. 27).

It should be noted — and indeed stressed — here, that the application of his theories to literary interpretation might be dismaying to Popper himself. He is very emphatic in insisting that his line of demarcation in terms of falsifiability is between scientific and non-scientific, not between meaningful and meaningless, discourse (see *Conjectures and Refutations*, p. 39):

The problem which I tried to solve by proposing the criterion of falsifiability was neither a problem of meaningfulness or significance, nor a problem of truth or acceptability. It was the problem of drawing a line (as well as this can be done) between the statements, or system of statements, of the empirical sciences, and all other statements . . .

Yet the principles whereby its irrefutability may constitute the major weakness of a theory, while falsifiability may constitute a major strength (since a good scientific theory — like Einstein's gravitational theory — is in principle falsifiable, although as yet unfalsified), could itself prove of methodological use to literary criticism in helping us to distinguish between differing kinds of interpretations.[21]

In any case, the methodology advocated by Popper would encourage us, as Norman Rabkin suggests, to take into account our own 'haunting sense of what doesn't fit the thesis we are tempted at every moment to derive', and, while 'rejecting narrow conclusions drawn by other critics, to learn from the assumptions that led to their conclusions' (*Shakespeare and the Problem of Meaning*, pp. 22, 25). It would also allow us to agree that there can be no definitive interpretation (any more than a definitive production) of a play by Shakespeare, and, simultaneously, acknowledge that critical or directorial interpretations which will stand up against the strongest arguments that can be levelled against them are likely to be sounder than conjectures which require acceptance, purely on faith, of the authority of the critic, or director, or psychoanalyst who propounded them. For that matter, what have we to lose by adopting a critical (as opposed to a defensive) attitude towards our own best efforts – as well as those of others?

The texts themselves, the responses they have historically elicited from audiences down through the centuries, and the facts of theatrical life provide our most obvious sources of 'negative feedback' concerning critical interpretations of Shakespeare's plays. For instance, the common laws of Shakespearian communication which call into question Bertrand Evans's new reading of *Antony and Cleopatra* also render suspect certain views propounded by A. L. French, who has announced (to a hitherto unsuspecting world) that Claudio was lying to Shakespeare's audience, as well as to Lucio, when he claimed to have a true precontract with Julietta, and that Kent and Cordelia were prejudiced, and speaking on the basis of their vested interests, when they reported that Goneril and Regan threw King Lear out into the storm. In this case, Shakespeare's characters are said to tell the truth *only* when their statements confirm the critic's own theories. Otherwise, they are proclaimed to be lying, or biased, or deceived. Enobarbus is, therefore, said to speak with the 'voice of the play' when he criticizes Antony (criticisms with which French concurs). But his final lines praising Antony's magnanimity (praises which French believes are unfounded) are alleged to demonstrate that 'even Enobarbus dies deceived'.[22]

Yet if French is, in fact, correct in concluding that Claudio's expository lines informing us about his relationship with Julietta are not to be believed, and that the last words of Enobarbus are not to be credited,[23] and that we should not trust even Kent and Cordelia (characters whom Shakespeare took some pains to establish as speakers of truth at any cost), then there would seem to be no character in the complete works of Shakespeare whose testimony can be considered reliable. For the same principles with which French impugns the testimony of these witnesses (e.g. that they are speaking on the basis of a vested interest, or lying, or deceived) could be used to discredit any statement ever made by any character in (or by any critic of) any play ever written. One could, for instance, argue that Desdemona was lying — since she so obviously had a vested interest in doing so — when she claimed to be guiltless of adultery, and that the last of her lies was intended to deceive Othello into believing that she truly loved him and so to avenge herself by driving him to commit suicide out of remorse. By the same token, Emilia's passionate lines affirming Desdemona's innocence could be cited as evidence that she, too, dies deceived. On the other hand, someone else might argue that this interpretation itself demonstrated that the critic who propounded it was prejudiced against Desdemona, or had a vested interest in positing a radically unorthodox reading of *Othello*, etc.

But be that as it may. It is very difficult to see what, if anything, is gained by disregarding, or rejecting, the Shakespearian conventions and guide-lines whereby certain characters, during a few brief hours upon the stage, have quite effectively communicated, to a succession of audiences, the information and sentiments necessary for the understanding of the tragic, or comic, or tragicomic ironies involved in a given dramatic situation. It is, surely, Shakespeare's customary practice to let his audience know which characters are deceivers (like Richard III and Iago), and which (like Lady Anne and Roderigo) are deceived; which are the truth-tellers (like Kent and Cordelia), and which are hypocritical liars (like Goneril and Regan). So far as critical methodology is concerned, it is hard to see how we can possibly evaluate, or concur with, or criticize a latter-day commentator's distinctions between reliable and unreliable testimony, if neither we, nor the commentator, can rely on Shakespeare's own, most dramatic, distinctions between characters who are to be, or not to be, believed. And it is even more difficult to see what vested interest Shakespeare himself might conceivably have had in misleading, or confusing, his own audience concerning the true nature of Antony's magnanimity, Lear's treatment at the hands of Goneril and Regan, or Claudio's sexual and legal relationship with Julietta.

The fact that certain critical interpretations cannot be communicated in performance to an intelligent spectator who is unfamiliar with the script renders those interpretations suspect (since that is the kind of spectator Shakespeare wrote for). It would, for instance, take a great effort to mount a production of *All's Well That Ends Well* which would dramatically confirm John Edward Price's theory that Shakespeare commends Bertram's rebellion against the 'pious platitudes' and 'nearly suffocating restraints' of the Countess and the King.[24] One might sympathize with any character who is forced into marriage, but this critic goes further than that. The Countess's advice, 'Love all, trust few/Do wrong to none' is said to be 'blandly conventional', the 'kind of advice young people will react against'. One wonders just how they will react — by loving few, trusting none, and doing harm to all? This critic's arguments will not persuade those of us who find his elders more, not less, sympathetically portrayed than Bertram, who, given (for instance) his behaviour towards Diana, might best be defended as Shakespeare's most definitive portrayal of a stinker. If Shakespeare intended our sympathies to go to Bertram, but failed in his efforts to elicit them, then that is just too bad. No critic can put things right for him without rewriting the play.

As a rule, the more drastic the alterations to the text required to produce it, the more likely a directorial or critical interpretation is to be wrong. It is, for instance, possible to imagine a performance of *Romeo and Juliet* conceived in terms of those scholarly arguments in fashion several years ago which dismissed the prologue and denied the emotional impact of the poetry to argue that Shakespeare's hero and heroine got just what was coming to them for their passionate misdeeds.[25] Still, the prologue and the poetry would have to be cut, radically adapted, or spoken in very peculiar ways in order to turn the play into an indictment of the two young lovers. We cannot know how Shakespeare felt when he was writing *Romeo and Juliet* (or any other play), but the odds are that he worked on his 'wording' until he thought his play would elicit the kind of response he wanted it to elicit from his audience. For all we know, he might have worked on a comedy until reading it over very much amused him, and worked on a tragedy until he, personally, was moved by the re-reading of it.[26] In any event, the words on the page are what provide the starting-point for the critic's, the reader's, the actor's, or the director's interpretation of them. In this sense, the play's the thing, whether it is being read for the purposes of directing it, acting in it, or writing about it, and it is therefore easy to spot those critical essays and productions that mandate the substitution of some scholar's, or critic's, or director's frames of reference for the dramatic co-ordinates provided us by Shakespeare's own expository scenes, prologues, and poetry.

For those who set out to produce them in conformity to a dictatorial theory, the richness of the scripts may prove an obvious liability. As Edith Holding observes in her discussion of Charles Johnson's adaptation of *As You Like It*, 'The variety of intellectual and emotional life which Shakespeare offers' may be more than a given adapter, or director, can handle. The selective version of the play produced may be coherent and effective in its own right, but none the less represent an 'enormous reduction of Shakespeare's own breadth of vision'.[27] Yet again, our knowledge of the scripts themselves is our best check against one-sided or reductive interpretations of them on the stage. After all, to adopt a reverently respectful attitude towards the loony and inane interpretations sometimes posited in performance (I most vividly remember seeing Mariana swilling booze on the haystack at the moated grange), seems no less absurd than to adopt an uncritical attitude towards all theories propounded in scholarly books and journals. The odds, alas, are that other people's brain-children, as well as one's own, are more likely to be Gonerils and Regans than true Cordelias. Why, though, are Shakespeare's works so consistently richer than so many critical and directorial interpretations of them?

It is, I believe, his practice of admitting refutations which most distinguishes Shakespeare's own dramatic practice from critical approaches and directorial interpretations wherein any evidence that might appear to refute or to contradict the reigning theory is either disregarded, or discounted, or reinterpreted in the light of that theory, and thus alleged to confirm it. In the works of Shakespeare, precisely the reverse holds true. If, say, in *King Lear*, he most profoundly affirms the humane values of kindness, generosity, self-sacrifice, he does so by taking into account, as opposed to denying, the fact that those who act with best meaning may, thereby, 'incur the worst'. For that matter, whole plays and sonnets, as well as any number of individual characters, are constantly asking, or finding out, 'If this be error'.

Hamlet, for instance, considers himself obliged to seek out evidence against the insights of his own 'prophetic soul'. Therefore, although he absolutely loathes his uncle, he decides to subject the spectral evidence against Claudius to a critical test. If the King's 'occulted guilt' does not manifest itself in the play-scene, then Hamlet will have to admit that his own 'imaginations' were as 'foul as Vulcan's stithy'. Likewise, in other plays and in sonnets alike, a given theory, premiss, or argument has to be re-examined in the light of whatever evidence there is against it ('Moor, she was chaste; she lov'd thee, cruel Moor;... Nay, lay thee down and roar;/For thou hast kill'd the sweetest innocent/That e'er did lift up eye'; 'Hermione is chaste; Polixenes blameless; Camillo a true subject; Leontes a jealous tyrant; his innocent babe truly begotten; and the King shall live without an heir, if that which is lost be not found.').

Thus Shakespeare's works never cease to remind us that – like all human beings – all theories, all arguments, all our reason and our imagination, all our sources of insight and knowledge, are poignantly, tragically, comically, dangerously, fallible and vulnerable to the extent that 'men may construe things after their fashion,/Clean from the purpose of the things themselves.'

Part iii.
Some Dramatic and Critical Constructions and Misconstructions: The Problem of the Obvious

Perhaps because there is no other way to assure that the audience will know when a character has construed things correctly (like Paulina and Emilia) or has misconstrued everything (like Othello and Leontes), Shakespeare's own dramatic co-ordinates are, for the most part anyway, made obvious to his audience. In this sense, at least, although he may have had small Latin and less Greek, Shakespeare seems more classical than some of his avowedly neo-classical contemporaries and successors: like the ironies of a Greek tragedy, Shakespeare's dramatic ironies tend to depend on information possessed by – not withheld from – his audience. Thus Coleridge rightly placed first of the 'Characteristics of Shakespeare' that the major impacts of his plays derive from 'Expectation in preference to surprise'.[28] In Shakespeare's works, as compared to certain works by Ben Jonson or Beaumont and Fletcher, surprise (like the resurrection of Hermione) is the exception, not the rule. As a rule, Shakespeare's characters, not his audience, are the ones who are surprised. We know that Sebastian is safe in Illyria, that Friar Lawrence's letter to Romeo was not delivered, that Desdemona is chaste. When the necessary information cannot be assumed (as knowledge concerning the assassination and its consequences can be assumed in *Julius Caesar*), it is supplied. When necessary, prologues may let us know what to expect, and how to think, about the characters and events portrayed. By means of the prologue to *Romeo and Juliet*, for instance, we are informed that (unlike Brooke's cautionary story condemning lovers who abused the honourable name of lawful marriage) Shakespeare's play will treat his star-crossed lovers with great sympathy. We are to see them as tragic victims, as children whose misadventured, piteous overthrow finally ends their parents' strife. And so it goes, for the most part, throughout the works of Shakespeare.

The general outline of the action, the major co-ordinates with which to pinpoint the hero and the heroine, the victim and the villain, would be clear enough even to a doltish or inattentive playgoer. This is why Richard Levin is surely right to argue that the 'burden of proof' should rest upon those who reject the most obvious and reasonable hypothesis in interpreting a given play. Thus the critic advocating a radically 'new reading' would have to confront the 'old reading' fairly and squarely, and 'show that it is less probable than his own'. This does not mean, Levin adds, 'that an informed and sensitive spectator will not see more in the play than a groundling', but we would expect these further insights 'to represent an enrichment of the common experience of the play — not something quite different from that experience and certainly not its opposite' (pp. 202–4).

Speaking of groundlings, in spite of the mid-twentieth-century controversy about it, one wonders if even an Elizabethan numbskull would have had serious difficulty with the exposition in *Hamlet*. That ghost is *there* to tell him what he needs to know about past events, about carnal, bloody, and unnatural acts, and deaths put on by cunning. Its independent existence is affirmed by the soldiers and Horatio, and its testimony is later confirmed by the murderer himself. For the purposes of tragic irony, Shakespeare thus makes sure that we in the audience will have no lingering doubts concerning Claudius's guilt. Having identified the King as the murderer of his brother, Hamlet's father, before the end of the first act, Shakespeare contrives to set other obstacles in the way of Hamlet's revenge. Indeed, he may have raised serious questions about the validity of spectral evidence in order to keep things from being *too* easy for his hero, or for the audience. For although the ghost tells us what we need to know about what has already happened, Shakespeare makes certain that, like Hamlet, we remain uncertain what will, or should, happen next, not knowing how, or when, the right moment for retribution will come.

As a rule, surely, Shakespeare's expository speeches and scenes serve to assure that the various problems in his plays (like Claudio's sexual, emotional, and legal relationship with Julietta) are, as Chekhov would put it, 'correctly posed'. They may also serve to make certain that the audience knows what kind of comic, or tragic, or tragicomic action to expect. Could there be more blatantly expository lines than the ones Shakespeare gives to Prospero, who commands the audience, even as he urges Miranda, to pay attention while he explains exactly how he lost his dukedom? Here informing us that 'there's no harm done', here identifying the villain, there telling us what has happened and why, Shakespeare's lord of *The Tempest* (rather like the Deity in the medieval cycle-plays) directs, intervenes in, watches, comments upon, and finally ends his show when all fulfilled is his forethought, his judgements given, his 'dukedom got'. 'I am determined to prove a villain' boasts Richard III, who goes on to indicate some specific forms his villainy will take. Richard also tells us groundlings, in no uncertain terms, how to think about other characters like 'simple, plain, Clarence'. So does Queen Margaret. This walking ghost of the House of Lancaster who, with witch-like power, prophesies the downfall of her enemies, very effectively supplies us with crucial information about the past history of the various characters, about the old scores to be settled and old debts to be paid, along with a grimly satisfying foreknowledge of retributions yet to come. Departing from his sources, Shakespeare brought Queen Margaret back from France to serve his scene, and she serves it, both technically and metaphorically, as an instrument of exposition and as a living symbol of Nemesis.

For that matter, what better instruments of exposition are there than those supernatural beings in Shakespeare's plays? There is Oberon, King of Shadows, who assures us that 'all things shall be peace'; there are those witches who prophesy future developments to us, as well as to Macbeth and Banquo; and there is that ghost in *Hamlet* who, in the upshot, tells us what we need to know about the world the characters inhabited before the tragedy began. These figures could hardly be more potent as instigators, as overseers, as portents. What better instrument of exposition, in a tragedy obsessed by the past, than a ghost? Could Tom Stoppard be right in concluding that the ghost 'of course' was 'not a problem' to Shakespeare? Does it not give the audience pretty much what they might expect from a dramatic ghost? And does it not say, to Hamlet, very much what his murdered father, if he could communicate from beyond the grave, would most likely have said to his son?

On the most obvious of all symbolic levels, Shakespeare's familiar, compound ghost — rather like Queen Margaret in *Richard III* or like the ghost in *The Spanish Tragedy* (and, for that matter, very like certain ghosts in plays by Ibsen, Strindberg, and Yeats) — simultaneously recalls and embodies truths about the past that cannot be permanently suppressed. It thus may be seen as the perfect dramatic manifestation of past passions and past crimes that, in life itself, may sometimes rise 'though all the earth o'erwhelm them, to men's eyes'. 'Remember me!' it urgently, repeatedly insists. In fact, from beginning to end, this particular tragedy is haunted by the remembrance of things past, by the *status quo ante*, by the way things were before the play began. Moreover, various characters in this ghost-ridden play seem to be walking shadows, or spectres, of their former selves. Rosencrantz and Guildenstern, Hamlet's old friends, are now the instruments of his enemy. Gertrude, so loving to Hamlet's father, now honeys and makes love with his murderer. Hamlet, who loved Ophelia, treats her rudely and cruelly. Images from the past filter through this tragedy like ghosts, suddenly intruding upon the present, or like Yorick, grinning from his grave. These buried truths may be tragic, but there is no way of making certain that they will not, for the bane and the enlightenment of the present, break loose from their confines. Thus the influence of the ghost of Hamlet's father seems far more richly analogous to the pervasive pressures exerted upon the present by the past (pressures felt by all of us, as well as by the various characters in *Hamlet*) than to the case of demonic possession portrayed at the Royal Court (or in *The Exorcist*). Although the influence of the past upon the present would seem an undeniable fact of all our lives, the consequences of that influence, for good or evil, for the individual, or for a nation, for us, as well as for Hamlet, are essentially problematical. So is the influence of the future. And in a tragedy as obsessed by the future as *Hamlet* is possessed by the past, what better instruments of exposition than those three weird sisters? In *Macbeth*, as in *Hamlet*, Shakespeare, by way of supernatural beings, supplies his audience with the information necessary for an appreciation of his tragic ironies. Like Queen Margaret, the witches officially prophesy subsequent events to us, as well as to the characters on the stage, but, like Macbeth, we groundlings remain uncertain how the prophecies will be fulfilled. Ironically enough, characters in *Richard III* ignore the curses of Shakespeare's bitter Cassandra. Macbeth, of course, acts upon the prophecies of the witches. In doing so, he enables Shakespeare to raise all sorts of questions about free will, fixed fate, foreknowledge absolute. Indeed, watching *Macbeth*, we may observe the operation of that principle, whereby in history as in the drama, human expectations, whether for good or evil, may play a crucial role in inspiring people to bring about what has been expected or imagined. On both literal and symbolic levels, Shakespeare's witches dramatically remind us how, in life itself, prophecies may incite, if not force us, to bring about their fulfilment. And the tragic fulfilment of their prophecies serves to remind us with what cruel irony fate may keep the word of promise to our ear — and break it to our hope.

Thus in the greatest works of Shakespeare, as in the masterpieces of other major playwrights down through the ages, dramatic form and content are fused. The symbolic significance of his instruments of exposition – whether they are instruments of darkness, ministers of grace, honest ghosts, or juggling fiends – serves to reinforce and complement, not to contradict, their technical function. In the hands of a master-playwright, the technical instruments of the drama itself may constitute instruments of discovery effectively designed to inquire into, even as they hold the mirror up to, our own, most strange, estate.

Of course, it could be argued that even as an interpretation of, say, the ghost of Hamlet's father as a demon with the power to assume a pleasing shape is too facile, too reductive, my emphasis on it as an instrument of exposition, as a dramatic metaphor of the never-quite-buried past, seems equally facile and reductive. If either interpretation of the ghost is credited, the other can be attacked for having (on the one hand) over-simplified, or for having (on the other hand) over-complicated the dramatic and moral issues involved. As we shall see in the next chapter, quite a number of one-sided interpretations that, in the past decades, have over-simplified the plays, are now being challenged by counter-arguments that sometimes tend to over-complicate them. How to avoid doing either (and how to avoid either labouring, or failing to take into account the obvious) is now – as it always has been, and probably always will be – the most ubiquitous of the methodological problems that a critic of Shakespeare must face.

Notes

1. See Bertrand Evans, *Shakespeare's Tragic Practice* (Oxford, 1979), pp. 241–69.

2. 'To make the Spectators Understanders' is the epigraph to Jonson's *Love's Triumph Through Callipolis* (1630). Good, and even great, plays that fail to do this will fail until they finally do. Jonson's own experiments with dramatic form and characterization caused *The New Inn* to fail in performance (see Anne Barton's fascinating discussion of '*The New Inn* and the Problem of Jonson's Late Style', *English Literary Renaissance*, 9 (1979), ·395–418). Likewise, the greatest comedy of manners ever written in English, Congreve's *The Way of the World*, failed when it opened because the audience wasn't able to tell the difference between a Truewit and a Fainall. By contrast, when Shakespeare's plays, or scenes, prove unpopular, it is not because they are not understood, but because readers or audiences do not approve of what they clearly see to be going on (even

as the death of Cordelia was disapproved of by eighteenth-century critics and producers). The reason *Troilus and Cressida* was long unpopular was because people found its bitter views of love and war distasteful. And regardless of whether one likes them or not, the plays that seem most offensive nowadays – *The Merchant of Venice* and *The Taming of the Shrew* – are clearly comprehensible, however differently individuals may respond to, or interpret them. *The Merchant of Venice* has been staged as an anti-Semitic play (see above, pp. 53–4, and also see D. M. Cohen, 'The Jew and Shylock', *Shakespeare Quarterly*, 31 (1980), 53–63); conversely, it has been interpreted as a pro-Shylock, anti-Christian-hypocrisy play (see Frank Whigham, 'Ideology and Class Conduct in *The Merchant of Venice*', *Renaissance Drama*, 10 (1979), 93–115). (I, personally, would interpret the Shylock plot as a case-study of the nature and consequences of ancestral tribal grudges, of religious and racial prejudices – on both sides.) Likewise, the *Shrew* could be interpreted as a virulently anti-feminist farce; or as a pro-feminist protest against the breaking of a proud spirit; or as a kind of Spencer Tracy – Katherine Hepburn, *Kiss Me, Kate,* love story wherein two people, who are obviously 'made for each other', must work their way through combat to truce, etc. The crucial disagreements in these instances have to do, not with an understanding of what is going on, but with how what goes on should be interpreted and judged – see E. D. Hirsch's discussions of the issues of interpretation and understanding in *Validity in Interpretation* (New Haven and London, 1967). By contrast, Bertrand Evans's disagreement with everyone else is about what is actually going on in *Antony and Cleopatra*. His assertion that Antony never really loved Cleopatra is equivalent to asserting that Shylock never really intended to cut into Antonio in Act IV of *The Merchant of Venice*.

3. See Michael Steppat, *The Critical Reception of Shakespeare's 'Antony and Cleopatra' from 1607 to 1905, Bochum Studies in English* (Amsterdam, 1980).

4. In Benchley's review of the production starring Tallulah Bankhead, he thus rebuked the star for her tendency 'to wax unintelligible in the clinches' – a fault 'shared by several of her team mates' – 'all of which is too bad, considering the hard work that Shakespeare must have put in on his wording' in *Antony and Cleopatra.* See Brendan Gill, *Tallulah* (London, 1972), p. 61.

5. Reviewing Adrian Noble's production of *King Lear* in the *Observer* (4 July 1982), Robert Cushman (who otherwise admired it) regretted the cutting of Edmund's repentance, and the deplorable behaviour of the servants who 'shove the blinded Gloucester while pretending to pity him'. In this, of course, the director followed the play-as-previously-adapted by Peter Brook (see below). If art is often influenced more by other art than by 'nature', and criticism often owes more to previous criticism than to art, certain directorial interpretations of Shakespeare nowadays often owe as much (whether by development or reaction) to previous directorial interpretations as to Shakespeare's scripts themselves.

6. Contrast the refreshing frankness of the film credits to *Carry on Cleo* ('Based on an Idea by William Shakespeare') and *The Boys from Syracuse* ('After a play by William Shakespeare. Long, long after.').

7. Tom Stoppard, *Is It True What They Say About Shakespeare?* International Shakespeare Association Paper No. 2 (Oxford, 1982).

8. See Kenneth Burke, 'Psychology and Form', in *Perspectives by Incongruity*, ed. Stanley Edgar Hyman (Bloomington, Indiana, 1964), pp. 20–1.

9. See David O. Selznick, as quoted by Roland Flamini in *Scarlett, Rhett and a Cast of Thousands* (New York, 1975), pp. 197–9. The same holds true of any popular work. See Gore Vidal, 'Who Makes the Movies?' in *Pink Triangle and Yellow Star* (London, 1983), pp. 169–87: 'The plot of *Ben-Hur* is, basically, absurd and any attempt to make sense of it would destroy the story's awful

integrity'. Vidal also makes important points about the dependency of a film director on the script writer: Paddy Chayefsky's 'early career in films perfectly disproves Nicholas Ray's dictum: "If it were all in the script, why make the film?" If it is not all in the script, there is no film to make.' 'Recently', Vidal observes, 'a movie critic could not figure out why there had been such a dramatic change in the quality of the work of the director Joseph Losey after he moved to England. Was it a difference in the culture? the light? the water? Or could it – and the critic faltered – could it be that perhaps Losey's films changed when he . . . got Harold Pinter to write screenplays for him? The critic promptly dismissed the notion.' For that matter, 'Few directors . . . possess the modesty of Kurosawa, who said, recently, "With a very good script, even a second-class director may make a first-class film. But with a bad script even a first-class director cannot make a really first-class film".'

10. See *Hamlet*, III. ii. 39–40. And see also Evert Sprinchorn, *Strindberg as Dramatist* (New Haven and London, 1982), pp. 252–3.

Strindberg was not one of those playwrights who regard their scripts as sacrosanct and inviolable. . . . He wrote to his German translator: – 'You may certainly insert a few lines if you want to, but it would be better to have the actor smooth out his entrances and exits by repeating a line or by . . . adding a few words of his own. . . .' [But] in return, Strindberg wanted the spirit of his play to remain inviolate.

The advice Hamlet gives to the actors would suggest that Shakespeare felt the same way about the spirit of his play. Sprinchorn also observes that, at its greatest, drama may transform the audience from witnesses to participants in the tragic or comic recognition (p. 45). As Tom Stoppard observes, this transformation was achieved, quite by accident, in a production of *Hamlet* wherein 'the Ghost was supposed to be a bright light shining from the back of the auditorium, and on the night I was there, some member of the audience unfortunately having to leave the theatre at that point, got in the way of this light – and a shadow passed over the audience; and my blood, and I think everybody's blood, went cold' (see Stoppard, p. 5).

11. For a discussion of the way in which the spirit of the play seemed honoured in Peter Brook's production of *A Midsummer-Night's Dream*, but violated in other recent productions, including Brook's *Lear* (which was nothing like such a triumphant critical or commercial success as the *Dream*), see Helen Gardner, 'Shakespeare in the Directors' Theatre', in *In Defence of the Imagination* (Oxford, 1982), pp. 55–82.

12. See Margot Heinemann, 'Modern Brecht', *London Review of Books* 5–18 August 1982, pp. 22–4. If, as Brecht observed, the playwright may not wish – and need not have – 'to have the *last* word', then (arguably anyway) neither should his director, or his critic. You can't devise a drama – or a criticism – to make people think for themselves, and then insist on doing all their thinking for them (see Heinemann, p. 24).

13. In Malcolm Bradbury's *The History Man* (London, 1977), pp. 65, 81.

14. See the *Spectator*, 27 June 1981, p. 30.

15. The first two quotations are from Elizabeth Sacks, *Shakespeare's Images of Pregnancy* (London and Basingstoke, 1980), pp. 19 and 43, the third quotation is from Simon Stuart's *New Phoenix Wings: Reparation in Literature* (London, 1979), p. 167. Perhaps significantly, none of these points would be easy to communicate in production. And what about the costuming, etc. required to communicate this one (see *Shakespeare's Images of Pregnancy*, p. 59)?

[In *Measure for Measure*] the Duke's penetration of the city limits, the opening gates, the holy fountain a league below, all contribute to a powerfully sexual atmosphere. His homecoming is metaphorically portrayed in terms of a vaginal penetration.

16. See Bernard Beckerman, 'Explorations in Shakespeare's Drama', *Shakespeare Quarterly*, 29 (1978), 133–45.

17. See Karl R. Popper's essays, 'On the Sources of Knowledge and of Ignorance' and 'Science: Conjectures and Refutations', in *Conjectures and Refutations: The Growth of Scientific Knowledge* (London, 1969). Page references are inserted parenthetically in the text.

18. See Popper, *The Open Society and its Enemies*, Vol. 2 (5th edition, London, 1966), pp. 217–18:

> Everyone who has an inkling of the history of the natural sciences is aware of the passionate tenacity which characterizes many of its quarrels. No amount of political partiality can influence political theories more strongly than the partiality shown by some natural scientists in favour of their intellectual offspring. If scientific objectivity were founded, as the sociologistic theory of knowledge naïvely assumes, upon the individual scientist's impartiality or objectivity, then we should have to say good-bye to it. . . . [The fact is] that science and scientific objectivity do not (and cannot) result from the attempts of an individual scientist to be 'objective', but *from the friendly-hostile co-operation of many scientists*.
>
> Two aspects of the method of the natural sciences are of importance in this connection. Together they constitute what I may term the 'public character of scientific method'. First, there is something approaching *free criticism*. A scientist may offer his theory with the full conviction that it is unassailable. But this will not impress his fellow-scientists and competitors; rather it challenges them: they know that the scientific attitude means criticizing everything, and they are little deterred even by authorities. Secondly, scientists try to avoid talking at cross-purposes. . . . They try very seriously to speak one and the same language, even if they use different mother tongues. . . . In order to avoid speaking at cross-purposes, scientists try to express their theories in such a form that they can be tested, i.e. refuted [by other scientists].

This is the best case I know of for clarity in critical exposition. It is impossible to refute an argument if you can't be certain what the argument is.

19. See Jonathan Howard, *Darwin* (Oxford, 1982), pp. 86–7: 'A popular misconception is that scientists invariably withhold assent from statements which purport to be scientific until something called "proof" is provided. It would be more accurate to say that scientists have an inclination to believe any tolerably sound argument of a scientific character until something called "disproof" is provided. There is, however, an important distinction betwen a scientific argument and other deductive arguments of equal logical precision, which rests on the contact that scientific arguments make with the real world. The real world does provide the possibility of disproof.'

20. See Rabkin, *Shakespeare and the Problem of Meaning* (Chicago, 1981), pp. 19–20.

21. For instance: Maynard Mack's theory that 'Hamlet's world is pre-eminently in the interrogative mood' is falsifiable. Anyone who has a copy of the text can put it to a critical test. Moreover the play, and our responses to it, would be identifiably different if it were pre-eminently conceived of in, say, the imperative, and *not* the interrogative, mood. Therefore, Mack himself goes on to suggest precisely what difference various questions do, in fact, make to the hero and his world, and to our responses to the tragedy (certain questions 'seem to point not

only beyond the context but beyond the play, out of Hamlet's predicaments into everyone's'). By contrast, the interpretation (recently propounded in several different discussions of *Measure for Measure*) whereby 'Claudio's sentence of decapitation is, in Freudian terms, a symbolic castration' is unfalsifiable. Yet the questions, 'What of it?' and 'What, if any, difference would it make (to us, or to the play) whether this interpretation is, or is not, correct?', have, so far as I know, gone unanswered.

22. See A. L. French, *Shakespeare and the Critics* (Cambridge, 1972), pp. 17-19, 152-4, 220-1. On pp. 221-2, French argues that Antony's ostensibly gentle and generous adieus and greetings to his old friend and comrade-in-arms were, 'in fact', strategically 'calculated' to make Enobarbus hate himself. And so, according to French, Enobarbus not only dies broken-hearted, he dies all the more deceived.

23. As a rule, the statements and sentiments of dying characters in Elizabethan drama tend to carry a special choric weight and credibility. See *Richard II*, II. i. 5-16:

> *Gaunt.* O, but they say the tongues of dying men
> Enforce attention like deep harmony.
> Where words are scarce, they are seldom spent in vain;
> For they breathe truth that breathe their words in pain.
>
> . . . .
>
> Though Richard my life's counsel would not hear,
> My death's sad tale may yet undeaf his ear.

For very much the same reasons that John of Gaunt gives us, the statements of persons who know they are dying are still presumed true in Anglo-American law, and thus the rules against admitting hearsay evidence are suspended in the case of a 'dying declaration'. If the statements of a dying character in a play by Shakespeare are not to be credited, or presumed to be true, then the playwright, as in the case of Desdemona, *very* dramatically presents the reasons why they should be seen as false. Indeed, Desdemona may have been depending on the traditional presumption of truth concerning death-bed testimony in her dying effort, as it were, legally, to exonerate Othello.

24. See John Edward Price, 'Anti-moralistic Moralism in *All's Well That Ends Well*', *Shakespeare Studies*, 12 (1979), 95-111.

25. See the critics cited by Richard Levin (*New Readings vs. Old Plays*, pp. 151-2). One critic thus equates the 'sins' of Desdemona and Juliet: 'as with Juliet so here we must allow for the weight given by Shakespeare to the sin of disobedience to parents.' Another critic explains that Juliet's behaviour would have 'shocked' Shakespeare's audience, because in 'boldly asserting her own will she violates a sacred canon of Elizabethan life; namely that children, and especially daughters, owe obedience to the wishes of their parents'. Another critic has asserted that 'a prolonged study of a cache of Elizabethan social documents' left him with the 'overriding impression' that 'the average audience of *Romeo and Juliet* would have regarded the behaviour of the young lovers as deserving everything they got'. As Levin points out, critics who are horrified at the behaviour of Juliet and Desdemona tend to overlook the fact that very little, if any, weight is given by Shakespeare to the 'sin' of disobedience to parents in certain comedies and romances.

26. See E. H. Gombrich, 'Focus on the Arts and Humanities', *Bulletin of the American Academy of Arts and Sciences*, 1981, on 'engendered creativity': 'It is the form which engenders the emotion, not the emotion which is turned into form' (p. 20). Gombrich, by the way, is the best advocate for Popper's

methodology in the humanities (see the Preface to *Art and Illusion* (London, 1968), p. ix): 'I should be proud if Professor Popper's influence were to be felt everywhere in this book'.

27. See Edith Holding, '*As You Like It* Adapted: Charles Johnson's *Love in a Forest*', *Shakespeare Survey*, 32 (1979), 37–48.

28. See Coleridge's *Lectures*, in *Shakespeare Criticism*, ed. D. Nichol Smith, p. 236.

Chapter 4

Some Current Themes for Critical Disputation

How seriously should we take Shakespeare's comedies? Can the characterization of his plays best be explained in terms of their construction — or vice versa? Should the plays be studied as poems, or can they only be understood in performance? Does Shakespearian drama affirm, or challenge, the political, social, moral, and sexual orthodoxies of his time — or our own? Are 'moral ambiguities' invariably to be preferred to moral clarities — especially when female sexuality is involved? Recent commentators on Shakespeare's plays and poems give us diametrically opposite answers to all these questions. Representative feminist and anti-feminist arguments about Shakespeare's treatment of female virtues and vices can serve to illustrate some of the best and worst features of Shakespearian studies at the present time, as well as to encapsulate some of the major critical problems discussed in the previous chapters.

Part i.
Female Virtues and Vices in Shakespearian Drama and Criticism

> For that which all men then did virtue call,
> Is now called vice; and that which vice was hight,
> Is now hight virtue, and so used of all;
> Right now is wrong, and wrong that was is right,
> As all things else in time are changed quite.
>
> Spenser

Kenneth Muir has observed that 'the temptation to enrol Shakespeare in one's own party is almost irresistible':

It is only possible to do this, without falling into manifest absurdity, by ignoring much of the evidence. The negative capability possessed by

Shakespeare made his opinions fluid. His mind, as Keats said of his own, was a 'thoroughfare for all thoughts' – not a select party.

'It is', Muir concludes, 'very difficult to point to any opinions in [Shakespeare's] works which were certainly his own', and critics who attempt to do so have tended to arrive at mind-numbingly obvious conclusions – e.g. that Shakespeare disliked flatterers, traitors, 'meanness, and ingratitude' and 'loved generosity and loyalty'.[1] Or that 'Shakespeare's attitude is that alcoholic drinks are good things when used in moderation, but bad things when used to excess.'[2] Likewise, the answer to the question, 'What were Shakespeare's conclusions about men and women, and about the relationships between them?' would seem to be that 'It takes all kinds to make a world.' Yet in so far as this cliché is equally applicable to Shakespeare's treatment of characters of both sexes, then it is rather less banal than it might appear to be. For if it does, truly, take all kinds of women to make Shakespearian drama what it is, then this sets that drama at odds with countless commentaries on the plays that have tended to insist or to imply that there really is only one kind of woman, or that there are only two kinds of women (see below), and that in any event, there is only one set of criteria by which the women in Shakespearian drama may be 'morally' judged, and that is in terms of their effects upon, and sexual responses to men.[3]

The Renaissance itself produced counter-arguments on practically every issue, including the nature of women (who were held to be either morally worse, or morally better than men).[4] But on the nature of man himself, there was at least some agreement. As Pico della Mirandola and Hamlet alike remind us, man's nature is essentially, perhaps even quintessentially, Protean.

At last, the Supreme Maker decreed that this creature ... should have a share in the particular endowment of every other creature. Taking man, therefore, this creature of indeterminate image, He set him in the middle of the world and thus spoke to him:
'We have given you, Oh Adam, no visage proper to yourself, nor any endowment properly your own, in order that whatever place, whatever form, whatever gifts you may, with premeditation, select, these same you may have and possess through your own judgment and decision. The nature of all other creatures is defined and restricted within laws which We have laid down; you, by contrast, impeded by no such restrictions, may, by your own free will, to whose custody We have assigned you, trace for yourself the lineaments of your own nature. . . . We have made you a creature neither of heaven nor of earth, neither mortal nor

immortal, in order that you may, as the free and proud shaper of your own being, fashion yourself in the form you may prefer. It will be in your power to descend to the lower, brutish forms of life; you will be able, through your own decision, to rise again to the superior orders whose life is divine.'

Pico goes on to extol the 'wondrous and unsurpassable felicity of man, to whom it is granted to have what he chooses, to be what he wills to be':

The brutes, from the moment of their birth, bring with them, as Lucilius says, 'from their mother's womb' all that they will ever possess. The highest spiritual beings were, from the very moment of creation . . . fixed in the mode of being which would be theirs through measureless eternities. But upon man, at the moment of his creation, God bestowed seeds pregnant with all possibilities, the germs of every form of life. Whichever of these a man shall cultivate, the same will mature and bear fruit in him. . . . Who will not look with awe upon this our chameleon, . . . this creature, man, whom Asclepius the Athenian, by reason of this very mutability, this nature capable of transforming itself, quite rightly said was symbolized in the mysteries by the figure of Proteus.[5]

And quite in spite of innumerable ancient — and modern — arguments to the contrary, Pico's most interesting generalizations about the volatile, mutable, Protean nature of the least specialized of all created beings seem obviously, and equally, applicable to Eve as well as to Adam, to the females of the species, as well as to its males. For that matter, if one were to judge solely by the behaviour, motivation, and morality embodied in the various women created by the mortal equivalent of Pico's 'Supreme Maker', the nature of woman would appear to be just as indeterminate, and as 'capable of transforming itself', as the nature of man. Like the various men in Shakespearian drama, individual women may choose to be kind or cruel; to be faithful or fickle; to obey, or to defy, authority; to be proud or humble; vindictive or merciful. Sisters in Shakespeare may behave with transcendent virtue (like Cordelia) or with heartless cruelty (like Regan). They may choose to act like Kate, or like Bianca, or may learn to behave like Luciana — or Adriana.

Shakespeare, of course, deals with certain stereotyped images of feminine (and masculine) virtues and vices that are to be found in art through the ages. The chaste and fair heroine, the loyal wife, the manipulative wife, the termagant, the temptress (along with the jealous husband, the clever servant, the braggart soldier, the conniver, and the seducer), appear in classical literature, *The Arabian Nights'*

Entertainments and the Bible as well as in Elizabethan drama. In contemporary pamphlets polemically designed (on the one hand) to condemn female vice, or (on the other hand) to extol female virtue, these (and other) stereotypes were hurled back and forth against each other. If pamphleteer X cites the shrewish Xanthippe, pamphleteer Y counter-cites the long-suffering Griselda. What is most interesting about certain paradigmatic types of 'naturally' or 'unnaturally' feminine — and masculine — virtues and vices is that they have a great deal more in common with each other than with other stereotyped images of members of the same sex, even as the Griselda-type of woman has more in common with the Job-type of man than with the Xanthippe-type of shrew (in the pamphlets, as well as in Chaucer, Griselda is the feminine counterpart of Job, even as Mary is the counterpart of Christ, etc.). Time after time, the vices (or virtues) alleged to be typically feminine, or characteristically masculine, turn out to be identical. It therefore seems pointless to discuss Shakespeare's women (or women in any other major literature) solely with reference to characters of the same sex, with whom they may have nothing in common except their gender. As often as not, the characters with whom men and women in literature (as in life?) have most in common are members of the opposite sex. For instance, the feminine counterpart to the shrew-taming husband, Petruchio, is the husband-taming Wife of Bath;[6] the masculine counterpart to the provoked wife is the hen-pecked and cuckolded husband; the female counterpart to the Satanic seducer of women is the Eve-like temptress of men, and so on.

The same holds true throughout Shakespearian drama wherein individual men and women often are shown to have infinitely more in common with each other than with members of their own sex. Looked at in terms of their behaviour, their motivation, and their morality, Cordelia has everything in common with Kent, and nothing in common with her sisters, Goneril and Regan; seen in terms of their passions, actions, values, and fates, Antony and Cleopatra have a great deal more in common with each other than with Octavius and Octavia; Tamora has more in common with Aaron the Moor than with Lavinia. Isabella has more in common with Angelo than with Mistress Overdone. Coriolanus has as much in common with Volumnia as with Aufidius. And so on and on. This is why it would seem just as futile to seek a common denominator in women as different as Venus and Lucrece, Cordelia and Regan, Cleopatra and Octavia, Volumnia and Gertrude, as it would be to seek the common denominator in Shakespeare's portrayals of men as different as Kent and Cornwall, or the Lord Chief Justice and Falstaff, since the only one that exists is of no poetic, or dramatic, or moral significance compared to the obvious differences between them.[7]

Is there any cardinal virtue, or vice, in Shakespearian drama that does not manifest itself in male and female characters alike? If Cressida is fickle, so is Proteus. If Adonis is repelled by the assaults of Venus, Lucrece is repelled by the assaults of Tarquin. If Cleopatra is beguilingly devious, so is Falstaff. If Prospero concludes that the rarer action is in virtue than in vengeance, so do Portia and Isabella and Cordelia. Queen Margaret is ruthlessly vindictive, but so is Shylock. Women like Cordelia, Cleopatra, Queen Margaret, and Joan of Arc, who actively engage in war or politics are exceptional, but there they stand, alongside Judith, Boadicea, and Queen Elizabeth as exceptions that might (on the one hand) be said to prove the rule, 'It is unnatural for women to participate in politics or war', but could, with more justification, be said to refute it: 'It may be unconventional, but it cannot be "unnatural" for women to engage in politics or war, since some women have historically, and as it were quite naturally, done so.' If, as has been observed, Shakespeare offers us no model of a heroine who is a complete success in coping with the world independently of men,[8] it is difficult to think of a Shakespearian hero who is shown to be a complete success in coping with the world independently of women (even Henry V needs his Kate). Certain traditionally 'masculine' vices show themselves more fiend-like in a woman, but that presumes that they were horrible vices to begin with. The kind of 'manly' behaviour that both of the Macbeths determine to act in accordance with, is judged, by Shakespeare, to be neither manly nor womanly but brutish, demonic, profoundly inhumane.[9]

I have laboured the obvious similarities between masculine and feminine actions and motives and virtues and vices in Shakespearian drama because what may emerge from them (*pace* Freud and his disciples) is the interesting possibility that biological gender, in and of and by itself, may not *necessarily* determine the motives or the behaviour of a given individual. Thus, the answer to Freud's unanswered question, 'What do women want?' would be the same as the answer to the question, 'What do men want?' And that is that 'Different ones may want any number of different things' — they may want kingdoms and power and glory and revenge as well as marriage and children, or romantic love. If this is true, then the psychological and behavioural traits traditionally identified with one sex or the other (pride/humility; cruelty/compassion; aggression/passivity; vanity/modesty; sadism/masochism; the will-to-power/the slave mentality, etc., etc.) whether they act, or whether Shakespeare portrays them, in opposition to or in isolation from each other, or in various internal fissions and fusions, may best be seen as fundamental components of the psychological and moral make-up of human beings in general, any of which may manifest itself, or not manifest itself, in individual entrants in the human race regardless of their gender.[10] Arguably, anyway, it is for this reason that whatever vices and virtues and motives and behaviour that are theoretically deemed to be characteristic of (or unnatural to) either sex will inevitably manifest themselves in characters of both sexes in any literature attempting to hold the mirror up to human nature (as opposed to a body of fiction attempting to confirm reigning theories about the nature of 'woman' as if it were morally, or psychologically, less indeterminate than the nature of man). The individual women in Shakespearian drama could thus be used to challenge, or to refute, rather than to confirm, virtually any theory, or idealism, concerning the essentially angelic, or bestial, or pure, or promiscuous, or masochistic 'nature' of womankind.

In marked contrast to the Protean nature of womanhood in Shakespearian drama itself, critical commentaries on Shakespeare's tragic heroines often insist that they all should be morally judged and critically placed in terms of their conformity to, or deviation from, whatever stereotyped image of womanhood the commentator thinks they ought to have behaved in terms of. In these critical commentaries, the nature of woman would seem to have been unalterably fixed, 'from the moment of creation', in the 'mode of being which would be theirs through measureless eternities'; as if women were unlike men ('those creatures neither of heaven or earth', whose 'nature is capable of transforming itself') but very like Pico's angels, who differ from men in their physical and spiritual purity; or like Pico's beasts, who bring with them from their mother's womb 'all that they ever will possess' – i.e. a congenital promiscuity. It was because of these either/or, angel/whore, categories that Desdemona died, and it is because of the same stereotyped images of the nature of woman that she has been judged woefully wanting by mid-twentieth-century critics.

'It is', H. A. Mason concedes, 'a delicate matter to use the word "guilty" for Desdemona's guiltlessness',

But we can say that she falls short in two respects of being the human symbol of divinity. She is too self-confined, when it behoved her to forget herself and understand Othello . . . But the damage to her symbolic value is greater when we see her passively *leaving everything to Heaven.* She ought in a sense to have *embodied* Heaven, given us a human equivalent that would 'make sense' of Heaven'.[11]

Conversely, Desdemona has been severely castigated for her 'proud denial of the body's claims', for her failure to face up to 'her own feminine frailty', and her tendency to shrink from 'the reality of the whore within her' (see above, p. 21). And of course, the same old stereotypes can be made to sound modern by positing them in Freudian terms. The identical arguments used to condemn Desdemona's failure to live up to the standard of ideal femininity extolled in Elizabethan courtesy books may thus be used to condemn her as a 'masculine' woman with a 'castrative' need to 'dominate Othello in terms of phallic rivalry'.[12]

Given these contradictory stereotypes, those of Shakespeare's tragic heroines who are chaste, or are faithful to their husbands, can always be charged with the sin of pride, since they refuse to acknowledge the 'reality' of the 'whore which exists within all women', even as those who acknowledge their own sexual desires can be got up on charges of bestiality (in her epithalamion, Juliet 'comes very close to panting like an animal'). However faithful or well-meaning, or however sexually forthright or forthcoming, Shakespeare's tragic heroines may be, and in whatever different ways they may behave, they can *all* be proved guilty of having failed to conform to one or the other stereotype. As various critical arguments concerning the rape and suicide of Shakespeare's Lucrece can serve to demonstrate, no female character, be she 'as chaste as ice, as pure as snow' can hope to escape critical calumny. Thus, S. Clark Hulse asserts, as if it were a foregone conclusion, that the suicide of Lucrece 'returns us to Shakespeare's [*sic*] misogyny, for while Lucrece is not to blame, she is clearly guilty'.[13] Critically speaking, however, this seems on all fours with insisting that the suicide of Madam Butterfly 'returns us to Puccini's misogynistic racism'. What is Lucrece so 'clearly guilty' of?

Part ii.
The Poetic and Critical 'Rape of Lucrece'

There is no possible way out: If she is adulterous, why is she praised? If chaste, why was she put to death? (*Si adulterata, cur laudata; si pudica, cur occisa?*)

Augustine, *The City of God*

No man inveigh against the withered flow'r,
But chide rough winter that the flow'r hath kill'd.
Not that devour'd, but that which doth devour,
Is worthy blame. O, let it not be hild
Poor women's faults that they are so fulfill'd
  With men's abuses! those proud lords to blame
  Make weak-made women tenants to their shame.

Shakespeare, *Lucrece* (ll. 1254–60)

Is there any such thing as an innocent victim in Shakespearian poetry or drama? If there is, she would seem to be Shakespeare's Lucrece. No one would argue that *The Rape of Lucrece* is one of Shakespeare's greatest works. Yet without it, certain forms of human suffering and experience would be absent from the canon. Moreover, as Ian Donaldson's remarkable study of the myth of Lucretia has demonstrated, emergent from critical reactions to the fate of its heroine are certain culturally, theologically, and dialectically determined arguments about rape and suicide (e.g. 'Did the victim incite or enjoy the rape?' 'Is suicide a sin?') that are as ubiquitous and controversial here and now, as they've ever been in art or history.[14]

Also emergent from Donaldson's study of *The Rapes of Lucretia* is a dialectical dichotomy between an artistic tradition, wherein victims of sexual injustice (e.g. the Roman Lucretia, Shakespeare's Lucrece, Richardson's Clarissa, Hardy's Tess) are portrayed as sinned against, not sinning, and a tradition of moral and critical commentary holding that the reverse is true, or ought to be true, and that literature's Lucretias are more to be censured than pitied. No book gives better pictorial and literary examples of a central tradition of art in which victims of rape, seduction, and sexual slander have been treated — at least by their creators — with unqualified sympathy and respect, and in which the biological vulnerability of the heroine is often, if not always, emblematic of the vulnerability of life's victims in general. However much works in this tradition may differ in quality or in kind, there is never any doubt who is to blame for the heroine's predicament; suffering, death: the villain is injustice, and the victim — justice — is always the same. And there is not the slightest question where the art or artist stands: they are on the victim's side. I believe this explains why

Donaldson has found 'no painting' of a 'lascivious, or vainglorious Lucretia' (p. 167).

A superfluity of such Lucretias is, however, to be found in theological and critical commentaries on the Roman prototype and her Shakespearian counterpart. For in seemingly eternal opposition to art's sympathies for life's victims, is a line of literary criticism that (rather like Inspector Javert hounding Jean Valjean) is generally determined to find art's victims guilty, and is so determined to find its female victims *sexually* guilty that the artist's emphasis on the injustice actually perpetrated on the heroine is lost sight of altogether. Here, for instance, are some of the sexual questions currently being put to literature's Lucretias:

Doesn't the sweat on the hand of Shakespeare's Lucrece serve as evidence of her 'subconscious preparation' for Tarquin's visit? Isn't her long plea to him just a way of 'escaping from calling for help'? Was Tess (Thomas Hardy's 'spiritual Lucretia') *really* raped or (as if that would have made any difference to the President of the Immortals) 'was she seduced'? Isn't Imogen (the Lucretia of Shakespearian romance) 'susceptible, and almost seduced'? And wouldn't Imogen make a far better 'heroine for all ages' if she were not (as she was 'once thought to be') the 'embodiment of all that is straightforwardly good', but was in fact as 'morally ambiguous' as Iachimo?[15]

Thus any heroines who might have served to challenge it are held to have confirmed the universally acknowledged truth — 'When a lady says "no", she means "maybe"; and if she says "maybe" she means "yes"; and if she says "yes", she ain't no lady' — that is the burden of this critical lay. Odder still is the fact that whatever sexual 'susceptibilities', proclivities, subconscious desires, feelings of irrepressible bliss while being raped, etc., that the commentator can voyeuristically project onto the rapist's, or seducer's, or culminator's — or fate's, or hypocrisy's — victim are proclaimed to be of paramount 'moral' concern.

Two questions are raised by this particular strain of literary criticism: how did it arise, and why does it still exist? Ian Donaldson's book can help us answer them both. The determination to prove literature's Lucretias sexually guilty entered the critical tradition via a historical confrontation between Roman and Christian beliefs concerning suicide, shame, and guilt, and those fates held to be, or not to be, worse than death. Because we still live with the moral, sexual, and critical consequences of the original conflict between them, I shall posit the obvious reasons why the same old arguments that were initially devised to divest the Roman Lucretia of her virtue are currently being reiterated in critical essays on her Shakespearian successor. For it is, as it were, in dialectical opposition to the most sympathetic portrayals of the type in literature that twentieth-century commentators (just like their precursors, Augustine and Tyndale) have felt it their 'moral' duty to consign the victim of Sextus Tarquinius to critical fates worse than death. Here is a brief account of the historical context of the controversy.

The story of the rape of Lucretia first emerged as the principal component of a 'powerful aetiological myth' designed to exemplify the moral values and heroic idealisms traditionally associated with the ancient Roman republic, and (as Ian Donaldson demonstrates) its political reverberations make it easy to see why this particular myth subsequently proved especially popular in times of revolution. In major Roman versions of the story, the sexual tyranny of Sextus Tarquinius (what better Linnaean taxonomy for a rapist?) was equated with the political tyranny of his father, Tarquinius Superbus, even as the ravaged Lucretia was seen as a symbol of Rome and its neighbouring cities. Thus Tarquin infiltrated himself into Lucretia's confidence in the same way he had previously infiltrated himself into the confidence of the people of Gabii (who, to their cost, had also given him a friendly welcome): *Cepimus audendo Gabios quoque*, Ovid's Tarquin boasts to himself, 'By daring we captured Gabbia too.' Comparable analogies were established between the way Lucretia achieved personal liberation ('in a sense that Seneca, and later David Hume, would have understood and approved') and the way that Lucius Junius Brutus freed Rome from tyranny, as he vowed to do while 'holding the dagger with which Lucretia killed herself' (pp. 8-9). Although she was obliged, as an ideal female, to leave vengeance to her menfolk, and could take up the sword 'only against herself', Lucretia's exemplary refusal to live on in shame was what inspired the men who witnessed it (including Brutus, who, for the purposes of survival, had previously feigned idiocy) to refuse, henceforth, to suffer under the Tarquinian yoke.

In dying in order to affirm her virtue as a woman – her guiltlessness, her moral inviolability ('let no adulteress use my precedent as an excuse'), the Roman Lucretia, like Shakespeare's Lucrece, can, of course, be seen as a victim of the very code of honour she embodied. But, *mutatis mutandis*, so can all those Roman heroes who commit suicide to protest against tyranny, or to affirm, or reaffirm, their 'manly' virtue, honour, integrity, etc. (e.g. Cato of Utica, Jonson's

Silius, Shakespeare's Antony) — the very noblest Romans of them all do it. For that matter, Lucretia/Lucrece's suicide is what most notably distinguishes her from her sister-victims, Virginia and Lavinia, who were killed, and so delivered from shame by their male relatives.[16] By contrast, Lucretia takes the traditionally 'masculine' prerogative of action into her own hands, and claims the ultimate freedom to choose the time and way to die. In any event, when looked at in terms of Roman concepts of human heroism, the original Lucretia's suicide seems of more potent propaganda-value than the suicide of a man, since her sex allows her to serve, both as a symbol of all victims of oppression, and as a model of transcendent virtue and integrity. But, of course, there are altogether different ways of looking at Lucretia's, or Lucrece's — or anyone else's — suicide. Hasn't the Almighty 'fixed his canon 'gainst self-slaughter'? Might it not be nobler in the mind to suffer the oppressor's wrong, the proud man's contumely (or whatever outrages that fortune might inflict on you and yours) than to follow Lucretia's example, and, by opposing, end them with a bare bodkin? In subsequent centuries, the Roman dictum, 'Better far it is to die/ Than to live in Ignomy', was countered by the Christian premiss that it is 'truly better to undergo all the Shame and Contempt in the World than for any to embrue their hands in their own Blood' (see Donaldson, p. 35).

Early Christians had extolled Lucretia as a pre-Christian model of the chastity and wifely fidelity on which they, too, set the highest of all premiums; and so her image lived on — as 'Lucrece for her chastity'; 'sad' Lucrece for 'modesty' (see *The Taming of the Shrew*, II. i. 288, and *As You Like It*, III. ii. 138). But should it have? Arguing in moral support of Christian nuns who had been raped by the Goths, but had determined not to commit suicide, St Augustine had used Lucretia's legend (1) to ask why an innocent victim should condemn herself to death; (2) to condemn suicide as a sin equivalent to murder; (3) to argue against over-valuing chastity for its own sake (since virtue is essentially a matter of the will); and so launched the most concerted of all attacks on the whole complex of values embodied in the Roman heroine.

Ian Donaldson thus summarizes Augustine's line of reasoning concerning rape and suicide: if spiritual virtue is the essential thing, then those 'accidents which overtake the body, however regrettable and distressing they may appear, are ultimately trivial. They are not fates worse than death or necessitating death. Life is not to be thrown away

upon such trifling pretexts' (p. 31). So far as I am concerned, the
insistence that you should not feel shamed, or commit suicide, on
account of something done to you against your will, would, in theory
anyway, seem equally consoling to all victims of those regrettable, yet
ultimately trivial, accidents that occasionally overtake the body — to,
say, male victims of castration as well as to female victims of rape
confronted with its biological and social consequences (enforced
pregnancy, social ignominy, ridicule, scorn, etc.). On the other hand,
given a cultural equation between feminine — or masculine — 'virtue'
and a given biological state (whether female chastity or male potency),
it is easy to understand why an irrevocable violation of that biological
state, through rape or castration, might well seem, *to the one who has
suffered it*, to represent a fate worse than death itself. For, alas, the
psychological and social facts are that, even if they have no reason to,
people do feel violated, polluted, contaminated, defiled, stigmatized,
and shamed, and, worse still, have often been blamed and shamed by
others (even as Lucretia has been blamed and shamed by successive
commentators, including Augustine) on account of what was done to
them by others, or what they felt forced to submit to for the sake of
others, or were forced to endure at knife-point, or whatever. Both
biological and social forms of shame actually exist, and may cause
extreme suffering, quite independently of guilt. And these forms of
shame: trauma; confusion; fear of ignominy; loathing of the world and
of the self; and, above all, a desire to spare her husband comparable
shame, suffering, ignominy, and ridicule, are, arguably anyway, what
Shakespeare's *Lucrece* is all about.[17] But in the vehemence and
brilliance of his attack on the Roman Lucretia, Augustine equated a
sense of physical shame with moral guilt. 'If chaste', he asked, as it were
rhetorically, 'why was she condemned to death?' Thus his moral argument against suicide turned into a case for the sexual prosecution of
Tarquin's victim. On the grounds of Augustine's humane intentions,
Donaldson disputes William Empson's use of the word 'caddish' to
describe his attack on the Roman Lucretia.[18] Yet the interpretative
tradition derived from that attack would seem to deserve Empson's
epithet. The cat that Augustine let out of the bag was a Tom.

After Augustine, a chorus of commentators insisted that Lucretia
'must have killed herself out of guilt'. 'One common speculation' was
that she killed herself 'because she had not been able totally to suppress
all feelings of pleasure when Tarquin raped her'. Thus her suicide, 'So
far from being proof of her innocence', was held as evidence of her

'moral corruption'. When cleared of charges of lechery, Lucretia was accused of an even deadlier sin. By glorying in her chastity, Tyndale concluded, Lucretia manifested a pride that 'God more abhorreth than the whoredom of any whore' (see pp. 34-6). Thus there is, as Augustine put it, 'no possible way out' for a Lucretia: you will be damned, by one set of commentators, if you do consider rape a fate worse than death; and you will be damned, by another set of commentators, if you don't. Three queries: (1) Would this line of critical speculation ever have arisen with reference to a 'manly' victim of homosexual rape or castration? (2) Who seems most markedly unable 'totally to suppress all feelings of pleasure' while contemplating rape − or while casting stones at its victim? (3) Which attitude towards Lucretia is finally the more moral, or the more profoundly Christian − the compassion of an artist or the merciless censoriousness of the critic? Who here would appear to be of the Devil's party without knowing it?

Unless sexual injustice is a legitimate subject for art, there is no defence of Shakespeare's poem as it stands. For, on the surface anyway, Shakespeare's *Lucrece* looks like a poetically unambiguous portrayal of virtue outraged. The Roman emphasis on the revolutionary ramifications of Lucretia's suicide is played down, since Shakespeare's Lucrece is herself the victim of a revolution against all laws of hospitality, kinship, and kind (see Donaldson, p. 16). Shakespeare's poem is pervaded by a sense of the pity of it, the suffering of it, the injustice of it, but the political and heroical impact of the heroine's suicide is muted. The primary effect of the poem is pathetic, not tragic. Should Shakespeare's heroine, therefore, be left to rest in peace as a paradigmatic victim? Or would his poem be more profound if an Augustinian subtext provided us with critical perspectives by which Lucrece's 'crimes' could be seen as 'reciprocal with Tarquin's', as a 'little beyond forgiveness'? Wasn't her suicide, like Lucretia's, prompted by the kind of pride in her 'maculate body' that is more abhorrent 'than the whoredom of any whore'?[19]

Is Shakespeare's ostensibly sympathetic portrayal of Lucrece poetically countered by Augustinian and post-Augustinian condemnations of its heroine? Some scholars say yes; some say no (the possibility that Shakespeare's poem might have been designed to counter *them* has, so far as I know, never been seriously considered).[20] Donaldson believes that the answer to this question is by no means clear. He cites terminology suggesting that the poem was rendered 'morally ambiguous' by Augustinian perspectives on its heroine, yet some of the same

quotations could be used to show that it wasn't. If Lucrece is described as a 'castaway' ('the common theological term for a lost soul',
p. 46), so is Shakespeare's 'most choice, forsaken' and 'most loved'
Cordelia (*King Lear*, I. i. 251). But if *The Rape of Lucrece* is *not*
rendered 'morally' ambiguous by Augustinian perspectives on its
heroine, how can we save it from critical damnation as a tedious depiction of outraged chastity? One critic cited by Donaldson attempts to
save it from this critical fate worse than death by arguing that 'the
significant rape is the rape of Tarquin's soul'. Lucrece, after all, is left
with only the 'material' (physical, domestic, and social) consequences
of the rape, while Tarquin, who violated his own better self, bears (as
well he might) the burden of a guilty mind. Shakespeare himself, of
course, insists that Lucrece's is the greater burden. But that is why the
poem lacks the 'moral' force it might have had.[21]

It would be most interesting to know whether, and how, these
critical conclusions about the issues might differ if the sex of the victim
and the villain had been reversed in a cognate myth wherein:

A happy, proud, wife, while visiting relatives out of town, boasts
of the fidelity of her handsome husband, Lucretius, who is heir to a
family fortune in precious jewels. An accomplished seductress, Sexta
Tarquinia, hears the boasts and determines to have Lucretius for herself. She goes to the city, introducing herself to Lucretius as a friend
and relative of his wife. He receives her politely, but all her attempts to
seduce him fail. Furious, she sneaks a powerful aphrodisiac into his
glass. While he is under its influence, they have sexual intercourse. She
absconds with the jewels, and leaves behind a note informing him that
he now has syphilis. Primarily for his wife's sake, he commits suicide.
Sexta Tarquinia subsequently feels guilty, and when the truth is known
her family is forever banished from the town.

Would the question, 'Might Lucretius himself have enjoyed the act of
sex?' be considered of any 'moral' importance (given the fact that he
did not engage in it of his own free will)? And would the physical,
economic, and domestic consequences of the seduction be considered
'ultimately trivial', merely 'material'? Arguably, anyway, physical and
emotional suffering that is the result of someone else's desire to exert
power, or simply to show off (see The Book of Job), may be harder to
bear than a burden of shame and guilt resulting from having done what
one chose to do. This, I believe, could explain why Shakespeare insists
that Tarquin leaves 'his spoil perplex'd in greater pain' than his (l. 733).

I, for one, am not persuaded that Shakespeare's poem would be of
any more 'moral' profundity if it had been, primarily, concerned with

the spiritual 'rape of Tarquin'. Nor am I convinced that it would be more profound if Augustinian frames of reference had provided explicit criticisms of Lucrece – or if the sweat on her hands actually had evinced her subconscious preparation for Tarquin's visit. If outraged chastity is a literary and artistic cliché (see Ovid's account of the rape of Lucretia), so, surely, is *Casta est quam nemo rogavit* ('Chaste is she who never gets asked') – see Ovid's *Amores*, I. viii. 43.

Literature, obviously would be as boring as it would be unrealistic if all its heroines were paragons of chastity and wifely fidelity. Happily, however, it also provides us with a sparkling succession of wantons, adulteresses, Lady Wishforts – and many a Sexta Tarquinia. So why don't our moral and sexual and critical beadles direct their energies towards them? Why bother to look for blemishes on the lamb, Lucrece, when her creator also painted the stripes of the tigress, Tamora? Unless – could it be? – that 'modesty' may more provoke our sense 'than woman's lightness'? If so, the critical 'desire to raze the sanctuary/And pitch our evils there', is very much like Angelo's – or Tarquin's ('Haply that name of "chaste" unhap'ly set/This bateless edge on his keen appetite' (ll. 8-9). The difference is that the critical rapes of Lucretia were once committed in the name of Christian morality, and are currently being committed in the name of 'moral' ambiguity. But whatever else in time has changed quite, and whether the rape is accomplished by force, by fraud, or by casuistical skill, the position of the victim remains exactly the same.

In the case of Lucrece, we have a clear-cut dichotomy between the realities and the moralities reflected in art and in criticism. Artists, like Shakespeare, who show a remarkable tolerance of, and sympathy towards, practically everything else on earth, and who argue the case on both sides of practically every other issue, often tend to take unequivocal and unambiguous stands against injustice. Conversely, their critics who are most unsympathetic and uncharitable towards practically everything else, are – in so far as they find its victims guilty – remarkably tolerant of injustice itself. Yet in none of the cases of egregious injustice that occur throughout the works of Shakespeare, does the poet himself insist that the victim is the one we ought to blame. Pity, combined with a sense of outrage, is the primary response aroused when Lucrece commits suicide as a result of rape, as when Cinna the poet, and Lady Macduff and her children are slaughtered on the stage. In *Romeo and Juliet* and in *Lucrece*, Shakespeare goes out of his way to insist that the young lovers and the ravished wife are tragic, pathetic, victims of pestilential hatred and sexual tyranny, and we are thus encouraged to condemn the forces that drove them to suicide: 'Not that devour'd, but that which doth devour/Is worthy blame.' It is in cases where that which doth devour others is itself devoured that the 'judgement of the heavens, that makes us tremble,/Touches us not with pity' (*King Lear*, V. iii. 231-2). In so far as a major goal of tragedy is, in fact, to touch us 'with pity', to portray characters who suffer and die as a result of unmerited misfortune would seem to be the easiest of all ways to do it. In the later tragedies, Shakespeare set himself a far more difficult task.

The most significant difference between Shakespeare's mature tragic practice and Aristotle's tragic theory is that while Aristotle at one point says that 'pity is aroused by unmerited misfortune,' Shakespeare insists on eliciting audience sympathy for characters who, to a greater or lesser degree, have brought their misfortunes on themselves. Shakespeare seems to ask his audience to understand, to empathize – even to forgive. In the later tragedies, Shakespeare seeks audience sympathy for inherently unsympathetic figures – a stubborn and mentally infirm octogenarian, a murderer, a misanthrope, a mama's boy, and (most difficult of all) a disreputable woman. As Willard Farnham points out in *Shakespeare's Tragic Frontier*, such an attempt involves great risks – what is gained in granting characters some say in their own destiny might easily be lost in diminution of audience sympathy. It seems to have been a risk that Shakespeare deliberately elected to take. In his last few tragedies, he made increasing demands on the humane tolerance (or perhaps on the Christian charity, in the most radical sense) of his audience. We are not expected to agree, in every case, that the protagonist is more sinned against than sinning; we are expected, on the basis of our common humanity with the offending protagonist, to offer sympathy unqualified by the necessity for exoneration.[22]

What the early and later tragedies have in common is that, whether the hero or heroine is portrayed as an innocent victim (like Juliet), whose suffering is the result of external forces, or as a character whose tragic flaws, errors, and frailties are made obvious from the outset, Shakespeare's compassionate portrayals of his tragic protagonists could be said to evoke *our* charity, in the most profoundly Christian sense of that term. This is why a 'Christian approach' that judges even Lucrece to be 'a little beyond [our] forgiveness' might appear to involve a contradiction in terms. If the casting of stones at his heroes and heroines really were, or historically might have been, or morally ought to be, the proper response to Shakespearian tragedy, then Shakespeare himself is, surely, the one who has proved to be of the Devil's party. For in cases of sinners far more culpable than poor Lucrece, Shakespeare, having confronted us with the worst that can be known or said about his protagonists, proceeds to encourage us to understand, to empathize, to respect their suffering, to admire their courage, and even to forgive them their trespasses.

Like the various critical conjectures and refutations cited throughout this book, certain critical arguments concerning the feminine (and masculine) vices and virtues portrayed in Shakespearian drama seem dialectically devised to counter previous critical arguments: Imogen would 'make a better heroine for all ages' if she were *not*, 'as she was once thought to be', the 'embodiment of all that is straightforwardly good'; Lucrece's crimes are *not*, as certain critics have alleged them to be, 'reciprocal with Tarquin's'. Yet in so far as it takes into account the most obvious poetic and dramatic effects involved in Shakespeare's works themselves, a sympathetic as opposed to a censorious approach to his tragic protagonists (of both sexes) effectively 'saves the phenomena' that otherwise tend to be critically disregarded, discounted, discredited, or explained away. For another instance: in innumerable performances and critical essays alike, it is taken for granted that Gertrude is a vain and self-satisfied woman. Thus Shakespeare's meaning – or so it has been argued – was, most effectively, augmented in the New York staging of *Hamlet* by Gielgud, where 'Gertrude's mink coat' served as 'an almost perfect expression of her complaisant vulgarity'.[23] But what does this have to do with the far more interesting woman who emerges from the poetry Shakespeare gives her? As Rebecca Smith has reminded us, what Gertrude's 'own words and actions actually create is a soft, obedient, dependent, unimaginative woman who is caught miserably at the center of a desperate struggle . . . her "heart cleft in twain" by divided loyalties to husband and son'.[24] So why not play, and discuss, her as such? The softness, sweetness, and vulnerability of the woman who once hoped to bedeck Ophelia's bridal bed with flowers, as well as her dependence upon (and undeniable appeal to) strong men might better be conveyed by an actress with the poignant charm and helplessly, essentially innocent voluptuousness of the late Marilyn Monroe, than by the complaisantly vulgar and contemptuously cynical portrayals of her in recent productions and critical essays. For whatever else she may lack, Gertrude certainly seems to have had 'It': however much they differ in other respects, the ghost, the villain, and the hero are as one in their affection for Gertrude –

Ghost. Taint not thy mind, nor let thy soul contrive
  Against thy mother aught.

  But look, amazement on thy mother sits. . . .
  Speak to her, Hamlet.

Hamlet.   . . . Once more, good night
  And when you are desirous to be blest,
  I'll blessing beg of you.

Gertrude. The Queen carouses to thy fortune, Hamlet.
King. Gertrude, do not drink.

These and other lines throughout the play would seem incomprehensible if all there is to Gertrude is a complaisant vulgarity.

As I believe the counter-arguments cited above must have already demonstrated, a sympathetically feminist – as opposed to a misogynistic – approach to Shakespeare's characterization has enabled certain critics to say something old, something new, something borrowed, and something true about Shakespeare at one and the same time – e.g. if the world that survives at the end of a Shakespearian tragedy 'tends to exclude greatness', it also tends to exclude women. 'There is no difference between the tragedies and comedies more striking than this – the comedies *must* have women present and alive at the end, the tragedies virtually can not.'

In fact, in all the tragedies, only one named woman . . . is both onstage and alive at the end of the play – Lady Capulet, who, though her age may be computed at under thirty, gives the impression . . . of being old and ready to think of dying.[25]

Far from precluding further speculation, these indisputably valid observations (even Coriolanus's wife and mother are not allowed onstage at the end) serve to raise a series of interesting questions about life and art, as well as about Shakespearian tragedy and comedy. How important is longevity, or survival, *per se*? Whatever their age, Shakespeare's tragic heroes and heroines seem to have lived more of life while they were living it – they may have 'seen more' because they 'tried more, confronted more' – than those, 'of whatever age', who survive. Does death come to Shakespeare's heroes and heroines (if not to his tragic victims) as a punishment for their misdeeds? Or is this traditional view rendered suspect, since so many of them finally 'seek [death], either as a rest from suffering or as the only thing consistent with their integrity'? Since women, in real life, are often among the survivors left to pick up the pieces after the battle or after the war is over, why must the endings of Shakespeare's tragedies exclude women along with greatness ('if anything has been superhuman in the world, it has died out along with the tragic energy and those individual men and women who embodied it')? Perhaps strong female characters cannot be included among the survivors at the end of a heroical tragedy because their presence might imply that the heroic energy embodied in its protagonists can, and will, be transmitted to another generation. So their absence may contribute to a sense of irrevocable loss, of sterility, of a tragic vacuum, or gap, that's left in nature when the hero, or the heroine, leaves the stage.

These speculations about Shakespeare's tragic endings and characterization raise cognate questions about the characterization and structure of Shakespeare's comedies wherein (for instance) not every Jack gets his Jill, but there is not a single Jill who does not get a Jack. Why should this distinction exist? What (if anything) does it signify? For that matter, why are Shakespeare's comic heroines generally so much more attractive than Shakespeare's comic heroes? As the numerous books and articles on them testify, whatever 'It' is, heroines like Viola and Rosalind have that certain something which appeals to the imagination of generations with very different concepts of ideal womanhood — and which sometimes carries over to the actresses who play them.

As Russell Jackson has observed, the depiction of Rosalind, Beatrice, and Viola as 'Perfect Types of Womanhood' in Victorian criticism and performance had serious limitations. Yet Dorian Gray raises a fascinating question in his description of Sybil Vane's appearance as Imogen, Juliet, and Rosalind:

I have watched her wandering through the forest of Arden disguised as a pretty boy in hose and doublet and dainty cap. . . . Ordinary women never appeal to one's imagination. . . . Why didn't you tell me that the only thing worth loving is an actress?[26]

Perhaps significantly, the identical conclusion was arrived at by a man who told me that he had fallen forever in love with Vanessa Redgrave, as Rosalind.

Discussing Helen Faucit's Rosalind, Carol J. Carlisle defends the romantic interpretation that finally prevailed against the saucy, robust interpretations by Mrs Jordan and Mrs Nisbett, who 'seem to have played the boldness of the swagger and the impudence of the wit for all they were worth'. By contrast, Faucit's Rosalind was characterized by the good taste and elegance suitable to a Duke's daughter.[27] Given heroines who are alternatively, or simultaneously, capable of being portrayed — and admired — as elegant and impudent, gentle and bold, passionate and sensible, merry and pensive, one cannot but wonder what roles for women created before or since have seemed so authentically attractive yet so adaptable to varying tastes. *Why*, then, are so many of Shakespeare's comic heroes comparatively unappealing? Who could possibly claim that Proteus and Valentine, Lysander and Demetrius, Bassanio and Orsino, or Posthumus or Bertram ever were, or ever might be deemed to be 'perfect types of manhood'? With the exceptions of Benedick and Petruchio — who are not exactly 'juvenile leads' — Shakespeare's comic heroes cannot compete, in dramatic vitality, with his comic heroines. So why do those golden girls themselves find them so attractive? Looks cannot be all there is to it. Given extreme cases, wherein male characters are portrayed as duplicates of each other, there seems no good reason why, say, Hermia should prefer Lysander to Demetrius, and Helena prefer Demetrius to Lysander — any more than there is any clear reason why Hermia's father should prefer Demetrius to Lysander. For that matter, *scilicet Hermionen Helenae praeponere posses?* — 'Why on earth would any man prefer Hermia to Helena?'[28] It could be that Ovid's great question receives as good an answer in Shakespearian comedy generally, and in *A Midsummer-Night's Dream* in particular, as it ever is likely to get: there is no reason why.

This is why a major point gets lost when Helena (as she nowadays often is) is portrayed as plain, and Hermia as pretty (see *A Midsummer-Night's Dream*, I. i. 226–31):

Helena. How happy some o'er other some can be!
　　Through Athens I am thought as fair as she.
　　But what of that? Demetrius thinks not so;
　　He will not know what all but he do know.
　　And as he errs, doting on Hermia's eyes,
　　So I, admiring of his qualities.

The men and women in these comedies think each other 'best' for exactly the same non-reason: they think them so because they think them so (see *The Two Gentlemen of Verona*, I. ii. 21–4). See also IV. iv. 180–92, where Julia compares herself to her rival, Sylvia:

　　　　　Here is her picture; let me see. I think,
　　　　　If I had such a tire, this face of mine
　　　　　Were full as lovely as is this of hers;

　　　　　. . . . .

Her hair is auburn, mine is perfect yellow;
If that be all the difference in his love,
I'll get me such a colour'd periwig.
Her eyes are grey as glass, and so are mine;
Ay, but her forehead's low, and mine's as high.
What should it be that he respects in her
But I can make respective in myself,
If this fond Love were not a blinded god?

Sex appeal, in Shakespearian comedy and tragedy (as in life?) seems to have more to do with imagination than with anything else. Looked at from the perspective of anyone over, say, 45, there seems no reason why teenager X (Demetrius) should moon for teenager Y (Hermia), when equally attractive teenager Z (Helena) is mooning over him – or her (as Juliet's Nurse observes, Paris is at least as handsome as Romeo). It is also hard to see any reason why anyone, of any age, should suffer from the pangs of unrequited love ('If she be not fair to me, what care I how fair she be?'). Yet reason and love keep as 'little company' nowadays as they do in Shakespearian drama. When the imagination is activated, 'love looks not with the eye'. What everyone else sees as obnoxious, or grotesque, is perceived as admirable – even as Titania admired those furry ass's ears. Conversely, it would be of no help to her if everyone else in Athens thought blondes, like Helena, to be more attractive than brunettes, like Hermia, so long as Helena's own beloved Demetrius 'thinks not so'. Moreover, there is *absolutely nothing* that Lucrece herself could have done, or said, to avert the rape. For Tarquin's determination to 'girdle with embracing flames the waist/Of Collatine's fair love, Lucrece the chaste', was activated, before he ever laid eyes on her, by a whole complex of challenges to his imagination: by Collatine's pride in 'the possession' of such 'a peerless dame'; by the very name of 'chaste'; by resentment that 'meaner men should vaunt/That golden hap which their superiors want', etc. etc. (see *Lucrece*, ll. 1–42). It seems to me that in his treatment of these issues, Shakespeare is worth studying in terms of behavioural psychology alone. 'Rape begins in the rapist's mind'; and power, 'possession' and property are his primary considerations: like robbery, rape 'is an act of acquiring property'; the 'intent is to "have" the female body in the acquisitory meaning of the term'. These quotations are from Susan Brownmiller's profile of real-life, 'police-blotter' rapists – in *Against Our Will: Men, Women and Rape* (Harmondsworth, 1976), pp. 185-6 – but the identical conclusions could be derived from Shakespeare's account of Tarquin's motives in the opening lines of *The Rape of Lucrece*.

Whatever approach the individual critic might have adopted as a starting-point, the best of all recent discussions of Shakespeare's plays (like the best of the earlier ones) invariably transcend the critical dialectic, and thus bring us back to the psychological and artistic facts, effects, and problems emergent from the plays and poems themselves. The reason I have here emphasized the virtues of feminist discussions of Shakespeare, in dialectical opposition to the vices of anti-feminist discussions of Shakespeare, is that they so dramatically demonstrate the various ways in which Shakespeare's works themselves may serve as our ultimate weapon, shield, defence, witness, evidence, proof *against* those critical and psychological dogmas (concerning the 'nature' of woman, or of man, or of art) that every age is heir to.

As we have seen, the processes of critical action and reaction, whereby one generation's dogma becomes another generation's taboo, and one generation's guru becomes the next generation's straw-man, have long been in operation. But the fact that these processes currently operate at an unprecedented speed poses unprecedented problems for modern critics. This is why it seems important, if we are to be its beneficiaries, and not just its unwitting instruments or victims, to take the dialectical process itself into critical account.

Part iii.
Some Recent Examples of the Dialectical Process

About thirty years ago there was much talk that geologists ought only to observe and not theorize; and I well remember someone saying that at this rate a man might as well go into a gravel-pit and count the pebbles and describe the colours. How odd it is that anyone should not see that all observation must be for or against some view if it is to be of any service.

Charles Darwin

'There is in fact no longer any such thing as a universal education in Goethe's sense. But that is why today to every thought we also have a counter-thought and to every tendency a counter tendency. Today, every act and its opposite are accompanied by the subtlest intellectual arguments, with which one can both defend them and condemn them. I can't understand how you can bring yourself to speak up for such a state of things!'

Ulrich shrugged his shoulders.

> . Robert Musil, *The Man Without Qualities*

We need look no further than this . . . for an explanation of many a complete revolution in opinion, politics, or literary feeling: it is enough that a view has been held for the opposite to be held afterwards.

> E. E. Kellett, *The Whirligig of Taste*

Towards the end of the time I served reviewing critical studies for *Shakespeare Survey*, it came to me, with the force of revelation, that, precisely because I had read so many Freudian interpretations of Shakespeare's poetry and characters, I, therefore, could hardly bear to look at another one. It had long since ceased to matter whether or not Claudio's fear of death might, like Coriolanus's entry into Corioli, ultimately represent a fear of castration.[29] Nor did I want to be informed, yet once more, of the phallic symbolism underlying a virtually infinite number of Shakespeare's lines (like 'The soldier's pole is fallen'). And if the imagery of Sonnet 4 ('spending upon' and 'trafficking with' himself alone) does, in fact, imply that the Young Man really ought to quit masturbating and start copulating, that, too, seemed a matter of supreme indifference to me.

What did seem important about this private moment of truth was the recognition that it had also ceased to matter whether the next Freudian interpretation I read might be brilliant or absurd, true or false.[30] By bringing to mind previous reactions like it, this experience appeared to suggest that one's personal exhaustion with a given thesis, interpretation, or approach, may outweigh any concern with its validity. Just hear the same arguments (regardless of whether they are true or false) repeated once too often, and the temptation to reject them out of hand, the desire to argue the opposite case, may become virtually irresistible. Boredom itself would seem to explain why its antithesis is almost inevitably bound to emerge at the point when, and indeed precisely because, a given thesis has been repeated too many times.

If indeed there is anything to the idea that sheer boredom (that is, a general exhaustion, culminating in a hostile reaction — often an over-reaction — to a given interpretation or approach) may be a crucial factor in changing critical attitudes, then the power of its influence, for good and ill, really should be taken into account. Boredom may, after all, be our best defence against critical dogmatism. Moreover, as Blake observed, 'without contraries' there can be no progression. On the other hand, as the author of *Wit and Science* long ago demonstrated, the Monster Tedium poses serious threats to those in pursuit of knowledge. For the fact is that (in certain cases, anyway), true interpretations may be, or may have been, rejected simply because everyone finally gets sick of hearing, or saying, the same things over and over again. In certain extreme cases of reaction and rejection, the worst things critics say – their real or imaginary defects – are what live after them, the best things are interred with their bones. Of course, the rejected truths may rise again when some future generation of critics gets sufficiently bored with hearing their opposite – and so on.[31] In any event, for these (and other) reasons, the odds are awfully good that today's reigning theories are going to be challenged tomorrow: We think our fathers fools, so wise we grow; our wiser sons, no doubt, will think us so. A quick survey of twentieth-century counter-arguments about Shakespeare's comedies, characterization, and construction can serve to illustrate these points.

In a review article introducing *Shakespeare Survey*, Volume 32, M. M. Mahood discusses a single 'generation of criticism' in which descriptions of the middle comedies as 'happy', 'gay', 'golden', 'festive', and 'joyous' have given way to accounts of the 'hard', 'abrasive', and 'aggressive' qualities of *Much Ado About Nothing* and *As You Like It*, while 'unnumbered critics stress the underlying sadness of *Twelfth Night*'. By now the critical vogue which tends, (rather like the melancholy Jaques) to moralize the spectacle, 'augmenting it with tears', has gone about as far as it can go. *The Merry Wives of Windsor*, one critic informs us,

is not a lighthearted midsummer romp, or a springtime celebration, but rather a record of the transition from fall to winter – an effort to put the house in order, to become reconciled to the passing of fertility from the old to the young. Just beyond the frivolity of the play's pranks and the 'innocent' revenge of its night-wandering spirits lie the gravity and earnestness of a sober New Year. Allhallow Eve must give way to the Feast of All Saints.[32]

And in an essay entitled ' "Wild Laughter in the Throat of Death": Darker Purposes in Shakespearean Comedy', another critic has insisted that 'Shakespearean comedy is really about death and dying': 'More precisely, Shakespearean comedy is about the initial avoidance or displacement of the idea of death . . . and then, crucially, the acceptance, even the affirmation, of that mortality.' Thus 'the revels moment of applause that marks its close is the comic theater's counterpart to the shared feast of the mourner.'[33]

Several interesting questions are raised by these grave interpretations of Shakespeare's comedies. Would the management at the Globe have advertised them in such gloomy terms? A modern producer might do so precisely because modern critics have imposed comparable interpretations on so many of the comedies that these sombre criteria of analysis have come to seem criteria of *comic* merit. Yet it is so obviously true that youth's a stuff will not endure, that winter winds will blow, and that death, a necessary end, will come when it will come, that one wonders why we need always make a Star Chamber matter of it when discussing Shakespeare's comedies. Even in *Volpone, The Alchemist,* and *The Silent Woman* – comedies that have a lot more to do with death and dying, and legacies, and bells tolling in time of pestilence, than, say, *As You Like It,* or *A Midsummer-Night's Dream* – there come times when 'gravity and earnestness' must give way to present mirth and present laughter. Need we forever deny the crucial differ- ences between Shakespearian comedy and other genres (like satires and sermons) in order to justify its existence?

And so the critical pendulum swings – and swings again: 'Not all readers', Mahood has correctly observed, will agree with the argument that 'Beatrice, after telling us she was born under a dancing star, leaves the stage in tears'.[34] But how can one write about Shakespeare's merriest comedies *without* sounding unduly solemn or pontifical, and, simultaneously, avoid rendering them utterly trite or meaningless? You can argue that the comedies are about nothing but their own ingenuity, yet that argument raises the questions, 'So why bother to write about them?' – *'Est-ce une image juste, ou "juste" une image?'*[35] The problems of style and substance involved in writing about Shakespearian comedy (it is easier to write about the world's worst tragedy than the world's best comedy) can go on the list of the most difficult ones that any commentator on Shakespeare has to face.

In any event, sweeping generalizations about what 'Shakespearian comedy' – or tragedy – 'is' ultimately about, often indicate that the critical dialectic (the thesis or counter-thesis) is what's determining the conclusions being arrived at. Another indication is that the major question raised by such sweeping assertions ('what follows if they are true?') is left unanswered. Assuming, for the purposes of argument, that any single one of these statements (or its dialectical opposite) is valid:

Shakespearian comedy is about death . . .
Shakespeare's comedies are about nothing but their own ingenuity . . .
Shakespeare's heroines are all sexually susceptible . . .
Shakespearian drama affirms the orthodoxies of the age . . .

then the plays would seem equally predictable and boring. Which they obviously are not. What is interesting are the dramatic conflicts operating in various plays which may, or may not, involve orthodoxies upheld or challenged;[36] female susceptibilities, or sexual fidelity; dramatic ingenuities displayed or concealed, etc. When looked at independently of the critical processes of action and reaction, to recognize the minor chords within them by no means precludes the recognition that the major key is dominant in Shakespeare's merriest plays. To see the processes of action and reaction for what they are is to see our critical totems and taboos for what they are. And ditto for literary and theatrical totems and taboos. By now, for instance, the reaction against previous depictions of ideally fair, chaste, and faithful heroines has gone so far that, unless she is a member of an oppressed racial or religious minority, it is virtually *verboten* to portray a chaste or faithful heroine in 'serious' modern fiction or drama. Thus the bright heroine of Malcolm Bradbury's *The History Man* was, finally, obliged to display her sexual susceptibilities to its anti-hero. By the identical token, Elijah Moshinsky concluded that Shakespeare's Imogen would 'make a better heroine' if she were presumed to be 'sexually susceptible', and, therefore, as 'morally' ambiguous as Iachimo. Yet Moshinsky's premiss would seem to reflect an oddly ambivalent attitude towards female sexuality itself. To qualify as a thoroughly modern heroine, an Imogen (or Lucrece) cannot *not* be sexually susceptible to Iachimo, or Tarquin, or whatever man might be sexually susceptible to her; conversely, whatever sexual susceptibilities — including non-existent ones — that can be discovered in the heroine are judged, in the most prurient, puritanical, and eminently Victorian of ways, as if they constituted prima facie evidence of a 'moral' culpability comparable to Iachimo's and 'reciprocal with Tarquin's'. Thus, a heroine is judged woefully wanting, by modern standards, if she is not 'sexually susceptible' enough to be judged blameworthy in terms of the old-time equation between female sexuality and female immorality. By contrast, Shakespeare endows his female creations with the right to say 'No', as well as to say 'Yes'; and to say 'Yes' to one man (Posthumus, Collatine, Romeo), and 'No' to another (Iachimo, Tarquin, Paris). He, therefore, portrays the violation of that right — by slander, rape, or by enforced marriage — as the moral and sexual outrage that it is.

Although the idols of our tribe, cave, marketplace, and theatre will continue to exact their tributes, to see them for what they are enables us to register complaints about the excessive tributes they demand, among the most absurd of which is the critical bowing and scraping currently required by the totem of the 'Shakespearian play in performance' — as it were in propitiation for the equally exorbitant tribute previously rendered to the 'Shakespearian play as poem'. Thus, as Susan Snyder has observed: 'Recent times have witnessed a new concentration on the direct imagery of stage production, and a corollary withdrawal from verbal imagery — for fear of committing the new cardinal sin, reading the play as a poem.'[37] Why is 'reading the play as a poem' our 'new cardinal sin'? And why do so many of us, nowadays, consider ourselves obliged to inform each other, over and over again, of the most obvious fact about the plays — that is, that they were 'written for performance'? The reason is that some of the most distinguished critics of the previous generation revealed certain blindspots, even as they derived major insights, through their concentration on Shakespeare's poetry.[38] In his Introduction to *Shakespeare's 'More Than Words Can Witness'*, an interesting anthology of essays on 'visual and nonverbal enactment in the plays', Sidney Homan provides several excellent illustrations of the dialectical processes currently at work. While acknowledging that, by now, it is 'beating a dead horse' (becoming dangerously boring?) 'to say that at times we treat the plays as if they were literary pieces not intended for the stage', Homan recommends to us the 'assumption that the playwright's glorious language is complemented, *enhanced*, indeed, totally dependent on the visual and non-verbal dimensions of production.'[39] The words 'indeed, totally dependent' are what give away this particular game. The processes of action and reaction whereby argument A (because the poetry was once too often discussed independently of it) leads to counter-argument B (therefore the poetry should now be seen as *totally* dependent on performance) causes the critic to overstate his case. Thus Homan virtually has to overlook the obvious facts that Shakespeare's 'glorious language' survived unscathed when performances were banned, and still blazes with light in places where opportunities to enjoy the 'visual and non-verbal dimensions' of a full-scale production are extremely rare. Why can't we frankly admit that, by now, it *does* seem too obvious to need saying that the various ways in which Shakespeare suits 'the word to the action' and the 'action to the word' may indeed be enhanced in a good production, and that (by exactly the same token) they may be garbled, obfuscated, or torn to tatters in a bad one. But in neither case are they totally dependent on the visual and non-verbal dimensions of that production. For that matter, nothing could be easier than to argue that all performances — from the best to the worst — are themselves 'totally dependent' upon the playwright's script, which has an independent reality of its own, and by which those performances can, and will, be judged by audiences and reviewers.

The moral to be derived from recognizing the critical dialectic that dictated it, is that the dichotomy between play-as-poem and play-in-performance is a false one. Except in terms of critical action and reaction, there is no reason why the two ever should have been, or should still be, considered in isolation from — or somehow opposed to — each other. After all, the director, the actor, the critic, and the student all start with the words on the page. Looked at from this angle, the play's the thing, and the starting-point is the same, whether the show is performed in the theatre, or we see it in the mind's eye. Thus to extol the play-in-performance *at the expense of* the play-as-poem is as pointless and misleading as the reverse. Their synergism — the positive or negative interaction between them — seems far more important than their separate claims to our attention.

The dialectical and hierarchical distinction between dramatic realism and symbolism may also be misleading. All great drama would seem to include some real toads within its imaginary gardens; and the greatest of realistic plays always have some symbolic overtones. In his book on *The Golden Age of English Drama*, S. Gorley Putt concludes that Eliot may have had a valid point when he found in the works of Shakespeare and his contemporaries an association of sensibilities and visions (a fusion of intellectual and emotional energies, of realistic and symbolic images of life, etc.) which may not have been 'dissociated' in the major art of subsequent periods, but which certainly *have* been dissociated in critical discussions of art. In drama, as in life, the most memorable of individuals always seem to symbolize, or embody, something important about, or typical of, human nature — whether that something be the will-to-power, sheer sexual or intellectual energy, absolute integrity, or, for that matter, incorrigible gullibility, pomposity, or greed. Cleopatra, for instance, is symbolically associated with the forces and powers of the Goddess Venus and the Goddess Isis. Falstaff is Elizabethan drama's King of Carnival and Lord of Misrule.

It's in this sense that Dr Johnson may have been right when he said that Shakespeare's individual characters seemed to represent a species of their kind as well. Likewise, Gorley Putt recommends Marston's 'Antonio' plays on the grounds of the impact that results when Marston's cardboard figures seem 'to become, for an instant, the living representatives of man's subconscious passions'. In *Antonio's Revenge*, 'the hideous ritual murder on full stage' excites genuine pity and terror in the recognition that 'behind all the Mannerist gestures of evil there is, all the time, genuine evil at work'.[40]

Gorley Putt also has illuminating things to say about the ways in which (comparably) lurid and sensational depictions of vice and violence in the works of Shakespeare and his contemporaries seem so markedly different from those in our own time. To modern fans of X-certificate films, the truly surprising thing about the most gruesome portrayals of man's inhumanity to man must, surely, be the fact that they were deemed stageworthy in-or-around 1601 rather than in-or-around 1979 (p. 78). Yet no one would think of describing the decades since World War II as a 'golden age' of literature or drama. Why not? One crucial difference is that (apart from obvious manifestations of superior individual talents) Elizabethan playwrights had at their command a language so flexible and powerful as to make most current expressions of dismay, despair, or defiance seem comparatively thin (p. 76). Another difference is here accounted for in terms of Eliot's distinction between an art wherein thought and feeling function synergistically, and one wherein they are dissociated, alienated from, or deemed to be essentially at odds with each other (p. 148). And it does seem manifestly true that, nowadays, we often get (on the one hand) primal screaming, or (on the other hand) – in literature, scholarship, and theatrical productions alike – we have critical, frequently clinical, judgements that seem utterly dissociated from any emotional engagement with, or sympathy for, the subjects under analysis.

Arguably, anyway, Eliot's distinction helps to explain one difference between certain major and minor portrayals of human vice and violence in any age. How many masterpieces are there wherein – in effect, if not in intent – emotional and intellectual energies do *not* seem intimately associated? As Gorley Putt observes, Nabokov's *Lolita* provides us with protagonists markedly comparable to those in, say, Middleton's *The Changeling*. Moreover, in its portrayal of Humbert's 'single-hearted brutality of devotion', his 'absolute absorption of soul and body by one consuming force of passionately cynical desire', as well as in its

alchemical fusion of sympathy and judgement, *Lolita* could be
described in much the same terms which Eliot and Swinburne used
in their tributes to Elizabethan dramatists and characters like De Flores
(p. 119). When (and only when?) comparable energies and fusions are
typical of a whole body of literature, as they almost (?) always are of
the isolated masterpiece, we have a 'golden age'. Asking how to achieve
such fusions is comparable to asking where to find the philosophers'
stone. Yet the dissociations between thought and feeling, and between
realism and artifice, that are often taken for granted, if not actively
encouraged, in much recent criticism and literature, as well as in
productions of Shakespeare's plays, may be doing serious damage to
drama and criticism alike by assuming that what Yeats called the
'masterful images' of art can, or should, survive independently of their
energy-sources down in the 'foul rag-and-bone shop of the heart'.

Today, as yesterday, the critical dialectic has, on the one hand,
resulted in formulaic application, chain-reactions, a fungus-like
fecundity, producing a succession of weary, stale, flat, and unprofitable
arguments; on the other hand, it has also resulted in new and truly
illuminating perspectives on Shakespeare's plays and poems, even as
some of the best, as well as some of the worst, twentieth-century
criticism has emerged· from a confrontation between diametrically
opposite accounts of Shakespeare's construction and characterization.

Part iv.
Shakespeare's Construction and Characterization:
The Questions of Technique and of Vision

I, too, dislike it: there are things that are important beyond all
    this fiddle. Reading it, however, with a perfect contempt for it,
    one discovers in it after all, a place for the genuine.
      Hands that can grasp, eyes
      that can dilate, hair that can rise
        if it must, these things are important not because a
high-sounding interpretation can be put upon them but because
    they are useful. . . .

                  . . . One must make a distinction
    however: when dragged into prominence by half-poets, the
    result is not poetry,
      nor till the poets among us can be
      "literalists of

the imagination" – above
insolence and triviality and can present

for inspection, "imaginary gardens with real toads in them," shall
we have it. In the meantime, if you demand on the one hand,
the raw material of poetry in
all its rawness and
that which is on the other hand
genuine, you are interested in poetry.

Marianne Moore, 'Poetry'

Here is a dialogue about Shakespeare's construction by Bertolt Brecht:

['Hamlet's] experiments lead straight to disaster.'
'Not straight. Zigzag.'
'All right; zigzag. In a sense the play has the permanence of some-
thing makeshift.'

'Shakespeare', Brecht concluded, doesn't 'need construction'. 'With him
everything develops naturally.' He 'wouldn't dream of giving a suitable
twist to a human life in Act 2' merely to 'prepare the way for Act 5.'
His plays are the 'unvarnished representations' of life by 'a great realist'
without any interest in making a pattern of it that will 'lend arguments
not drawn from life' to some 'principle that can only be prejudice'. In
the 'inconsequentiality of his acts' we see the 'inconsequentiality' of
human experience. 'He is naturally unclear.' 'He is absolute matter.'[41]

I have quoted Brecht's impressions about Shakespeare's craftman-
ship because they are historically representative and demonstrably accurate. Like Hamlet's deliverance by pirates, many things in Shakespeare
do seem 'inconsequential' in the sense that they do not, necessarily,
follow from what has gone before. There are accidental judgements,
casual slaughters, and purposes mistook. For instance, the fact that
Edmund falls, just as he rose, because of a letter, seems utterly, even
poignantly, inconsequential. So does the death of the County Paris.
And so does the death of Cordelia.[42] It has been argued, by Maurice
Morgann (among others) that in drama the 'impression is the fact'.
And the main impression conveyed by Shakespeare's construction is
that, at its best, it is not too good to be true to human experience.
Very like some of their greatest characters, the zigzag motions of
certain plays have resisted all critical efforts to clear them up, to
smooth out their depressions and elevations, or to lend arguments not
drawn from life to principles (or prejudices) that will shape, to tidy
ends, what Brecht called the 'lot of raw material' that Shakespeare
'shovels onto the stage'.

Consequently, Shakespeare's construction initially turned up on the debit side of the critical ledger. To many of his seventeenth- and eighteenth-century admirers, he prevailed in *spite* of the obvious facts that he failed to observe the unities, should have blotted a thousand lines, and neglected opportunities of instructing which the train of his story seemed to force upon him. While plays by Jonson and Fletcher were praised for their formal excellence and artful contrivances, Shakespeare was acclaimed as a natural genius: 'Some others may perhaps pretend to a more exact *Decorum* and *œconomie*', wrote Milton's nephew, Edward Phillips, but 'where the polishments of Art are most wanting', Shakespeare 'pleaseth with a certain wild and native Elegance.'[43] And so he did. For transcending any technical liabilities were the supreme assets: that high invention which allows the mind to contemplate well-nigh every possibility, the just representations of general nature, and – above all – those characters who, beyond any others, have the property of being believed in.

Like Brecht, Shakespeare's earliest critics point straight at the most obvious, yet surely the oddest, thing about Shakespeare's construction. And that is the fact that, in many of his greatest scenes and plays, you do not notice it. At the risk of seeming dim-witted, I might as well admit that, both while watching a good production of, or while reading some of his plays, I still don't notice it. Everything would seem to develop so naturally from the context and the characterization that (for instance) it took me years and years to notice how economically Shakespeare recycles the identical materials – so that, say, the gulling of Malvolio and the enlightenment of Benedick are effected by the same trick whereby Character X is persuaded that Character Y is in love with him. And it dawned on me only recently that Claudio, in *Measure for Measure*, is cousin-german to Costard, who, contrary to proclaimed edict and continent canon, was also taken with a woman; and that the laws against lovers in both their plays elicit a remarkably comprehensive range of responses to the same home truth: 'Such is the simplicity of man to hearken after the flesh.' What seem especially striking and significant, however, are not the technical similarities – which often go unnoticed even by readers and audiences familiar with the plays – but the differences between the characters and situations portrayed in *Twelfth Night*, *Much Ado*, *Measure for Measure*, and *Love's Labour's Lost*.

By contrast, no admirer of the drama could fail to notice the taut unities, the systematic liaison of scenes, the Fourth Act reversals and

Fifth Act resolutions in the works of Ben Jonson. As they operate synergistically with his glorious language and fine naturalistic gifts, his methods of construction are essential to the pleasure Jonson set out to give us. Hence, through the finely articulated exoskeletons of his own works, Jonson supplied subsequent generations of playwrights with object lessons in the art of dramatic construction: 'Something of Art was wanting to the Drama until he came', wrote Dryden in his *Essay of Dramatic Poesy*; and his rich legacy was put to good use by the many sons of Ben.

In contrast to Jonson, Shakespeare left no succession of heirs-apparent. For who then could (who now can?) tell anyone else how to construct plays like his? With Shakespeare at his best, construction is not an art but a secret; and the secret of organic form remains inviolable. As Maurice Morgann and Bertolt Brecht alike remind us, Shakespeare's construction is most telling and admirable when it is most concealed: 'We discern not his course', wrote Morgann. 'We are rapt in ignorant admiration and claim no kindred with his abilities.' 'Whilst we feel and are sensible that the whole is design', all the incidents, all the parts 'look like chance'. 'He commands every passage to our heads and to our hearts, and moulds us as he pleases, and that with so much ease that he never betrays his own exertions.' Consequently, 'it is that art in Shakespeare, which, being withdrawn from our notice, we more emphatically call Nature.' When Shakespeare's craftsmanship directs attention to itself, Morgann finds it wanting: the 'over-strict adherence [in *The Tempest*] to the Laws of Place and Time, by which he has almost strangled the Play, discovers either a Childish Ambition or a peasant-like Acquiescence in the Dictas [*sic*] of some pedantic school.'[44] Following these leads, successive commentators have argued that it is where his art seems most natural — that is, when he does not betray his own exertions — that Shakespeare seems most Shakespearian.

But perhaps the most important breakthrough in twentieth-century criticism has been the revolutionary change in assumptions concerning Shakespeare's craftsmanship. In a ground-breaking essay on *Construction in Shakespeare* (University of Michigan, 1951), Professor Hereward Price complained that critics and scholars spent all their time talking about Shakespeare's characterization and poetry without paying any attention to the construction of his plays. And I still remember how Price's brilliant discussions of the relationships between speech and speech, scene and scene, part and whole, in *Titus Andronicus, Love's*

Labour's Lost, and the Henry VI plays came to me with the force of revelation. For that matter, there is no question that some of the best twentieth-century discussions of Shakespeare have to do with the ways in which he developed modes of construction that originated in medieval drama.[45] As more and more critics jumped on the bandwagon, however, the principles of dramatic counterpoint and thematic unity, of analogous action and iterative imagery came to be treated, in certain circles, as if they were ends in themselves — in spite of the obvious fact that they may occur in the worst of Shakespeare's plays as well as in the best. For a time, it appeared that the situation deplored by Professor Price had been all too effectively reversed, as strict constructionists devoted any amount of time to Shakespeare's schematically thematic — or historically orthodox 'morality-play' structures — without paying much heed to his characterization. Indeed, it was, for a while, fashionable to sneer at 'character-analysis', as if Shakespeare's characterization (on which the survival of his plays had, historically, depended) were a subject unworthy of serious scholarly consideration. As William Empson observed, there was 'a kind of truth' in the recognition that Shakespeare's characters are not amenable to the kind of biographical and psychological scrutiny one might give people in real life, but in treating the subject as a critical taboo, the new emphasis on structure and imagery was 'dangerously liable to make us miss points of character'.[46] For after all, it is through characters who appear to be acting independently of him that Shakespeare constructed some of his greatest plays.[47]

In her book about *Shakespeare and the Story*, Joan Rees gives us an excellent account of the dialectical dichotomy between various critical conclusions concerning Shakespeare's construction and characterization.[48] In opposition to seventeenth- and eighteenth-century commentators, who conspicuously failed to recognize Shakespeare's consummate artistry, much modern criticism is characterized by an 'unwillingness to admit that the artistry ever fails' (p. 140). Whereas Dr Johnson found certain plays 'so loosely formed, that a very slight consideration may improve them, and so carelessly pursued, that he seems not always to comprehend his own design', Hereward Price concluded that 'Shakespeare's work is a strict intellectual construction developed from point to point until he brings us to the necessary and inevitable conclusion' (see Rees, pp. 2-3). Rightly acknowledging that Price's appreciative response to Shakespeare's construction had proved immensely fruitful, Rees points out that his assumptions have also led to numerous discussions that deaden the plays: 'by over-intellectualising and schematising [Shakespeare's] work they misrepresent the leaping life that is in it' (p. 4). Pausing to look at the stories as they are being turned into drama, Rees observes that Shakespeare's creative energies sometimes manifest themselves in ways that are destructive of any 'point by point development of a strict intellectual construction'. While he may be an 'inspired craftsman', and while 'his resourcefulness in an emergency often endows the plays with an extra dimension', there is also the Shakespeare 'whose management of his stories is sometimes mismanagement', producing problems 'which a purely efficient organiser of narrative would have avoided' (p. 233).

In her discussion of language and characterization, Rees comes close to concurring with the Romantic conclusion (still often deemed to be a Romantic delusion) that the organic life in them is what justifies the construction of Shakespeare's plays, not vice versa. The tendency for 'character to challenge story' is present from the beginning. The construction of *The Comedy of Errors* required that Adriana be a shrew and reproved as such by Luciana and the Abbess. But Shakespeare presents the other side of the case, and 'Adriana's dependence on the love she fears she has lost makes an appeal for sympathy which runs across the bias of the play' (pp. 14-15). *Much Ado About Nothing* 'has its neatly concluded story', but the life manifested in Beatrice and Benedick is 'far more satisfying' (p. 37). In *Measure for Measure* we have a play which shares with *The Merchant of Venice* the problems caused by an infusion of creative vigour into the original characterization which is 'in excess of the scope provided by the framework of the story' (p. 38). The stories of *Measure for Measure* and *All's Well That Ends Well* 'involve the same obvious difficulty': whereas 'the initial situation lends itself to characterization and subtle psychological treatment, the resolution does not' (pp. 38-9). One can 'only admire the wonderful manipulative and inventive facility' displayed in Shakespeare's solutions to these, and other, problems. Yet there is no denying that in his efforts to avoid leaving a play 'with just one or two brilliant figures, and desolation all around them', Shakespeare sometimes sacrifices character to structure and betrays his own exertions in conclusions that are improbably produced and imperfectly represented. Certain of his endings are firm enough, 'yet bland – and deceptive for, of course, the statement of the problems and their resolutions at the end does not match the situations as they were at the beginning' (pp. 70-1). Thus, on the one hand, Shakespeare may occasionally sacrifice structure to characterization; and, on the other hand, he may elsewhere sacrifice characterization to structure. And thus his slashing, individual, raids on the inarticulate would sometimes seem to confound — though they elsewhere would seem to create — the most perfectly ordered of structures for the thoughts and the feelings portrayed. This is why he was deemed by his admirer and rival, Ben Jonson, to have 'wanted art'.

In the greatest works by Ben Jonson, the characterization, however fantastical or grotesque, is generally consistent — taken as given — while the construction is the instrument of dramatic revelation and surprise as well as closure. By contrast, what can, for the most part, be taken for granted as given in some of the greatest works of Shakespeare is the subject, the story, the starting-point, the format, the construction if you will, but rarely the characterization, which appears to be a matter of inspiration and discovery. Moreover, the fact is that, regardless of whether we believe it ought to be, characterization can be an end in itself, and — occasionally anyway — Shakespeare's characterization appears to be just that. One might buy tickets to the histories solely to find out what will become of Queen Margaret or Falstaff. By contrast, dramatic construction is a means to meaning. Technically speaking, it is a means to an end, and the end has to justify the means. In some of the best of his works it does just that by *virtue* of the fact that the characters themselves appear to be making up the lines, and deciding what they are going to do next. When the playwright himself appears to be making up the construction, and arbitrarily adapting the characterization in accordance with it, as he does in, say, the last scenes of *The Two Gentlemen of Verona*, the resolution seems both improbably produced and imperfectly represented. Whatever the twists and turns of the plot, in the best of his comedies and tragedies alike, we are finally convinced that this, truly, *is* the promised end. In other cases, the question, 'is this the promised end?' hangs up in the air. Therefore, one critic can extol the structural ingenuities and the technical contrivances of the second part of *Measure for Measure*, and another critic can counter-argue that the continuing life of the play may well depend upon those characteristically Shakespearian characters who manage to survive in the memory and the imagination in defiance of the ever more constricting construction that comes close to choking the life out of them in the end. The internal dichotomy between the construction and the characterization can itself explain why, in recent years, Shakespeare's scholarly jury has been hopelessly split between those who will, and those who will not, accept the ending of *Measure for Measure*.[49] It also explains why both the case for the defence and the case for the prosecution of the play's ending can — depending upon which lines and incidents you chose to cite — be either supported, or refuted, by references to the script itself. What the critical deadlock concerning them generally serves to demonstrate is that, in the works of our King of Foxes, the construction and characterization alike are just as Protean and indeterminate, and occasionally as contradictory, as the nature of woman — or man. Perhaps inevitably so. For Shakespeare is that rarest of rarities, a comprehensive and representative poet, and not one of the 'brilliant partial poets who do justice, far more than justice, to a portion of reality, and leave the rest of things forlorn'.[50]

Therefore, the fact that the centuries-long search for some unified field theory — for some structural, or theological, or historical, or mimetic, or moralistic, or theoretical, or sexual, or psychoanalytical, perspective (or premiss) that can comprehend the organization and characterization of Shakespearian drama — has proved as futile as the search for the Fountain of Youth, or the Philosophers' Stone, or the Maltese Falcon (some very interesting discoveries have been made along the way), should be cause for general celebration, not despair. It suggests that we are far better off with a multiplicity of approaches, and so opens everything up by liberating critics, teachers, students, and directors alike from the obligation to confirm the ubiquitous applicability of any given approach — whether with or without reference to those works that might better serve to refute it. The inexhaustible range of Shakespearian subjects and styles also explains why anyone, from the beginning student to the greatest living Shakespearian critic (and the best in our kind are but his students) who looks to the plays as a source of personal delight and instruction is bound to find innumerable topics for fruitful speculation. Thus the triumphs, as well as the failures, the validity, as well as the refutability, of past and present theories and interpretations can, finally and fruitfully, be tested (by any one of us) against those works which might well be the best source we have of what T. S. Eliot described as the wisdom that we may have lost in knowledge and the knowledge we have lost in information.

But all this has already been said, as well as it can ever be said, in certain Proustian generalizations about the multiple forms of art that could as well have been made about Shakespeare's art in particular. Looked at in this light, Shakespeare's construction, his characterization, his differing comic and tragic perspectives and styles, can be seen to represent altogether different visions and revelations. Note Proust's crucial emphasis on difference, on otherness — for on it may rest the best of all critical cases for the defence of Shakespeare's 'real toads' and 'imaginary gardens' alike. 'Style', Proust concluded, 'is for the writer, as for the painter, a question, not of technique but of vision':

> It is the revelation — impossible by direct and conscious means — of the qualitative differences in the way the world appears to us, differences which, but for art, would remain the eternal secret of each of us. Only by art can we get outside ourselves, know what another sees of his universe, which is not the same as ours, and the different views of which would otherwise have remained as unknown to us as those there may be on the moon. . . .
>
> The only true voyage of discovery, the only fountain of Eternal Youth, would be not to visit strange lands but to possess other eyes, to behold the universe through the eyes of another, of a hundred others, to behold the hundred universes that each of them beholds, that each of them is . . . Thanks to art, instead of seeing only one world, our own, we see it under multiple forms, and as many as there are original artists, just so many worlds have we at our disposal, differing more widely from one another than those that roll through infinite space, and years after the glowing center from which they emanated has been extinguished, be it called Rembrandt or Vermeer, they continue to send us their own rays of light.[51]

Or, as Randall Jarrell puts it,

> From Christ to Freud we have believed that, if we know the truth, the truth will set us free: art is indispensable because so much of this truth can be learned through works of art and through works of art alone — for which of us could have learned for himself what Proust and Chekhov . . . [and] Shakespeare and Homer learned for us? and in what other way could they have made us see the truths which they themselves saw, those differing and contradictory truths which seem, nevertheless, to the mind that contains them, in some sense a single truth?[52]

Jarrell's observations seem pertinent, not only to different works of art and artists, but also to those 'differing and contradictory' truths that seem, in some sense, to merge into a single truth in an individual work like *King Lear*, wherein, to the anguished question raised by Kent, 'Is this the promised end?' the tragic thunder answers, 'This is the promised end.' And yet — '*Datta. Dayadhvam. Damyata. Shantih shantih shantih*' also seems part of what the thunder said throughout that play. If, in *King Lear*, it is undeniably true that

> Cruelty has a human heart,
> And Jealousy a human face,

Terror, the human form divine,
And Secrecy, the human dress.

It is also true that

Mercy has a human heart,
Pity, a human face,
And Love, the human form divine,
And Peace, the human dress.

And it is as if,[53] in *King Lear*, Shakespeare used the wisdom of the world itself to demonstrate that the wisdom of this world is not enough.

It seems to me that, in *King Lear*, Shakespeare confounds his interpreters in the same way that Job confounds his comforters (and that the Voice from the Whirlwind confounded Job himself): 'Canst thou draw out leviathan with an hook?' Time after time, poets and critics alike have agreed that all we can say about this tragedy must fall short, not only of the subject, but of what we ourselves conceive of it. It defies critical analysis, in the Keatsian sense that, 'on sitting down to read *King Lear* once more', all 'disagreeables' – all our theories and counter-interpretations and conclusions – tend to fuse, dissolve, evaporate, and finally to seem, as Job felt himself to be, not merely insufficient, but almost completely insignificant, as the play burns through.

Because it implies that the only reward of doing well may be the doing of it (at the cost of comfort, of eyesight, of life), and because it insists that the best of us all, like Cordelia, will meet the same fate as the worst, it is open to attack, on Platonic grounds, as the most immoral of Shakespeare's tragedies (the evil are shown to suffer not more, but less, than the good). Conversely, it could be argued that *King Lear* is the most profoundly moral tragedy ever written. Even as the truths and the falsehoods inherent in a cliché like 'virtue is its own reward' are dramatically countered by the falsehoods, as well as the truths, inherent in the contradiction of that cliché, there is, in *King Lear*, the dramatic negation of a negation, the *reductio ad absurdum* of expedience, as well as of unselfishness, of vice, as well as virtue, from which emerges the fiery, icy certainty that nothing but mercy, pity, peace, and love will do. By making it humanely understandable, and humanely un-understandable, *King Lear* enables us to perceive a dimension of reality that makes the wisdom of the world itself seem foolish:

When a wise man gives thee better counsel, give me mine again. I would have none but knaves follow it, since a fool gives it.

> 'That sir which serves and seeks for gain,
>   And follows but for form,
> Will pack when it begins to rain,
>   And leave thee in the storm.
> But I will tarry; the fool will stay,
>   And let the wise man fly.
> The knave turns fool that runs away;
>   The fool no knave, perdy.'

As Randall Jarrell has also observed, all that any critic can say about the *kind* of claims, and counter-claims, that occur throughout *King Lear* (and which may be the ultimate claims, and counter-claims, of artistic mimesis and morality, so far as worldly, and other-worldly wisdom is concerned) was summed up for us in the lines of fire with which he ended his own most famous lecture, and which comprise the only fitting conclusion to this particular book. All 'we can say' is 'that everything is arranged in this life as though we entered it carrying the burden of obligations contracted in a former life'.

There is no reason inherent in the conditions of life on this earth that can make us consider ourselves obliged to do good, to be fastidious, to be polite, even, nor make the talented artist consider himself obliged to begin over again a score of times a piece of work the admiration aroused by which will matter little to his body devoured by worms, like the patch of yellow wall painted with so much knowledge and skill by an artist who must forever remain unknown and is barely identified under the name Vermeer. All these obligations which have not their sanction in our present life seem to belong to a different world, founded upon kindness, scrupulosity, self-sacrifice, a world entirely different from this, which we leave in order to be born into this world, before perhaps returning to the other to live once again beneath the sway of those unknown laws which we have obeyed because we bore their precepts in our hearts, knowing not whose hand had traced them there — those laws to which every profound work of the intellect brings us nearer and which are invisible only — and still! — to fools.[54]

On this, the greatest of all artistic — and critical — footnotes to Plato, the case for the defence of art and criticism (and of criticism of criticism) alike may, finally, rest.

Notes

1. Kenneth Muir, *The Singularity of Shakespeare* (Liverpool, 1977), p. 57.
' 2. See Buckner B. Trawick, *Shakespeare and Alcohol* (Amsterdam, 1978), p. 56.
3. See the responses to Cleopatra that are quoted by L. T. Fitz (Linda Woodbridge) in 'Egyptian Queens and Male Reviewers', *Shakespeare Quarterly*, 28 (1977), 297–316.
4. For full discussion of the contemporary controversy about the nature of women, see Linda Woodbridge, *Women and the English Renaissance: Literature and the Nature of Womankind, 1540-1620* (Urbana and London 1984), and the commentaries on the pamphlets printed in *Half Humankind: Writings from the Controversy about Women in Renaissance England*, ed. Katherine Usher Henderson and Barbara F. McManus, forthcoming at the University of Illinois Press.
5. See Giovanni Pico della Mirandola, *Oration on the Dignity of Man*, translated by A. Robert Caponigri (Chicago, 1956), pp. 7–9. See also Hamlet's account of Pico's 'paragon of animals' (II. ii. 300–4).
6. Compare, for instance, the remarkably similar endings of *The Taming of the Shrew* ('Come on and kiss me, Kate', etc.) and the Wife of Bath's *Prologue*:

> And whan that I hadde geten unto me,
> By maistrie, al the soveraynetee,
> And that he seyde, 'Myn owene trewe wyf,
> Do as thee lust the terme of al thy lyf,
> Keep thyn honour, and keep ekk myn estaat' –
> After that day we hadden never debaat.

– and her *Tale*:

> 'Thanne have I gete of yow maistrye,' quod she,
> 'Syn I may chese, and governe as me lest?'
> 'Ye, certes, wyf,' quod he, 'I holde it best.'
> 'Kys me,' quod she, 'we be no lenger wrothe.'

It would be impossible for me to feel unduly upset or offended by Shakespeare's ending without – *mutatis mutandis* – being equally offended by Chaucer's endings, which I for one find eminently satisfying (see also David M. Bergeron, 'The Wife of Bath and Shakespeare's *The Taming of the Shrew*', *University Review*, 35 (1969), 279–86).
7. For further discussion, see 'Egyptian Queens and Male Reviewers' (note 3 above). Shakespeare's male characters are not compared with each other simply because they are men, but his women characters are often compared only with each other. Plato seems light-years ahead of his time in concluding that the anatomical differences between the sexes have no bearing on the fact that both sexes share 'the same nature'. See *The Republic*, trans. Desmond Lee (Part VI, Book 6), pp. 233–5:

> . . . 'if the only difference apparent between them is that the female bears and the male begets, we shall not admit that this is a difference relevant for our purpose, but shall maintain that our male and female Guardians ought to follow the same occupations . . . [and that there is] no administrative occupation which is peculiar to woman as woman or man as man; natural capacities are similarly distributed in each sex, and it is natural for women to take part in all occupations as well as men, though in all women will be the weaker partners.'

[Plato none the less acknowledges that a 'good many women, it is true, are better than a good many men at a good many things'.]

'Are we therefore to confine all occupations to men only?'

'How can we?'

'Obviously we can't; for we are agreed, I think, that one woman may have a natural ability for medicine or music, another not. . . . And one may be good at athletics, another have no taste for them; one be good at soldiering, another not.'

'I think so.'

'Then may a woman not be philosophic or unphilosophic, high-spirited or spiritless?'

'She may.'

'Then there will also be some women fitted to be Guardians: for these natural qualities, you will remember, were those for which we picked our men Guardians.'

'Yes, they were.'

'So men and women have the same natural capacity for Guardianship, save in so far as woman is the weaker of the two.'

'That is clear.'

'We must therefore pick suitable women to share the life and duties of Guardian with men, since they are capable of it and the natures of men and women are akin. . . . And the same natures should follow the same pursuits, shouldn't they? . . . So our proposed legislation was no impossible day-dream; we were legislating in accordance with nature and it is our present contrary practice which now seems unnatural.'

'It looks like it.' . . .

'Well then, to make a woman into a Guardian we presumably need the same education as we need to make a man into one, especially as it will operate on the same nature in both.'

'True.'

Contrast the programme of education outlined for women by the 'Sex-Directed Educators' cited in Betty Friedan's *The Feminine Mystique* (New York, 1963), pp. 142-73. From her survey of American education, Friedan concluded that the 'stunting of able girls from nonsexual growth [was] nationwide' (p. 154).

8. See Clara Claiborne Park's lively discussion of Shakespeare's heroines as 'role-models' in 'As We Like It: How a Girl Can Be Smart and Still Popular', in *The Woman's Part: Feminist Criticism of Shakespeare*, ed. Carolyn Ruth Swift Lenz, Gayle Greene, and Carol Thomas Neely (Urbana, Chicago, London, 1980), pp. 100–16 – hereafter cited as *The Woman's Part*.

9. Whether you look at them as essentially 'feminine' values, or as humane virtues traditionally associated with women, the fact is that 'The values that emerge from [Shakespeare's] plays are, if anything' the ones commonly deemed to be 'feminine' – as opposed to the traditionally 'masculine' priorities of power, force and politics. See Madelon Gohlke, '"I Wooed Thee With My Sword": Shakespeare's Tragic Paradigms', in *The Woman's Part*, pp. 150–70.

10. This point is confirmed by the classic printer's error (if it never really occurred it certainly should have): when setting Nietzsche's famous line, 'When thou go'st to woman, forget not thy whip', the printer inserted an 'e' between the 'h' and the 'y' of the penultimate word.

11. See H. A. Mason, *Shakespeare's Tragedies of Love: An Examination of the Possibility of Common Readings of 'Romeo and Juliet', 'Othello', 'King Lear' and 'Anthony and Cleopatra'* (London, 1970), pp. 146-7. Juliet also gets

clobbered on p. 46: in the balcony scene she 'is doing something that ranges from the naughty through the improper to the downright immoral'. By declaring her love, and eloping with her lover, Juliet does nothing that Perdita, Imogen, and Anne Page do not also do, but I suppose that, given Mason's exacting standards, they, too, could be said to be 'downright immoral'. In fairness, however, it should be noted that Mason is equally severe in his judgements of Shakespeare's heroes.

12. See the critical discussions of the indiscretions of Desdemona and the misdemeanours of the Duchess of Malfi that are cited by Richard Levin in *New Readings vs. Old Plays*, pp. 99, 151. For the psychoanalytic portrait, see Robert Dickes, 'Desdemona: An Innocent Victim?' in *American Imago*, 25 (1968), 287, 293. For a far more complex view of the issues, see Edward A. Snow, 'Sexual Anxiety and the Male Order of Things in *Othello*', *English Literary Renaissance*, 10 (1980), 384–412.

13. See S. Clark Hulse, ' "A Piece of Skilful Painting" in Shakespeare's *Lucrece*', *Shakespeare Survey*, 31 (1978), 13–22.

14. See Ian Donaldson, *The Rapes of Lucretia: A Myth and its Transformations*, (Oxford, 1982). Subsequent page references to this book are cited parenthetically in the text.

15. On Lucrece, see the various critics cited by Richard Levin in 'The Ironic Reading of *The Rape of Lucrece*', *Shakespeare Survey*, 34 (1981), 85–92, and quoted by Coppélia Kahn in her article on 'The Rape in Shakespeare's *Lucrece*', *Shakespeare Studies*, 9 (1976), 45–72. On Tess, see the critical arguments cited by Donaldson (p. 80) and countered by Mary Jacobus in her detailed discussion of 'Tess's Purity', *Essays in Criticism* (1976), 318–38. On Imogen's sexual susceptibilities, see Elijah Moshinsky (the director of the BBC production of *Cymbeline*) as quoted in *Radio Times*, 9–15 July 1983, p. 4.

16. See *Titus Andronicus*, V. iii. 46–52:

Titus. Die, die, Lavinia, and thy shame with thee;
And with thy shame thy father's sorrow die!
. . . .
I am as woeful as Virginius was,
And have a thousand time more cause than he
To do this outrage; and it now is done.

17. See *Lucrece*, ll. 1058–71:

'Well, well, dear Collatine, thou shalt not know
The stained taste of violated troth;
I will not wrong thy true affection so
To flatter thee with an infringed oath;
This bastard graff shall never come to growth;
   He shall not boast who did thy stock pollute
   That thou art doting father of his fruit.

'Nor shall he smile at thee in secret thought,
Nor laugh with his companions at thy state;
But thou shalt know thy interest was not bought
Basely with gold, but stol'n from forth thy gate,
For me, I am the mistress of my fate,
   And with my trespass never will dispense,
   Till life to death acquit my forc'd offence.'

The best account of Lucrece's predicament that I know of is Coppélia Kahn's 'The Rape in Shakespeare's *Lucrece*' – she is driven to death by her determination to spare her husband shame.

18. See Donaldson, p. 29, citing Empson's Introduction to the Poems of Shakespeare in *The Complete Signet Classic Shakespeare*, ed. Sylvan Barnet (New York, 1972), p. 1670.

19. See Roy Battenhouse, *Shakespearean Tragedy: Its Art and Its Christian Premises* (Bloomington, 1969), pp. 3–41, Don Cameron Allen, 'Some Observations on *The Rape of Lucrece*', *Shakespeare Survey*, 15 (1962), 89–98, and the other critics cited by Levin and Kahn.

20. Deploring historical injustice in his *Apology for Poetry*, Sidney asked, 'See we not virtuous Cato driven to kill himself'?, and one *could* protest about sexual injustice in the same terms: 'See we not virtuous Lucrece driven to kill herself'? Certain lines in Shakespeare's poem would seem to forestall, even as they anticipate, the various arguments designed to sully her good name:

> 'Let my good name, that senseless reputation,
> For Collatine's dear love be kept unspotted;
> If that be made a theme for disputation,
> The branches of another root are rotted,
> And undeserv'd reproach to him allotted
> That is as clear from this attaint of mine
> As I ere this was pure to Collatine.'
>
> (ll. 820–6)

It's as if his modern critics were determined to subject Shakespeare's Lucrece to the very calumnies she killed herself to preclude.

21. See Donaldson, pp. 52–3, and Sam Hynes, 'The Rape of Tarquin', *Shakespeare Quarterly*, 10 (1959), 451–3.

22. See L. T. Fitz, 'Egyptian Queens and Male Reviewers', *Shakespeare Quarterly*, 28 (1977), 313–14.

23. See Maurice Charney, '*Hamlet* Without Words', in *Shakespeare's 'More Than Words Can Witness': Essays on Visual and Nonverbal Enactment in the Plays'*, ed. Sidney Homan (London and Lewisburg, 1980), pp. 23–42. As Charney also observes, Shakespeare's meanings may be distorted in production. 'The Elizabethan word "closet" means simply a private apartment ... It does not mean "bedchamber", and the ponderous bed that often dominates performances of the "closet scene"' may be 'entirely out of place'.

24. See Rebecca Smith 'A Heart Cleft in Twain: The Dilemma of Shakespeare's Gertrude', in *The Woman's Part*, pp. 194–210.

25. See Walter C. Foreman, Jr., *The Music of the Close: The Final Scenes of Shakespeare's Tragedies* (Lexington, Kentucky, 1978), p. 21. Subsequent quotations are from pp. 3, 6, 27, and 28.

26. See Russell Jackson, '"Perfect Types of Womanhood": Rosalind, Beatrice and Viola in Victorian Criticism and Performance', *Shakespeare Survey*, 32 (1979), pp. 15–26. Dorian Gray is quoted in full on pp. 25–6.

27. See Carol J. Carlisle, 'Helen Faucit's Rosalind', *Shakespeare Studies* 12 (1979), 65–94.

28. See T. Walter Herbert, *Oberon's Mazèd World* (Baton Rouge and London, 1977), p. 19.

29. Here are some examples of Freudian interpretations quoted (for their typicality) from, or in, various works received for review.

The circus clown's costume 'retains from the medieval fool's many symbols of castration'. The outsized necktie, baggy pants, etc. 'all symbolize the father, who was once big and fearful, but is now depreciated, castrated and ridiculed'.

The 'Oedipus complex is experienced by the anti-Semite as a narcissistic injury, and he projects this injury upon the Jew who is made to play the role of the father. His choice of the Jew is determined by the fact that the Jew is in the unique position of representing at the same time the all-powerful father and the father castrated.'

Coriolanus's fear of castration may 'help to account for the enthusiasm with which he characterizes Valeria, in strikingly phallic terms, as the icicle on Dian's temple . . . the phallic woman may ultimately be less frightening to him than the woman who demonstrates the possibility of castration by her lack of a penis.'

'It is characteristic of Coriolanus's transformation of hunger into phallic aggression that the feared castration is imagined predominantly in oral terms: to be castrated here *is* to be a mouth.'

'Otto Fenichel discusses the derivation of acting from exhibitionism'; like 'all such derivatives, it is ultimately designed to protect against the fear of castration'.

Claudio's fear of beheading 'is, in Freudian terms, a fear of castration'. 'We have it on Freud's authority that beheading occurs frequently in dreams as a substitute for castration.'

'Wilson suggests that Corioli represents defloration; specifically, that it expresses the equation of coitus with damaging assault and the resultant dread of retaliatory castration.'

To assert that the same phenomenon is 'ultimately' responsible for the aetiology of anti-Semitism, the aetiology of acting, the circus clown's costume, Coriolanus's entry into Corioli, and Claudio's fear of the executioner's axe is comparable to saying that solar energy is ultimately responsible for activating muscular contractions. If it is true, to say so is pointless, since the same explanation can, 'ultimately', be held responsible for virtually everything else that happens under the sun, including scholarly essays designed to propound or refute it. The same thing Fenichel says about the derivation of acting could be said about his conclusions about the derivation of acting, and so on, *ad infinitum*. The one thing this theory does not account for is the anti-Semitism, or enjoyment of clowns, occasionally manifested by females of the species, who, as loyal Electras, would, presumably, not wish to see their own fathers castrated or humiliated. And if certain women, in similar circumstances (Mary Stuart, Anne Boleyn, and Katherine Howard) could, conceivably, have had nightmares about beheadings quite independently of a fear of anything else, then so could Claudio. If 'fear of castration' is a psychoanalytical metaphor for the general human fears of a loss of integrity, of identity, of face, of life, then it cannot, simultaneously, be used to account for the phenomena that it metaphorically describes. The threat to 'splay' and 'geld' the young men of Vienna (II. i. 219) is not the ultimate danger that Claudio confronts. To equate Claudio's account of all that men (and women) have feared of death with his 'fear of castration' seems logically comparable to arguing that a fear of the diagnosis, 'syphilis', ultimately explains a young patient's reaction to the diagnosis: 'It's terminal cancer'.

30. For a sympathetic (but not uncritical) account of various Freudian interpretations of Shakespearian drama see Meredith Anne Skura, *The Literary Use of the Psychoanalytic Process* (New Haven and London, 1981). The best psychoanalytic discussions I've read have to do, not with sexual tags, but with the dream-like qualities of certain plays. See Barbara Freedman, 'Egeon's Debt: Self-Division and Self-Redemption in *The Comedy of Errors*', *English Literary*

Renaissance, 10 (1980), 360-83, and Naoe Takei da Silva, 'The World of Shakespeare's Last Plays', in *Poetry and Drama in the English Renaissance*, ed. Koshi Nakanori and Yasuo Tamaizumi (Tokyo, 1980), 33-59.

31. Back in the 1940s, it was fashionable to sneer at Bradley, and to begin your article with a quotation from T. S. Eliot. By now, the wheel has come full circle: Bradley is highly esteemed (as grandfathers usually are), while yesterday's hero is rarely cited except in rejections of his conclusions about *Othello* and *Hamlet*. Yet Eliot's essays, like Bradley's, sparkle with insights ignored to our loss. In both cases, the reaction had to do with their influence, as their theories and approaches tended to harden into dogma.

32. See Jeanne Addison Roberts, *Shakespeare's English Comedy: The Merry Wives of Windsor in Context* (Lincoln and London, 1979), p. 83. In cases where the arguments are determined by the critical dialectic, as they are in this chapter, the quotations are, too – Roberts has a lot more to say about *The Merry Wives* than this. But the whole point of this chapter is to illustrate the way the process of reaction operates.

33. See Marjorie Garber, '"Wild Laughter in the Throat of Death": Darker Purposes in Shakespearian Comedy', in *Shakespearian Comedy*, ed. Maurice Charney, *New York Literary Forum* (1980), pp. 121-6.

34. For criticisms of unduly solemn and pontifical interpretations of Shakespeare's comedies, see Helen Gardner, 'Happy Endings: Literature, Misery, and Joy', *Encounter*, 57 (1981), 39-51; John K. Hale, '"I'll Strive to Please You Every Day": Pleasure and Meaning in Shakespeare's Mature Comedies', *Studies in English Literature*, 21 (1981), 241-55; and A. P. Riemer, *Antic Fables: Patterns of Evasion in Shakespeare's Comedies* (Manchester, 1980). As Riemer reminds us, Elizabethan comedies were frequently promoted as 'mirth-provoking, jesting, pleasant, and conceited'. On the other hand, criticism 'is most at home where literary texts stand for something other than their particular preoccupations' and where 'exegesis, explanation and explication' seem indispensable tools: 'The habits of criticism are, therefore, fundamentally allegorical' (pp. 5, 13). So far as allegories are concerned, it seems uncanny how succinctly Shakespeare's own characters encapsulate various critical responses to his works. Richard Levin has described the school of critics who follow Fluellen's methodology (see *New Readings vs. Old Plays*, pp. 210-11) and so ignore all differences between the various objects they are equating ('even if a census of the Wye turns up cod, dace, hake, pike, and salmon, while the nameless Macedonian river yields only gudgeon, lamprey, spichcock, umbrina, and salmon' the Fluellenist can still claim they are alike because 'there is salmons in both'). As we have seen, the melancholy Jaques speaks for numerous critics who moralize Shakespeare's comedies, augmenting them with tears. 'Providentialist' critics, like Duke Senior in *As You Like It*, can find 'Sermons in stones, and good in everything'. And whenever the question 'Do you see nothing there?' is posed with reference to some alien interpretation of Shakespearian drama, the answer given to it by the Gertrudes of criticism is virtually bound to be, 'Nothing at all, yet all that is I see.' Regan has a host of critical counterparts, who agree with everything their sister-and-brother critics have already said – 'only [it] comes too short'. And there are those of us who must needs contemplate the fate of Polonius ('Thou wretched, rash, intruding fool, farewell!') with heartfelt pity and terror.

35. See Riemer, *Antic Fables*, p. 108, '*Cymbeline* is finally a vehicle for nothing but its own ingenuity.' It always seems a let-down when critics conclude that Shakespeare's comedies are 'nothing but' flamboyant 'theatrical extravaganzas concerned with largely abstract and formal preoccupations' (see p. 54). For discussion of the increasingly fashionable tendency to emphasize the 'self-reflexive

and metadramatic signals in the comedies and romances', see Norman Rabkin, *Shakespeare and the Problem of Meaning* (Chicago and London, 1981), p. 119. Rabkin is especially good on the 'take up the sword again, or take up me' phenomenon in criticism. As Richard III knew, nothing more effectively confounds wisdom (or criticism) than a false antithesis.

36. Shakespeare's challenges to, and affirmations of, Elizabethan orthodoxies are the subject of continuing debate. For lively discussions of the major points of contention, see Robert P. Merrix, 'Shakespeare's Histories and the New Bardolaters', *Studies in English Literature*, 19 (1979), 179-96; L. C. Knights 'Shakespeare and History', *The Sewanee Review*, LXXXVI (1978), 380-96, and John Wilders, *The Lost Garden* (London, 1978).

37. See Susan Snyder, 'Patterns of Motion in *Antony and Cleopatra*', *Shakespeare Survey*, 33 (1980), 113-22.

38. See S. Viswanathan, *The Shakespeare Play as Poem* (Cambridge, 1980).

39. See Sidney Homan, *Shakespeare's 'More Than Words Can Witness'*, pp. 10-11.

40. See S. Gorley Putt, *The Golden Age of English Drama* (Cambridge, 1981), pp. 77, 79. See also J. L. Simmons, 'Diabolical Realism in Middleton and Rowley's *The Changeling*' in *Renaissance Drama*, New Series 11 (1980), ed. Douglas Cole, pp. 135-170.

41. See Bertolt Brecht in *The Times Literary Supplement*, Thursday, 23 April 1964, p. 333 (the German texts are in his *Schriften zum Theater*, vols. 1 and 5).

42. Fredson Bowers has argued that the catastrophe of *King Lear* is inevitable from the time he decides to split the kingdom ('The Structure of King Lear', *Shakespeare Quarterly*, 31 (1980), 9-20). The 'division of the kingdom' is the 'true turning-point' for 'the story and its action, including the tragic fate of Lear'. Yet if Edmund's message had got through, Cordelia would have been spared, and Lear would have survived, as in the sources.

43. See Edward Phillips, extract from *Theatrum Poetarum*, 1675, in *Shakespeare Criticism*, ed. D. Nicol Smith, p. 26.

44. See Maurice Morgann, *Shakespeare Criticism*, ed. Daniel A. Fineman (Oxford, 1972), p. 291. The earlier quotations are from pp. 170-1.

45. Among the pioneering critics in a most distinguished list are Erich Auerbach, E. R. Curtius, and Willard Farnham; for examples of the continuing fruitfulness, of this approach, see Emrys Jones on 'Shakespeare and the Mystery Cycles', in *The Origins of Shakespeare* (Oxford, 1977); K. M. Lea, on poetic imagery derived from the morality plays, in 'Shakespeare's Inner Stage', in *English Renaissance Studies Presented to Dame Helen Gardner* (Oxford, 1980), pp. 132-40; and O. B. Hardison, Jr., 'Logic Versus the Slovenly World in Shakespearian Comedy', *Shakespeare Quarterly*, 31 (1980), 311-22.

46. See William Empson, *Milton's God* (London, 1961), p. 69.

47. See John Bayley, *The Characters of Love* (London, 1960), *The Uses of Division* (London, 1976), and *Shakespeare and Tragedy* (London, 1981).

48. Joan Rees, *Shakespeare and the Story: Aspects of Creation* (London, 1978).

49. Critics who cannot accept the ending tend, primarily, to be concerned with the characters, and with the emotional responses they elicit. Critics who admire the ending tend to be primarily concerned with the play's structure. For various points of controversy, see Arthur C. Kirsch, 'The Integrity of *Measure for Measure*', *Shakespeare Survey*, 28 (1975) 89-106; Darryl J. Gless, *Measure for Measure: The Law and the Convent* (Princeton, 1979); and my article, '"The Devil's Party": Virtues and Vices in *Measure for Measure*', *Shakespeare Survey*, 31 (1978), 105-13.

50. See Randall Jarrell, 'To the Laodiceans', in *Poetry and the Age*, p. 69.

51. See Proust's *The Captive* and *The Past Recaptured*, trans. C. K. Scott Moncrieff and Frederick A. Blosson (New York, 1932), pp. 559, 1013 (the quotations are conflated). I have quoted this translation of *Remembrance of Things Past* because the theories of Randall Jarrell, on which my own conclusions are based, were derived from it.

52. Jarrell, 'The Obscurity of the Poet', in *Poetry and the Age*, p. 31.

53. When Marvin Rosenberg put the text of *King Lear* through a computer, he noticed that the word 'if' showed up over a hundred times. 'In *Lear*, many of the play's hundred-plus "ifs"' come from the king himself, culminating in the most tragic of all uses of the conditional: 'if it be so,/It is a chance which doth redeem all sorrows/That ever I have felt.' Shakespeare's great 'ifs' force critics to use the word themselves. Discussing the ending of *King Lear*, Joseph H. Summers quotes Bradley: 'If to the reader . . . that scene brings one unbroken pain, it is not so with Lear himself.' Summers then argues that, 'If at the end we respond to Lear's death as heroic rather than merely pathetic', it is because 'his final powerful fluctuating responses cast doubt on the "realities" which we often assume as "objective" or "self-evident".' See Marvin Rosenberg, 'Shakespeare's Tragic World of "If"', *Deutsche Shakespeare-Gesellschaft West, Jahrbuch* (1980), pp. 109–17, and Joseph H. Summers, '"Look there, look there!" The Ending of *King Lear*', *English Renaissance Studies, op. cit.*, pp. 74–93.

54. Proust, *The Captive*, pp. 509–10.

Index

Adams, Robert M., 102n2
Aeschylus, 73
All's Well That Ends Well, 8, 130, 177
Allen, Don Cameron, 186n19
Andrews, John F., 75-8, 104n18
Anna Karenina (L. Tolstoy), 79
Anne Boleyn, Queen of Henry VIII, 187n29
Antony and Cleopatra: and Platonic criticism, 16-17; moralistic views of 21, 40; passions in 33-4; character of Cleopatra, 38, 40; Structure of, 83-4; reality and illusion in, 92; Bertrand Evans on Antony's motivation in, 109-12, 129, 138n2
Arabian Nights' Entertainments, The, 145-6
Archilocus, 1, 6
Aristotle: influence, 15, 46; and Plato's *Republic*, 51-2, 54; and sympathy for protagonist, 76; and catharsis, 89-90; on comedy, 98; on pity, 158; *The Poetics*, 46, 59n24, 76, 89, 93
As You Like It: ruling class in, 7; on poetry, 17-18; virtues in, 85; Charles Johnson's adaptation, 131; on Lucretia, 153; as comedy, 166-7, 188n34
Asclepius, 145
Aspects of Shakespeare's 'Problem Plays' (ed. Kenneth Muir and Stanley Wells), 103n8
Auerbach, Erich, 58n15, 189n45
Augustine, St, 89-90, 107n34, 150, 152-7

Bacon, Francis, 11, 13n14, 58n16
Bankhead, Tallulah, 35, 58n18, 138n4
Bardot, Brigitte, 100
Barish, Jonas, 59n24
Bate, Walter Jackson, 59n24

Battenhouse, Roy W., 23, 57n10, 186n19
Bayley, John, 102n2, 189n47
Bear, Andrew, 107n36
Beaumont, Francis and Fletcher, John, 133
Beckerman, Bernard, 123, 140n16
Bellette, A.F., 56n6
Benchley, Robert, 111, 138n4
Bentley, Eric, 77, 104n19
Bergeron, David M., 183n6
Berlin, Sir Isaiah, 6, 94
Berry, Ralph, 59n25
Bible, Holy, 146
Birth of a Nation, The (Griffiths film), 53
Bismarck, Otto von, Count, 73
Black, James, 12n5
Blake, William, 24-5, 51, 53, 62, 123, 165
Bloom, Harold, 83, 105n26
Boadicea, 147
Bogdanov, Michael, 74, 118
Borges, Jörge Luis, 61-2, 87, 102n1
Bowers, Fredson, 189n42
Boys from Syracuse, The (film), 138n6
Bradbrook, Muriel, 103n5
Bradbury, Malcolm: *The History Man*, 139n13, 168
Bradley, A.C., 2, 22, 42, 188n31, 190 n53; *Shakespearean Tragedy*, 36-7
Brando, Marlon, 100
Brecht, Bertolt, 8, 119, 139n12, 173-5, 189n41
Bronowski, Jacob, 106n28
Brook, Peter: production of *Lear*, 113-14, 121, 138n5, 139n10; production of *A Midsummer-Night's Dream*, 139n10
Brownmiller, Susan: *Against Our Will*, 163
Brucher, Richard, 104n19
Brutus, Lucius Junius, 152

Burke, Kenneth, 28–9, 32–3, 58*n*14, 114–15, 138*n*8
Burton, Robert: *The Anatomy of Melancholy*, 61, 70–2, 104*n*12

Campbell, Lily Bess, 59*n*23
Cantor, Paul A., 104*n*19
Carlisle, Carol J., 161, 186*n*27
Carry on Cleo (film), 138*n*6
Cato of Utica, 152, 186*n*20
Charney, Maurice, 186*n*23
Chaucer, Geoffrey, 27, 146, 183*n*6
Chayefsky, Paddy, 139*n*9
Chekhov, Anton, 78–9, 82, 105*n*21, 134, 180
Choderlos de Laclos, Pierre A.F., 34
Cibber, Colley, 106*n*32
Cohen, D.M., 138*n*2
Coleridge, Samuel Taylor, 1, 45, 70, 104*n*9, 133, 142*n*28
Collier, Jeremy, 55*n*3, 98
Comedy of Errors, The, 72–3, 177
Congreve, William: *The Way of the World*, 107*n*38, 137*n*2
Cooke, Alistair, 6, 12*n*4
Coriolanus, 8, 85
Count of Monte Cristo, The (Alexandre Dumas), 105*n*19
Curtius, E.R., 189*n*45
Cushman, Robert, 138*n*5
Cymbeline, 22, 188*n*35

Darwin, Charles, 164
Davies, Howard, 118
Davies, Robertson, 102*n*2
Dean, James, 100
Dennis, John, 26–7, 58*n*12, 96
Dickes, Robert, 185*n*12
Dinesen, Isak (Baroness Karen Blixen), 14
Donaldson, Ian, 13*n*8, 150–6, 185*nn*14, 15, 186*nn*18, 21
Dostoevsky, Fyodor, 6
Drake, James: *The Antient and Modern Stages Survey'd*, 74, 104*n*17
Dryden, John, 35, 93–4, 97; *Essay on Dramatic Poesy*, 94, 107*n*37, 175
Duthie, G.I., 27

Einstein, Albert, 128
Eliot, T.S., 2, 170–2, 179, 188*n*31
Elizabeth I, Queen of England, 147

Empson, Sir William, 154, 176, 189*n*46
Epimenides, 17
Eugene Onegin (Pushkin), 79
Evans, Bertrand, 109–11, 129, 137*n*1, 138*n*2
Exorcist, The (film), 136

Farnham, Willard, 23, 158, 189*n*45
Faucit, Helen, 161
Faulkner, William, 119
Fenichel, Otto, 187*n*29
Fichter, Andrew, 57*n*8
Fielding, Henry, 13*n*8
Fish, Stanley, 59*n*25
Fitz, L.T. (Linda Woodbridge), 183*nn*3, 7, 186*n*22
Flamini, Roland, 138*n*9
Flaubert, Gustave: *Madame Bovary*, 92
Fletcher, John, 174; *see also* Beaumont, Francis and Fletcher, John
Ford, John, 23; *The Broken Heart*, 32
Foreman, Walter C., Jr., 186*n*25
Freedman, Barbara, 187*n*30
French, A.L., 59*n*22, 129, 141*n*22
Freud, Sigmund, 5, 10, 122, 125, 147, 165, 186*n*29
Friedan, Betty, 184*n*7

Garber, Marjorie, 166, 188*n*33
Garbo, Greta, 100
Gardner, Dame Helen, 12*n*1, 57*n*9, 139*n*11, 188*n*34
Gielgud, Sir John, 159
Gill, Brendan, 58*n*18, 138*n*4
Girard, René, 105*n*20
Gless, Darryl, 189*n*49
Godshalk, W.L., 23, 57*n*10
Goethe, J.W. von, 164
Gohlke, Madelon, 184*n*9
Gombrich, Ernst H., 37, 59*n*19, 141*n*26
Gosson, Stephen, 98; *The School of Abuse*, 16
Gray, Dorian *see* Wilde, Oscar
Grene, Nicholas, 13*n*10
Griffiths, D.W. *see Birth of a Nation, The*
Gross, John, 12*n*1
Grudin, Robert, 106*n*29

Habicht, Werner, 53, 60*n*28
Hale, John K., 188*n*34
Half Humankind (ed. K.U. Henderson and B.F. McManus), 183*n*4

Halliwell, Leslie, 107*n*35
Hamlet: varied views of, 19; moralistic views of, 22; unresolved vengeance in, 73–82, 104*n*19; reality and illusion in, 92; prayer scene, 104*n*16; ghost in, 112, 114–15, 117, 134–7, 139*n*10; Royal Court production of, 113–16; Gielgud's production of, 159; character of Gertrude, 159–60, 186*n*23
Hardison, O.B., Jr., 189*n*45
Hardy, Thomas: *Tess of the D'Urbervilles*, 150–1
Harlow, Jean, 100
Hartman, Geoffrey, 5, 12*n*3
Havelock, Eric A., 55*n*1
Havely, Cicely, 13*n*8
Hawkes, Terence, 83, 105*n*25
Hazlitt, William, 2, 23–4, 53
Heinemann, Margot, 119, 139*n*12
Heller, Erich, 93
Hepburn, Katherine, 138*n*2
Herbert, T. Walter, 186*n*28
Heywood, Thomas: *An Apology for Actors*, 97
Hill, Christopher, 68, 103*n*6
Hirsch, E.D., 138*n*2
Hitler, Adolf, 27, 45
Hobbes, Thomas: *Leviathan*, 61, 105*n*24
Holding, Edith, 131, 142*n*27
Homan, Sidney: *Shakespeare's 'More Than Words Can Witness'*, 169, 189*n*39
Homer, 31, 35, 51, 87
Horace: *Art of Poetry*, 93
Howard, Jonathan, 140*n*19
Hulse, S. Clark, 149, 185*n*13
Hume, David, 152
Hynes, Sam, 186*n*21

I.G.: *A Refutation of the Apology for Actors*, 97–8
Ibsen, Henrik, 135
I.M.S., 56*n*5
International Shakespeare Association Congress, 1976, 6

Jackson, Russell, 161, 186*n*26
Jacobus, Mary, 185*n*15
Jarrell, Randall, 1, 20–1, 56*n*7, 180, 190*nn*50, 52

Jew of Malta, The: see Marlowe, Christopher
Job, 146, 156, 181
Johnson, Charles, 131, 142*n*27
Johnson, Samuel: and neo-classical theory, 2, 95–6, 107*n*33, 121; and educational value of reading, 33; on Shakespeare's representation of nature, 35; on textual commentators, 36; on Hamlet, 75; on comedy, 97; on absence of moral design in Shakespeare, 99, 107*n*33; experiments with dramatic form, 137*n*2; on Shakespeare's characters, 171; on Shakespeare's construction, 176; *Preface to Shakespeare*, 26–7, 36, 95–6; *The Rambler*, 38, 107*n*33
Jones, Emrys, 189*n*45
Jonson, Ben 13*nn*8,10; characters, 42–4, 104*n*10; Dryden analyses *Epicene*, 94, 97; on making spectators understanders, 110; surprise in, 133; and Roman honour, 152; comedies, 167; formal construction, 174–5, 178; on Shakespeare's 'wanting art', 178; *The New Inn*, 137*n*2
Jordan, Dorothea, 161
Jud Süss (film), 53
Julius Caesar, 21, 133

Kahn, Coppélia, 185*nn*15, 17, 186*n*19
Katherine Howard, Queen of Henry VIII, 187*n*26
Keats, John, 2, 45, 53, 144
Kellett, E.E.: *The Whirligig of Taste*, 165
Kermode, Frank, 10, 13*n*13
King Kong (film), 12*n*2, 117–18
King Lear: class ideology in, 7; survival, 10; and mirror of nature, 18; on tragedy of 'betters', 82; contrarieties in 84, 180–2; audience's shared grief, 88; recent interpretations, 112–14, 120–1, 138*nn*2,5, 139*n*10; humane values in, 132; Cordelia as 'castaway' in, 156; pity in, 158; assessed, 181–2; structure, 189*n*42; word 'if' in, 190*n*53
Kipling, Rudyard, 38

Kirsch, Arthur C., 103n8, 189n49
Kiss Me, Kate (musical play), 138n2
Knights, L.C., 189n36
Koch, Georg August, 53
Kott, Jan, 13n9
Krauss, Werner, 53
Krieger, Elliot: A Marxist Study of Shakespeare's Comedies, 7, 13n7
Krouse, F.M., 55n2
Kuhn, T.S.: The Structure of Scientific Revolutions, 9, 13n11, 126
Kurosawa, Akira, 139n9
Kyd, Thomas, 46, 118; The Spanish Tragedy, 118, 135

Laclos, Choderlos de see Choderlos de Laclos, Pierre A.F.
Lamb, Charles, 86-7, 106n32
Lea, K.M., 189n45
Leavis, F.R., 3
Lee, Desmond, 56n4
Leonard, Nancy S., 106n27
Levin, Richard: 'The Ironic Reading of The Rape of Lucrece...', 60n26, 185n15, 186n19; New Readings vs. Old Plays, 20, 24, 57n8, 59nn21, 25, 60n26, 122, 134, 141n25, 185n12, 188n34
Lewis, C.S., 57n9
Lloyd-Jones, Hugh, 73, 104n15
London Review of Books, 4
Losey, Joseph, 139n9
Love's Labour's Lost, 7, 101, 174-7
Lucilius, 145
Lucretia, 149-59, 168
Lukács, Georg, 7, 12n7
Lyttelton, George, 1st Baron, 35, 58n17

Macbeth, 80, 106n30, 117-18, 136
McCanles, Michael, 106n29
Machiavelli, Niccolò: The Prince, 58n16
Mack, Maynard, 9, 13n12, 105n22, 140n21
McLellan, David, 8
Mahood, M.M., 166-7
Marlowe, Christopher: evil and pride in 23, 58n10, villains, 43; Bloom on, 105n26; Doctor Faustus, 80-1; The Jew of Malta, 43; Tamburlaine, 23
Marston, John, 171
Marvell, Andrew, 62

Marx, Karl, 6-8, 10
Mary Stuart, Queen of Scots, 187n29
Mason, H.A., 148, 184n11
Maxwell, J.C., 70, 104n11
Measure for Measure: chastity and charity in, 63-73; betrothal contracts in, 65-67, 103nn4, 5; structure, 83, 106n27, 177-9, 189n49; sexual connotations in, 103n8, 104nn9-10, 139n15; decapitation in, 141n21; Claudio in, 174
Medawar, Sir Peter, 59n20, 73, 104n14
Merchant of Venice, The: class hierarchy in, 7-8; revenge in, 29-30, 32; anti-Semitism in, 53-4, 60 nn27, 28, 105n20, 138n2; structure, 177
Merrix, Robert, P., 189n36
Merry Wives of Windsor, The, 7, 166
Middleton, Thomas, 43; The Changeling, 171
Midsummer-Night's Dream, A, 17, 24, 92, 139n11, 162, 167
Miller, Jonathan, 70
Milton, John, 2, 25, 52; 'L'Allegro', 62; Areopagitica, 124; Paradise Lost, 44, 62; 'Il Penseroso', 62
Minturno (Antonius Sebastianus), 98
Moby Dick (Herman Melville), 80-1
Modern Language Association of America: Newsletter, 4
Molière, Jean-Baptiste Poquelin de, 13n10
Monroe, Marilyn, 100, 159
Moore, Marianne, 173
Moore, Thomas, 93
Morgann, Maurice, 173, 175, 189n44
Moshinsky, Elijah, 168, 185n15
Much Ado About Nothing, 122, 166, 174, 177
Muir, Kenneth, 6, 13n6, 60n27, 143-4, 183n1
Murdoch, Iris, 55n1
Musil, Robert: The Man Without Qualities, 165

Nabokov, Vladimir: Lolita, 171-2
Napoleon Bonaparte, 45
National Theatre, London: production of The Spanish Tragedy, 118
New York Review of Books, 4
Nietzsche, Friedrich, 61, 184n10

Nietzshe, Friedrich, 61, 184n10
Nisbett, Louisa Cranstoun, 161
Noble, Adrian, 138n5

Okerlund, Arlene N., 59n25
Olivier, Laurence, Baron, 106n32, 107
    n35
Ornstein, Robert, 27, 57n10, 58n13
Othello, 21, 48, 85, 94, 130
Ovid, 34, 152, 157, 162
Park, Clara Claiborne, 184n8
Pasteur, Louis, 84
Paulin, Tom, 12n2
Pericles, 22
Phillips, Edward, 174, 189n43
Pico della Mirandola, Giovanni, 144-5,
    148, 183n5
Pinter, Harold, 139n9
Plato: on drama and poetry criticism,
    2-3, 15-16, 19, 23-6, 44, 47-
    52, 54-5, 92; on mimesis, 14,
    18; on morality, 15; on poetical
    fictions, 18, 46; on Theseus, 24;
    on revolt against authority, 25-
    6; on studying Homer, 31, 51;
    on admiring stage characters,
    41-2, 48; repressive proposals,
    42, 48, 50; influence, 46-7,
    87; on immorality in art, 49;
    on 'opposite impulses', 84, 88;
    and 'example' of drama, 88-90,
    92, 99; and subversive nature of
    art, 100; and tolerance of human
    failings, 101; on sex differences,
    183n7; The Republic, 14-16,
    24-5, 31, 38, 41-2, 46-51, 54-
    5, 55n1, 59n24, 88-90, 182,
    183n7
Pope, Alexander, 12n1, 95; Essay on
    Man, 44
Popper, Karl: on critical theory, 6; on
    refutation, 11, 109, 124-8,
    140nn17, 18; Conjectures and
    Refutations, 128, 140n17; The
    Open Society and its Enemies,
    55n1, 56n4, 140n18
Price, Hereward: Construction in
    Shakespeare, 175-6
Price, John Edward, 130, 141n24
Prosser, Eleanor, 79, 105n23
Proust, Marcel, 34, 56n7, 179-80,
    190nn51, 54

Puccini, Giacomo, 149
Putt, S. Gorley: The Golden Age of
    English Drama, 170-1, 189n40

Quinton, Anthony, Baron, 13n14

Rabkin, Norman, 13n7, 56n6, 106n29,
    140n20, 189n35
Rambler, The (Johnson), 38, 107n33
Rape of Lucrece, The, 149-59, 163-
    4, 185nn15-21
Ray, Nicholas, 139n9
Redgrave, Vanessa, 161
Rees, Joan: Shakespeare and the Story,
    176-7, 189n48
Re-Reading English (ed. Peter Widdow-
    son), 4, 12n2
Revenger's Tragedy, The, see Tourneur,
    Cyril
Richard II, 77, 141n23
Richard III, 21, 43, 47, 86-7, 106n32,
    135-6
Richardson, Samuel: Clarissa Harlowe,
    150
Riemer, A.P., 188nn 34,35
Roberts, Jeanne Addison, 188n32
Rochester, John Wilmot, 2nd Earl of:
    'A Satire against Mankind', 44
Romeo and Juliet, 21, 39-40, 67, 121-
    2, 131, 133, 141n25, 157
Rosenberg, Marvin, 190n53
Rowe, Nicholas, 86-7, 106n31
Royal Court Theatre, London, 113-16
    136
Royal Shakespeare Company, 118
Russell, Bertrand, 109
Rymer, Thomas, 94, 96

Sacks, Elizabeth, 139n15
Sade, Marquis de, 60n25
Salingar, L.G., 23, 57n10
Saxo Grammaticus, 46
Schleiner, Louise, 106n27
Scouten, Arthur H., 103n5
Selznick, David O., 116, 138n9
Seneca, 152
Shadwell, Thomas, 98
Shakespeare Criticism (ed. D. Nichol
    Smith), 56n5, 58n17, 106nn31,
    32
Shakespeare Survey, 165-6
Shelley, Percy Bysshe, 2, 24-5, 53-4,
    58n11

Sidney, Sir Philip, 16, 25; and Plato's criticism, 54; on inventing punishment for tyrants, 77; on comedy, 98; *Apology for Poetry*, 31, 55*nn*2,4, 98, 186*n*20; *Astrophel and Stella*, 31-2
Silva, Naoe Takei da, 188*n*30
Simmons, J.L., 189*n*40
Sinfield, Alan, 104*n*16
Skura, Meredith Anne, 187*n*30
Smidman, David, 60*n*27
Smith, Rebecca, 159, 186*n*24
Snow, Edward A., 185*n*12
Snyder, Susan, 169, 189*n*37
Some Like It Hot (film), 101
Sonnets, 18
Spanish Tragedy, The, see Kyd, Thomas
Speer, Albert, 76
Spenser, Edmund, 52, 143
Sprinchorn, Evert, 56*n*5, 139*n*10
Stalin, Josef, 27
Stavig, Mark, 23, 57*n*10
Stendhal (Marie-Henri Beyle), 34
Steppat, Michael, 138*n*3
Stoppard, Tom, 113-15, 120-1, 135, 138*n*7, 139*n*10
Strindberg, August, 135, 139*n*10
Stuart, Simon, 139*n*15
Summers, Joseph H., 190*n*53
Swift, Jonathan: *Gulliver's Travels*, 30, 99
Swinburne, Algernon Charles, 172

Tamburlaine, see Marlowe, Christopher
Taming of the Shrew, The, 138*n*2, 153
Tarquin (Sextus Tarquinius), 152, 154-7, 159, 163-4, 168
Tate, Nahum, 121
Tempest, The, 92, 104*n*19, 134-5, 175
Tillyard, E.M.W., 104*n*13
Times Literary Supplement, 4
Timon of Athens, 17-18
Titus Andronicus, 48, 54, 175, 185*n*16
Tolstoy, Leo, 6

Tourneur, Cyril, 23; *The Atheist's Tragedy*, 78; *The Revenger's Tragedy*, 23
Tracy, Spencer, 138*n*2
Trawick, Buckner B., 183*n*2
Troilus and Cressida, 138*n*2
Twelfth Night, 7, 59*n*25, 121-2, 166, 174
Two Gentlemen of Verona, The, 162, 178
Tyndale, William, 152, 155

Van Gogh, Vincent, 54
Vane, Sybil, 161
Vermeer, Jan, 57*n*7, 182
Vidal, Gore, 138*n*9
Virgil, 62
Viswanathan, S., 189*n*38
Voltaire, François-Marie Arouet de, 96

Waith, Eugene, 102*n*2
Warton, Joseph, 1
Watts, C.T., 27, 58*n*13
Way of the World, The, see Congreve, W.'liam
Webbe, Thomas, 68
Webster, John, 27
Whetstone, George, 104*n*10
Whigham, Frank, 138*n*2
Whitehead, Alfred North, 59*n*24
Wilde, Oscar, 26; *The Picture of Dorian Gray*, 161, 186*n*26
Wilders, John, 189*n*36
Williams, Tennessee, 119
Wit and Science (John Redford), 166
Woman's Part, The (ed. C.R.S. Lenz and others). 184*nn*8,9
Woodbridge, Linda, 183*n*4; *see also* Fitz, L.T.
World Congress (on Shakespeare), Stratford-upon-Avon, 1981, 117
Wright, G.H. von, 13*n*14
Wulf, Josef: *Theater und Film im Dritten Reich*, 60*n*28

Yeats, William Butler, 15, 135, 172